ENGLISH TRANSLATIONS
OF THE
SCANDINAVIAN MEDIEVAL BALLADS

ENGLISH TRANSLATIONS
OF THE
SCANDINAVIAN MEDIEVAL BALLADS

An Analytical Guide and Bibliography

Larry E. Syndergaard

The Nordic Institute of Folklore

Turku
1995

For my parents,

Edward Boysen Syndergaard and
Esther Cation Syndergaard,

who taught us to learn about the world and to
care about its folk

NIF Publications No. 30
©1995 by Nordic Institute of Folklore
Published 1995
Printed by Gummerus Oy in Jyväskylä, Finland

Cover: Henry Forssell
Layout: Kevin L. Glick

ISBN 952-9724-11-X
ISSN 0355-8924

Distribution:
    The Nordic Institute of Folklore
    c/o University of Turku
    FIN-20500 Turku, Finland

Distribution in North America:
    Medieval Institute Publications
    Western Michigan University
    Kalamazoo, MI 49008-3801 U.S.A.

Table of Contents

PREFACE

This book is the final outgrowth of a much more circumscribed project begun a number of years ago: a register of the translations into English of the traditional Danish ballads. That task seemed important in subject, limited in scope, conventional in demands, and capable of prompt completion—all desirable qualities for someone seeking an above all manageable research project amidst the fatigue of a recent and demanding stint in academic administration.

That project did provide a change in focus, but my assumptions about limits and manageability were (as so often happens) wrong. Various discoveries and surprises had new implications; these in turn led to a much more complex conception of what a guide (no longer a simple register) to the translations of this folk genre needed to provide. Only my convictions on the value of the Scandinavian ballads and the importance of translation as a cultural factor came through unchanged.

While the concept was thus expanding, the material I kept finding argued for a different kind of expansion. The search for translations from the Danish often led to translations of ballads from the other Scandinavian languages, often in the same source, and sometimes by the same translators. Given the pan-Scandinavian nature of this genre, to restrict the project to the Danish ballads came to seem artificial, in fact unnatural. Thus I expanded the scope to include all five languages (six with the Shetland Norn), though several interruptions accompanied the expansions.

This long pattern of expansion was finally (and paradoxically) ended by another expansion of my understanding: Because so many segments of anglophone culture have wished to translate the Scandinavian ballads, in so many and such unexpected venues and for so many purposes, one will never stop finding at least a few more translations as long as one keeps searching. If I did not stop searching, no one else would have the benefit of what I had generated.

My interests have long gravitated toward literary and cultural zones of intersection, border-crossing, and transition—resistance to boundary. A colleague provides the apt metaphor: cultural plate tectonics, with zones of interest where forces and entities come together. Thus if only because my initial project involved the intersections of some of the most important cultural "plates" of all, languages, my expectations for a limited and non-problematic project were naive.

The other part of the project focus, the ballad, brings its own "crossings" and related complexities. My long-standing interest in ballads (English-Scottish-American as well as Scandinavian) has not followed the historically dominant mode of sorting them into groups and accounting for their origins, evolution, and diffusion. I find ballads more interesting in their powerful scripts as works of art and in the fact that they transcend and challenge some of the prevailing ways in which we divide up the world: national boundaries, conventional cultural "periods," socioeconomic class, literary classifications, and language boundaries. They are one of the few voices of the "folk" which modern academe (apart from folklorists) has had to acknowledge.

Far more than most, a project such as this makes one aware of personal and institutional limitations, and it is reassuring to find, in an era of research as competitive performance, that scholarship can still be a remarkably cooperative activity. My work has enjoyed the help of people on two continents, whose contributions it is a pleasure to acknowledge.

In Scandinavia, colleagues Bengt Jonsson, Velle Espeland, Iørn Piø, and Reimund Kvideland have responded to a variety of inquiries and have volunteered helpful information. Grethe Jacobsen and Jens Christian Johansen generously researched the possible Danish antecedents of a translator. In this country, I have enjoyed advice for years in ballad and ballad-translation matters from colleagues W. Edson Richmond and Patricia Conroy, and David Josephson has oriented me to the complex activity of Percy Grainger. Dan Ben-Amos has provided advice on the strategy of the book, Mary Ellen Brown and Gary Kuris on its audience and distribution, André Lefevere on its Translation Studies dimension, and Sven Rossel on sources for its support. At a key stage Mariella Lansford suggested useful ways to deal with ballads in translation.

The research has depended upon the aid of librarians and archivists in scores of institutions. Notably helpful have been Kermit Westerberg and Dag Blanck, Swenson Swedish Immigration Research Center at Augustana College; David Bromwich, Somerset County (England) Library Service; J. A. B. Townsend, University College London; Barry Peter Ould, Music Archivist, the Percy Grainger Society; Stewart Manville, Librarian, Grainger House; David Meek, Sioux City (Iowa) Public Library; William A. Miles, Buffalo and Erie County (New York) Public Library; Peggy Daub and Margaret Berg, University of Michigan Libraries; S. M. Simpson, National Library of Scotland; Alice Loranth, Cleveland Public Library; Brooke Whiting, University of California, Los Angeles Library; Tue Gad, Det Kongelige Bibliotek, Copenhagen; and the staff of Føroya Landsbókasavn.

Similarly thoughtful assistance has come from the staff of the Swedish Institute and from Mary-Jo Kline of Sotheby's, New York.

I have relied extensively (one might say chronically) on the able help of the Resource Sharing Center of Western Michigan University's Waldo Library. (Such is the longevity of the project that when it began the service was still called Inter-Library Loan, and the volume of the project, I sometimes think, may be reflected in the move of the Center to larger quarters!) Colleagues notably capable and professionally patient with requests for seemingly exotic titles have been Bettina Meyer, Heidi Rawson-Ketchum, Judith Garrison, and Kirk Evans.

I have also had to rely occasionally on the generous help of representatives to do library work in locations from Minneapolis to London: Clifford Davidson, Edward (Mike) Jayne, Grace Shaw, Mary Syndergaard Bowles, Jane Rosegrant, Christian Syndergaard, Robert (Bo) Snyder, and Peg Small.

Books finally exist in the translation of concept to the printed page. Thus I am grateful to Juleen Eichinger of Medieval Institute Publications for advice on the printed presentation of complex information. Kevin Glick of Medieval Institute Publications has responded capably to the need for expert and sustained formatting and flexibly to the need for experimentation and revision. Deborah Oosterhouse and Paul Boldry, also of Medieval Institute Publications, have provided skilled computer entry and revision. I am also indebted to Jennifer Syndergaard Snyder for her skilled proofreading of sections of the book under difficult conditions.

Four people deserve particular thanks for their contributions to such merits as this study may have.

Niels Ingwersen of the University of Wisconsin has provided counsel at all stages and has shared my assumptions on the worth of the Scandinavian ballads. To questions from the theoretical to the practical he has unfailingly provided responses at once critical, insightful, and sympathetic.

Tom Seiler, Managing Editor, Medieval Institute Publications, has made editorial suggestions for improvements in everything from logic to graphic design, always leavened by humor ranging from the acerbic to the genial.

Erik Dal, Copenhagen, has directly aided the project with information, advice and encouragement from time to time. His indirect contributions have been even greater: his signal accomplishments in the publication of and research on the *folkeviser* have enabled many kinds of research by all who follow, and both explicitly and implicitly his thinking on ballad translation has opened doors for the rest of us.

My wife, Ardis Carr Syndergaard, has contributed in many ways. For the book itself she has entered text, scanned proof, done endless cross-checking, and avoided crowing over her husband's sillier mistakes. More importantly, she has uncomplainingly subordinated the routines of family life and patiently accommodated the many unexpected demands made by the completion of a book, even to ignoring the leaky bathroom plumbing.

The combined contributions of the many people named above have strengthened this work and indeed made it possible. Those inevitable aspects still in need of improvement are, of course, my responsibility.

Finally, I am grateful for financial support. Parts of the research for this project were undertaken on a sabbatical leave and on two grants of released time from Western Michigan University. Support for the production and distribution of the book has come from generous grants from the Nordisk Kulturfond and from Letterstedtska Förening.

Western Michigan University
1995

INTRODUCTION

DISCOVERIES AND PRINCIPLES

The traditional ballads of Scandinavia are a remarkable cultural and artistic resource. They span distances that elsewhere become discontinuities: from the origin of the form in the Middle Ages to its survival in the twentieth century; from the nobility to the humblest classes, among both of whom the ballad flourished; from illiterate rural singers among the ballad creators to the learned and middle classes who collected, printed, and consumed ballads so intently; from one nordic nation to another despite the alienation of war and struggles of domination, liberation, and national identity. The ballad is an acknowledged mutual Scandinavian heritage as is no other literature and perhaps no cultural feature except the languages themselves. In its great international narratives, in its forms shared across national lines, in its varying national flavors, the balladry of Scandinavia is a perfect reflection of the cultural linkages of and distinctions among the six lands: Denmark, the Faroe Islands, Iceland, Norway, Sweden, and Swedish Finland.

The traditional ballads are regularly called the chief ornament of medieval Danish literature and of medieval literature in Scandinavia, along with sagas and eddic poetry. A debate over "medieval" here—the roots, not the trunk of the genre are in the Middle Ages—does not change our understanding that the Scandinavian ballad is a major, complex genre of cultural performance, rich in varied scripts of human significance. Unlike most other genres it co-mingles men's and women's creations, and it is one of the few preserved voices of the great majority who were not targeted by, moved by, nor depicted sympathetically in the products of the literary establishment. In breadth of subject matter these works rival the novel and short story, ranging from ballads of an expanded, magical universe with eldritch creatures and bewitchment to more earthbound stories of love and armed conflict, from saga-descended ballads with heroes larger than life to pious Christian legends, from ballads of historical events to coarsely comic ditties. Some may

1

express societal norms and values. Many of the most powerful, below their essentialized surface narratives, treat the conflicts of wills, the transitions and conflicts of the human psyche in love and maturation, and the most fundamental familial ties and tensions. Some ballads offer discrete symbols in the modern sense; some are such distilled narratives that entire sections attain a kind of symbolism; some are compact but nonfigurative; others are discursive. The percentage of awkward, imperfectly realized, and fragmentary efforts is probably almost as high as in other kinds of poetry.

Those who are not familiar with the Scandinavian ballads may gain some sense of the scope of this cultural resource from numerical measure. These ballads comprise 837 recognized and (since 1978) indexed narrative types; many occur in just one of the six lands, some in all (and some outside Scandinavia). A great many of the types are recorded in multiple versions. For the smallest land, the Faroe Islands, population about 5000 at the beginning of the era of ballad collecting, the national edition of the ballads includes 236 ballad types in six large volumes totalling 2618 pages. For Denmark there are 539 ballad types and 6405 very full pages (forty pounds!) of texts and commentary, not including the music volume. There is even one ballad preserved in Norn, the Scandinavian language of the Shetland Islands (here treated in the Faroese section).

From late in the eighteenth century, England and Scotland responded to this Scandinavian trove with great interest, continual discussion, and, beginning with James Johnstone's *The Robbing of the Nunnery* in 1786 (*Danmarks gamle Folkeviser* 408 "Hr. Mortens klosterrov"), a stream of translations into English.

In part this interest and activity were driven by the same cultural forces that led to the "discovery" of the traditional ballad in England and Scotland and indeed across Europe. (Like America, of course, it had never been hidden.) Along with romanticism came interest in new dimensions of the supernatural, including ghost and bewitchment narratives; interest in "new" literary forms and a turning-away from rationally perfected works of orthodox poetics; a need for new notions of the simple; and a hesitant, even fearful approach to the possibility that the rural and lower classes might have language and *kulturgut* that deserved being taken seriously. The cultural centers began groping toward a modern nationalism that led them to use the cultural margins in developing a sense of national identity (Anttonen 21–32; see also Abraham).

Other factors encouraged a special interest in the Scandinavian, especially the Danish, ballads. War and the bombardment of Copenhagen in 1807 had intensified interest and evoked a mixture of unresolved feelings. Some English-speakers were discovering—or better, constructing—a "primitive" and germanic (or "gothic"), and indeed pre-Christian past with the help of these ballads in translation. England was at the peak of empire, and its experiences around the world required that, at some level, it deal with the reality of the "primitive" and non-Christian cultures that it was conquering and sometimes expunging. The world of the Scandinavian ballads was probably sufficiently exotic to provide a "realm of imaginative license [and] moral and political license" (Brantlinger 13) that could serve as one indirect outlet for this need. And with their brevity and assumed simplicity these ballads were well suited to appear in translation in the general-interest periodical literature. This literature grew astonishingly in cultural import during the nineteenth century, as did its target audience: an educated, intelligent, and curious middle class.

But above all what drove this nineteenth-century interest in the Scandinavian ballads was a double sense of kinship. People who knew something of the English and Scottish traditional ballads, which were themselves emerging as a collected and published canon during the century, made the exciting discovery that a number of ballad narratives in English were essentially the same as in the Scandinavian. Many more shared substantial features or motifs across the North Sea. Even more important to many translators and commentators was the sense of kinship of peoples before the Norman conquest. These texts were seen as representing England too, but in the vigorous, conquesting youth of the race, before the various deteriorations in spirit and fiber that some found in the present. This context of earlier ballad translation in fact has a dark and racist dimension (Syndergaard, "'An Amateur'" 85–90).

The interest and the translation have continued, cyclically but steadily, up to the present, with constantly evolving motives and contexts. The result has been a literature in translation of major proportion. Ballad translations are the most important Danish literature in translation after H.C. Andersen and Kierkegaard, with 260 of 539 national types having some kind of translation; the single type DgF 90 "Fæstemanden i graven" has twenty-two translations, in thirty-eight "appearances" counting reprintings. The proportion of ballads translated is lower for the other four languages, in part, certainly, because Danish ballads had been collected and published beginning in the late sixteenth century and ballads in the other languages not really until the nineteenth. But collectively they comprise a substantial literature, as the summary shows:

	Danish	Faroese & Shetland	Icelandic	Norwegian	Swedish
Numbered ballad types translated	259 (of 539)	38 (of 237)	98 (of 110)	44	71 (of 260)
Borderline ballads translated	20	3	1	6	12
Total appearances (with reprints)	1192	83	64	154	260
Translators	90	30	20	45	57
Original sources used	39	16	8	19	17
Venues for translations	183	43	30	57	73

It is an interesting paradox that the translators and presses and readers of the English-speaking world have made this a major Scandinavian literature in translation but that the scholars of that world have not. *Scandinavian Literature in English Translation 1928–1977* by Ng and Batts does not even mention the four most important collections of ballad translations published in its target period. Grönland's *Norway in English,* which essays to cover all Norwegian literature in translation from the eighteenth century to the mid-twentieth, lists five venues of ballad translations; there are at least forty. Elias Bredsdorff's *Danish Literature in English Translation* (1950) and Schroeder's *A Bibliography of Danish Literature in English Translation, 1950–1980* (admirable works) together list thirty-nine venues for translations of Danish ballads; the present bibliography notes 183. The situation is similar for the Faroese, Icelandic, and Swedish material. Even the indispensable *Ballad Scholarship: An Annotated Bibliography* by the respected scholar W. Edson Richmond, who has translated ballads, sees no necessity to include works of translation. A twelve-page, duplicated "Norwegian Literature in English Translation" circulated at the 1994 annual meeting of the Society for the Advancement of Scandinavian Study included only one source containing ballad translations (with no indication there were ballads there).

Some scholarly resources thus include translations of ballads but miss a good number; others perhaps consider that ballads do not count as literature. Whether we mis-take, or even misuse, the ballads when we treat them as literary texts (and there is a debate here), in fact they are very widely used and discussed in exactly that way. The real point is the marginalization of ballad translation in scholarly discourse, however accomplished. Adolph B. Bensen manages this perfectly in his "Translations of Swedish Literature": after giving chapter and verse for translations of other material, he states "in addition . . . a number of books on Swedish folklore have been translated and published" and then provides no citations (249–50). The translations are there and yet not there.

In short, an important intercultural reality is not well recorded by scholarship.

Three experiences in the early stages of this study helped me first to understand that there was a bibliographic shortfall and, more gradually, to understand something of what it means. I started recording translations where any academic would, in books in deserted storage stacks in the few academic libraries with major Scandinavian collections. The search produced modest results, though not in proportion to the dust inhaled. Then three things happened in fortunate proximity. In a public library I happened across Van Doren's *An Anthology of World Poetry* in its 1928 Literary Guild of America book club edition, and there to my surprise saw its reprint of one of the earliest translations, Jamieson's "The Mer-man, and Marstig's Daughter" (1806, DgF 39). Next, after I explained a little about my project to my high-school-age daughter, she said, "Oh, you mean stuff like *this*?" and produced her textbook for a class called "World Heritage." Here were five Danish ballads in translation. And within the year I received a family copy of *A World of Song*, the songbook of the Danish American Young People's League, within a context of comments about the Fredsville Danish Lutheran congregation in Iowa (where the songbook had been warmly used) and its pastors, including S. D. Rodholm. I knew that Rodholm had been an important figure in Danish-American life and culture, but only in *A World of Song* did I learn that the onetime pastor to my family was also a translator of the ballad.

In all this I was learning that translations of the Scandinavian ballads are all around us, albeit widely scattered, and that one finds translations close to home, literally and figuratively, if one looks. That looking later led me to the magazines of the nineteenth century, an important but overlooked venue for translations. Today those periodicals are only figuratively close to us, but the homes of the educated and curious middle class were indeed their destination. The same kind of search also led to ballad translations in folk song collections, songbooks for piano, and other "obscure" venues. (The reader with an ironic bent will note that to their intended users nothing could be less obscure than these venues and that obscurity to scholars often equates with accessibility to the populace.)

That bibliographers and other scholars have not captured major dimensions of this ballad translation is probably partly a matter of choosing the (valid) principle of selectivity over inclusiveness; partly the difficulty of being inclusive; partly scholarly suspicion of popular venues; and partly a matter of scholars being best at finding things that aim to be taken as scholarly. But implicit in each of these is also the factor of marginalization—of perceived lesser importance—of the ballad, of folk literature, and perhaps of translation itself. Scholars would not have overlooked the same portion of the translations of Ibsen's poems.

The "obscure" venues yielded sizable additions to the corpus—Kenealy's "Swedish Anthology" in *Ainsworth's Magazine* and a flock of translations in folk-song books, for example. But equally interesting, often, was the context of these translations, the commentary or the program they were to exemplify. I was sometimes astonished by the Scandinavia, the "folk," and the Middle Ages being constructed. And the effects foreseen for the translated ballads in some books of folk songs were as striking as the uneven and sometimes off-putting texts themselves. If Scandinavia was speaking through its ballads, the English-speaking world was speaking back through its translation and comments, and sometimes the scripts seemed quite different. Here was, in fact, not just an accumulation of translated poetry but an intercultural discourse.

With an increasing range of ballad translations identified I could begin to notice larger patterns. Anyone who works with folk materials in an academic context, and especially with scholarly editions of Scandinavian ballads, will have been sensitized to a preoccupation with genuineness (the absence of editorial reworking) and with version, a necessary common currency in ballad classification, given the variation in this and indeed all folk genres. Why then did so many translators of the Danish ballad choose to English not the texts of the "folk" but redacted texts instead, even after the model, "full disclosure" edition *Danmarks gamle Folkeviser* began to appear (Syndergaard, "Translations" 223–24)? Why did so many works of translation say nothing of the source *versions* chosen, and how could a reader know which version she was reading, in this folk genre that exists in nothing but versions?

The first response was a conventional academic harrumph over these translators' irresponsibility, but on second thought their collective choice seemed intriguing and undoubtedly significant, if only studied and interpreted. For example, might it mean that at some level the translators were giving themselves more freedom to construct the Scandinavia and the ballad folk that were important to them? In a persuasive analysis Pertti Anttonen has argued that folklorists have inevitably, if unknowingly, constituted "the folk" according to the assumptions they bring and the nationalizing cultural projects of their era ("Nationalism, Ethnicity"), and the parallels with the translation process are often striking. It became obvious that questionable translation may still be culturally significant.

And if translators' practices are problematic in failing to reflect the realities of folk literature, what of scholars' practices? For with few (but notable) exceptions bibliographers of translation into English are silent in matters of ballad genuineness and version. (Lansford's comprehensive account of early translations into German, on the other hand, is exemplary.)

Thus observations and surprises evolved into discoveries, discoveries into questions, and all, finally, into four basic principles that underlie this work and its projected applications:

1. Ballad translation (indeed any translation) should be seen as intercultural discourse.

2. Translation and its context are as significant as translations.

3. Bibliography of a folk genre in translation should reflect the basic nature of folk genres, variation.

4. Bibliography of a folk genre in translation should indicate the degree of access to genuine tradition given by translations.

A fifth principle, utility to many kinds of users, not academics alone, was present from the beginning.

These principles and other considerations gave rise to a dozen much more specific desiderata for a work intended to be both a bibliography and a guide—desiderata giving rise to specific features of the translation tables in this work. These are discussed on pages 20–41. But first a more general discussion of some important implications of the principles above and the work that has resulted.

IMPLICATIONS

One result of the principles is a bibliography that makes accessible for the first time substantially all of the written translation dialogue between two cultures for a major folk genre, the traditional ballad. But the analytical guide and the applications foreseen for the work go well beyond the usual implications of "bibliography" and "translation." Some of these differences have to do with the special nature of folk materials, others with the principle that translation represents an intercultural discourse at any level of the phenomenon—from the deliberative choice of a single word to the declared context and interpretation of translated texts to the patterns in collective translation activity over time to the unconscious and at least partly acculturated factors driving the process (Lefevere, *Translating Literature* 125–27).

The more usual concept is that translation is a series of linguistic and aesthetic choices made in an attempt to "realize" or re-create a given source text. We evaluate translations mainly as separate entities, and in terms of their linguistic "accuracy" and artistic fittingness. Almost by definition source texts are not problematized; there is a single best text of Ibsen's *Vildanden* (The Wild Duck). Translations become point sources for aesthetic and interpretive ("literary") experiences; "context" largely means received knowledge about the author or text translated.

In turn we tend to see a bibliography of translations as an accumulation of these point sources from which we take those we may need according to an agenda we bring from outside. Many bibliographies are comprehensive within their defined limits, but usually the compiler has selectively omitted what is stated—or often, understood—to be peripheral: amateurish or blatantly inaccurate work, fragments, "trivial" or fugitive sources, fakes, and the like. (Convenience and time priorities might also figure in the selection.) The compiler's selectivity may save us work, or it may arrogate certain of our decisions, depending on our viewpoint. The prevailing use of a bibliography is hunt-and-pick, and the whole is roughly the sum of the parts, that is, reliable individual texts.

An alternative model, which sees bibliography of translation as autonomous, with its own agenda of recording an entire cultural transaction, is developed in the present work. The prevailing bibliographic model is seriously inadequate for the translations of Scandinavian ballads. What distinguishes folk literature is that fundamental quality of traditional forms which is both potent and frustrating: variation within unity, difference within sameness. "There are text*s*; there is no text," and even the largest printed editions of ballads or other folk genres represent only a (statistically unrepresentative) sampling of an unknown but often very large number of versions which have circulated and will continue to circulate far beyond the geographical and temporal sites of collection. Thus existence in variants is a central reality of the original narratives which ballad translators bring into English. For conventional literature it is different; we know that every translator's *The Wild Duck* comes from virtually the same best text of Ibsen's *Vildanden*. And we know how to find that source text and find out a lot about its circumstances: date, place in the canon, intellectual cross-currents, Ibsen the man.

But if a bibliography leads us, for example, to "Ribold and Goldborg" in *A Book of Danish Ballads*, probably the most widely distributed "respectable" collection of translations of Scandinavian ballads, things are very different. We do not even know which Danish ballad type (number) has been translated, though if we reach the end of the introduction the statements, "Our own two volumes represent a selection from Grundtvig's work" and "*The Ancient Folk Ballads of Denmark*" (71) may lead us, with luck and labor, to *Danmarks gamle Folkeviser*, edited by Svend Grundtvig and others. Provided we are within reach of one of the few research libraries holding *DgF*, we might consult it and, even knowing no Danish, feel we had run our source to earth in DgF Type 82 "Ribold og Guldborg" (2: 338–90). We would still not, however, know which of the fifty-seven versions of DgF 82 Smith-Dampier translates into the ballad we read and thus would not know date (Danish ballads are attested from late medieval times to the twentieth century), class and outlook of the informant (which in Denmark may range from pauper to member of the lesser aristocracy), or geographic origin (life and world-view in a market town may be quite different from that on the Jutland heath). We would still, however, feel confident that the bibliography had brought us to a translation of some Danish ballad text from the great Danish national edition, whose very weight and bulk would attest its genuineness.

That confidence, however, would be mistaken. Most of the sources for the translations in *A Book of Danish Ballads*, despite the statement quoted from its introduction, are not direct from *DgF*; they are rewritings and combinations of *DgF* texts—products of the editor's study, not living tradition. And indeed with yet more labor we would finally establish that "Ribold and Goldborg" of *A Book of* Danish *Ballads* (my emphasis) translates a conflation, in Danish translation, of two *Icelandic* texts of the ballad! ("Ribold og Guldborg" is found in four of the five languages.) Has our leg been pulled? The bibliography citation has led us to a translation of a ballad written in Danish, but how much access has it given us to a Danish ballad?

In short, translation bibliography must acknowledge that *identity*—What's in a name?—may be problematic at every stage of the convoluted journey of a ballad from first performance to printed translation. We have always known that ballads in tradition are multivalent and elusive, but we have been slow to see that even in the formaldehyde of the printed page, the sources for ballad translation may be similarly problematic. (*The Wild Duck* lives in a much more placid pond.) There are plenty of sources of uncertainty, including, often, no identification of sources at all.

More specifically, for translations of folk literature, if a bibliography does not indicate version, source text, and the degree to which the source is rewritten before the rewriting that we call translation, the user will not know what he is finding. The odds are surprisingly high that someone who simply assembles a packet of translated Danish, Swedish, and Norwegian ballads from well-known translation sources for use in a college course would have her students reading mainly translation from texts given their final re-creation by a learned editor, not by tradition. Because translation study has been so preoccupied with "fidelity" of target text to source text, until recently we have not paid due attention to the problematics of source texts themselves. The practice in Erik Dal, *Danish Ballads and Folk Songs* is an admirable exception, but this is the most recent comprehensive collection to be published, and most of its predecessors do not see source-text identity as an issue. And only in Dal do we find full attention to the important distinction among source text traditions: common-person, lesser aristocracy, broadside.

We need, of course, to maintain perspective, to separate the important and valid concern for genuineness of source from the quest for pristinity or Eden that is never quite absent from ballad studies. A source we call "genuine" has still been constructed by certain choices at every step from tradition to the translation we read: the collector's choice of singer or manuscript, of song or text within the repertoire, of performance; the collector's or editor's unconscious smoothing of rough edges and exclusion of integral parts like music or accompanying commentary; the editor's surrounding commentaries; and the like. Moreover, the ballad version translated may be two or three editions "downstream" from the event of recording.

A prevailing metaphor, "mining," for the use of bibliographies implies extraction, carrying away a certain number of useful references to individual literary transactions. The bibliography is simply a source for other studies. Yet any complete bibliography of translation is also a construct worth study in itself as a record of some kind of intercultural dialogue. This dialogue is a collective, cumulative, and ongoing transaction which invites a variety of cultural analyses.

We have begun to see that the collecting and editing of the Scandinavian ballads (and other folk genres) is part of a problematic cultural project and not "neutral" disinterested scholarship (Anttonen 20–31; see also Chesnutt, "Svend Grundtvig"). Would Svend Grundtvig have initiated his standard-setting *Danmarks gamle Folkeviser* had he not been responding in part to the Danish sense of national loss and redefinition of nationhood in his era, and to the initiatives of the Grimms, who were themselves responding to the new paradigms of romanticism and philological study?

Just so has the translation of the Scandinavian ballads into English been a cultural project from the beginning, the study of which is one desirable use of any bibliography of translation. Study of transla*tions* alone will hardly accomplish this, but study of transla*tion*—text, context, and metatext—can. Pioneer translator Robert Jamieson offers his works not simply as interesting poems but as a window to a coarser past felt to be shared to a degree by the British (*Popular Ballads* 2: 86–94; *Illustrations* 234–48). And the most recent major collection, Dal and Meyer's *Danish Ballads and Folk Songs*, is co-published by the American-Scandinavian Foundation, implying a cultural agenda: awareness abroad of Scandinavian culture; international understanding. Wholesome and valid enough, the intent behind this refraction of Scandinavian traditional culture does not offer to destabilize anything.

But as we have seen, translators of the earlier and middle nineteenth century often projected onto the Danish ballads a disturbing Scandinavian past of conquest, "pre-Christian" intensity, and shared racial superiority, in some degree an anticipation of the horrific racism of twentieth-century Germany (Syndergaard, "'An Amateur'" 86–90).

Because they have been by far the most often and earliest translated, the Danish *folkeviser* (ballads) most often have carried such metatextual baggage. But the translations of Swedish ballads in the nineteenth-century British periodicals sometimes have carried their own burden of cultural projection:

> These Reliques of Olden Minstrelsy comprise the most choice specimens of ballad literature, and hurry us at once into the bosom of antiquity, when knights and ladyes faire were every-day personages, and stories of magical device, and glittering cavalcade and tourney, and many an exchanged feat on land and water, were ordinary occurences in life, repeated by the grayhaired to the young, in household epic, and working-day rhyme and listened to with all the trusting fidelity which Childhood accords to the tradition of Old Age. . . . [Certain ballads] belong to a very rude state of society.
>
> (Kenealy, "Swedish Anthology" 112–13)

This is a mishmash of romantic projections, airy vapidities, acknowledgment of oral transmission (though romanticized), and social Darwinism. It condescends in several ways to the "ballad" past. Moreover, the ballad translations illustrating this claim are not very skillful. But it will not do for us to condescend to the claim by ignoring it or smirking it away, for it is part of our past, read and to some degree assimilated by thousands. Notably, it also reveals something of the mind and heart of a man who helped direct the nation as a member of Parliament in addition to translating ballads.

These cultural dimensions of the translation phenomenon should disturb us with the shock of immediate recognition. The celebration of anglo/germanic conquest and the arrogant creation of a lesser but brighter past and of a "simple" folk culture are not merely quaint Victorian vagaries: they are active within our collective cultural heritage, as anyone who teaches a course in medieval epic or in folk culture soon finds out. Here is an arena for translation research at least as productive as the study of lexicon and syntax.

However, these troubling patterns may be surprising even to some who know a good deal about the English translations of Scandinavian ballads, for some of the translation metatexts referred to above occur in "obscure" venues like the nineteenth-century British magazines of literature and general interest, e.g., *Foreign Quarterly Review*, *Fraser's Magazine*, and *The London Magazine*. Probably because of our assumptions about "impermanent" sources (and perhaps compounded by the labor needed to track them down), translations in such venues are rarely known or cited. Silently, and partly unconsciously, we have selected against them and thus limited our ability to study and understand this intercultural discourse—one consequence of the marginalization adduced earlier. (Malmin's "A Bibliography" is a significant but unpublished exception.)

It is true that the numerous ballad translations in these periodicals are extremely variable *as* translations: some are hasty, some misleading (but others careful)—seemingly ephemeral works in a seemingly ephemeral vehicle. But culturally, the periodical is one vehicle no one should ignore: it is "the most powerful literary engine in Europe" to one nineteenth-century editor (Sanders 299). Twentieth-century scholars agree—not just for literature (if we seek the primary sources for much of the great nineteenth-century fiction, we read the magazines)—but for the culture at large. "Civilization may never again have so sensitive an instrument for registering its course as the Victorian periodical press" with its 50,000 titles (North 3–5), and the field has its own MLA research guide (Vann and VanArsdel). From the polysystems or systems perspective we are seeing here the result of a major change in "patronage," the reward system that controls what gets printed and translated in a culture (Lefevere, "Why Waste" 226–27). One of the paradoxes one comes upon in the study of ballad translation is that our (perhaps classist) assumptions about the worth of popular venues may lead us to ignore as obscure and ephemeral precisely what is vitally present and anything *but* obscure to an engaged and growing reading public. (How different, still, the force of the terms "folk," "popular," and "public.") At some level we may also fear the contamination of the literary in an environment of articles about politics, science, religion, economy, and travel.

An even more suspect and ignored venue for ballad translations is folk-song books: "songs for fellowship" and "folk songs of the world" might serve as generic titles for two common varieties. Some of these are indeed as casual or sentimental as the stereotype would have it, and such books sometimes seem cavalier with translations, trimming or amputating them to produce texts that may appear laughably incomplete or seem to sacrifice all sense of the full ballad narrative. But the context that some of these collections reflect—the idealistic mindset that hearing and performing songs from a variety of cultures may help heal a world that is cracking apart (People's Institute, *Six Centuries of Folk Songs*)—is important and admirable, and still unstudied by cultural historians.

Our routine academic neglect of folk song collections as translation venues rests in part on the incompleteness of their texts. There is a nice irony here in that the academy elsewhere routinely honors the principle of completeness in the breach. Bertrand Bronson has insisted that since the ballad is largely a sung genre its texts are not complete without their music, and he has never seriously been refuted ("Interdependence"; "On the Union"). But in practice we have performed our truncations from the moment of collection onward, rarely treating text and melody as an integrated whole. Whatever their limitations, the folk song collections are the only sources from which Scandinavian ballads in translation are routinely *sung*—and in that sense experienced "whole" as most often first performed. And the few occasions on which ballad translations are performed to music in ceremonial or symbolic (and thus inherently significant) cultural contexts—tours of "national" choral groups—are represented by program texts that fall within this category. In *Den norske Studentersangforeningens Koncerttourné gjennem det norske Amerika* we note the power of Norwegian-American audiences' response to the Norwegian Student Choral Union performances (the programs of which could contain ballads both in the original and in translation). The emotional context for a translated text here is very different from what it would be when pondered in the study—but no less important culturally, and probably no further from the emotional context of the performance in tradition.

In fact there may be no other genre in translation that appears in such a *range* of venues in English—from august tomes, to specialist academic articles, to polemic, to songbooks for diversion and fellowship, to an Agricultural Extension bulletin. One might dismiss this as confusion and a sign that the "real" qualities of ballads are widely misunderstood. But one might better see it as an indication of a significance waiting to be understood—as is often the case with apparent disorder.

Thus a central claim of the present work is that ballad translations in sources at all levels of perceived "seriousness" have their own potential significance for culture studies, just as they do for the recent empirical, descriptive emphasis in Translation Studies (to be discussed below).

This principle of inclusiveness is intuitively powerful and has extended itself into four other qualities of the present work.

First, there has been no selection against poetically "bad" translations, since context, if not aesthetics, may make them culturally important. Benedict Wood's translations from "Draumkvede" (Norwegian Type 54) in Eleanor Merry's *The Dream of Olaf Åsteson* are awkward, and Merry's own translation is far from re-creating the visionary intensity of the Norwegian materials. Moreover, both follow the mindset of Rudolf Steiner, who, though fascinated by this poetry, seriously mistook it (Barnes 34–36). But right or wrong, Steiner's mindset is culturally important in driving the entire Anthroposophical Movement (more important in Europe than in the United States) and the associated system of Waldorf Schools (very significant on both continents). Translations that serve or express this world-view become important by definition. Other world-views may assign translated ballads roles that read as faintly bizarre, such as their use in Danish folk dances meant to help rescue the traditional culture and character of the Appalachian highlanders in Olive Campbell's pattern-setting folk high school (Whisnant 78–79, 155–69). But like the Waldorf Schools the folk high school is a very important experiment in American education, and one not yet completed. Like initial confusion, a sense of the bizarre may point us toward cultural phenomena that are worth interpreting.

Second, the work seeks out translations of the comic ballads as assiduously as it does translations of the serious. The magic, heroic, chivalric, and historical ballads have had due academic attention, the legendary ballads somewhat less, the jocular ballads very little. One wonders why, since they have the vital elements, "sex, money, and class," that tend to drive society (Buchan 293). In its inclusion of the comic the present work follows recent scholarly reassessments of importance (Solberg, "Jocular Ballads" and "Norwegian Jocular Medieval Ballad").

Third, the present work, which by definition finds the crossing of language boundaries significant and interesting, extends a little past the conventional boundaries of genre and venue as well. For each language, translations of some ballads and songs outside the national canon are included. Conventionally we say that the borders help define the center, and thus the translation of ballad-like lyrics or ballad-descended singing games or comic ballads which have simply not been canonized should help us define "the ballad" at the core. Or perhaps there is a different potential value. The cultural performances we call "the ballad" are hardly the entity that the single appellation implies, and it may be that for a time we should try defining traditional works according to their positions on multiple axes. Under that model the non-canonical works may not be outside the pale but simply occupy different positions along key continuums (lyricism, literary influence, etc.).

Indeed the boundaries of "traditional Scandinavian ballad" are always somewhat under negotiation; Vésteinn Ólason (*Traditional Ballads of Iceland*) does not fully accept the canon which Jón Helgason (*Íslenzk fornkvæði*) in his turn enlarged from Grundtvig and Sigurðsson, *Íslenzk fornkvæði*.

Including some borderline ballads in translation also reminds us that ballad translation is one part of a much larger translation discourse, and not always the dominant interest. The ditty "Roselille," a relative of the ballads but not included here, has attracted so much translating and reprinting that to have included it would have lengthened the table of translations from Danish by two pages!

The listing of translation venues beyond the expected printed sources is necessarily incomplete, but the range is instructive: archives, dissertations, classroom materials, and (especially) sound recordings. All extend our understanding of the multiform nature of ballad translation.

Fourth, since transla*tion* is a focus and since translations in all places and all degrees of truncation have their own value as evidence, the work includes partial translations down, sometimes, to fragments of two stanzas or even one, and it includes most reprintings. Besides the partial texts in folk-song books discussed above, fragmentary translations may be significant for their translator (Child, Grundtvig), the presence of music (Cagner), the context (W. P. Ker's important discussions of the genre in "On the Danish Ballads" or Kingsley's lecture on the Norse discovery of America), or for illustrations of alternative translation strategies used by the same translator on the same material (Cox's translations in Steenstrup's *The Medieval Popular Ballad*). Sometimes the only translation for a ballad type is a fragmentary one.

The principle of inclusion does not require that we cite half a dozen reprintings in order to evaluate a translation; one would do. But it does ask us to cite all reprintings in order to understand translation in a culture. Longfellow's "The Elected Knight" (DgF 487) does not translate one of the most significant Danish ballads, but it is one of the two most significant Danish ballad translations in terms of readership: in the vehicle of the Literary Guild of America edition of Van Doren's *An Anthology of World Poetry* (and many other editions) it has gone into untold thousands of homes. Mangan's "Elveskud" (DgF 47) from Herder's German is an interesting translation partly in its departures from the Danish original. Its first venue could be called ephemeral, but it becomes many times more potent culturally when Longfellow's *Poems of Places* carries it into libraries throughout the English-speaking world. The reprintings of the translations in Scott's *Lady of the Lake* and Longfellow's *Tales of a Wayside Inn* are literally beyond counting.

The tendency of the inclusion principle to question established practice is not limited to the arena of generally acknowledged translations; it also interrogates our notions of what constitutes a translation. Prose translations, especially summaries, have been almost ignored in scholarship on ballad translation. They seem not quite to count, perhaps because prose is seen as an evasion or cheap expedient. However, access to the Scandinavian material is the point here, not chastisement, and the fact is that prose translations give access to the narrative armature and other key ballad components even if not to the metrical dimension. (And some are not much further, rhythmically, from the originals than are some translations into verse.) The question is not whether prose versions are translation, but what kinds of translations they are, and how they are significant. The prevalence of prose summary translations in the comparative context of Child would in itself make this form significant. And a prose translation may be all we have for some ballads, such as the internationally important DgF 341 "Den forgivne datter."

For the powerful reasons discussed above, then, the bibliography and guide follow the model of inclusiveness, regardless of the nature or associations of the source. There is no gatekeeping, aside from the combined limitations of time, travel, and inter-library loan. Indeed there is no better model for a bibliography of *ballad* translations, for it is Svend Grundtvig's prospectus to the first "scientific" ballad edition that articulates a fundamental principle of editing folk literature: "All that there is . . . all as it is" or *Alt hvad der er . . . alt som det er* ("Prøve" 33). This model still suits the bibliography to all conventional studies, of course, but also to a wide range of cultural and translation studies.

The translations of traditional ballads both share and compound the cultural involvement of the originals. Our material in both original and translation is knit into some of the most powerful cultural developments of the last two and a half centuries: the discovery of "the folk," various evolutions and manifestations of nationalism and national identity, the development of ethnic and regional European awareness, the rise of the middle class, and the evolution of race consciousness, among others. Most of these remain deeply ambiguous and culturally problematic (Anttonen).

Within this context we again see that the collecting and editing of the Scandinavian ballads have had multifaceted cultural and partly political agendas: Grundtvig's Danish initiative as part of a pervasive patriotism; Landstand, Bugge, and Moe's efforts in Norway and Svabo's efforts in the Faroe Islands to discover and cultivate a national identity apart from Danish hegemony; Afzelius' efforts, informed by the pandemic national-romanticism of the era and by membership in an international network of enthusiasts, to produce a comprehensive Swedish collection (Hustvedt 148–52, 161–68, 193–200; Chesnutt, "Aspects" 249–56; Dal, *Folkeviseforskning* 133–48, 177–89).

For the ballads as elsewhere the relationship between the intelligentsia and the "folk" is problematic and in fact would not exist in present form if our learned predecessors had judged that the "folk" were competent and sufficient proprietors of their own cultural performance. Folklore collecting abounds with the rhetoric of loss and rescue (Anttonen *passim*; 20). (In Denmark the early dominance of manuscript as opposed to oral sources complicates but does not erase this pattern.) Even the terms of this field of study have been imposed from the learned urban classes; ordinary people knew they sang *viser*, songs, but they did not know, until more powerfully placed people told them so, that they were *a folk* singing *folkeviser*. ("The folk" seems ever to be more of a protean concept than a unitary sociological reality.)

The intense project of ballad collecting, editing, and publishing associated with these several currents is in one sense an act of massive cultural conservation. But it also accomplishes massive, net *class transfers* of the ballads, from rural to urban, from peasant and lesser aristocracy to middle class, from less literate to more literate.

Ballad translation in its turn is a complex discourse in which these cultural materials are not only rewritten for another culture but also continue the class transfer. The publications presenting translations are largely directed toward a (paying) middle class, not the "folk."

In one sense all these projects—collecting, editing, publishing, and translating—are also colonial activities of discovery, definition, and appropriation, though not of direct removal, by a more powerfully placed group. Although it is a nonce-word one should not avoid using "hegemonic" for the class relationships here discussed. Even in collecting the learned world tends to intervene, defining what within the folk informant's cultural performance is worth recording: ballads, yes; ditties and dirty songs, often no. Although the process from collection to publication of the Scandinavian ballads was a truly remarkable cultural development involving much collective effort and some shared purpose, all involved did not bathe in the warm cooperative glow of common social and cultural vision. It is instructive to follow the relationship between Evald Tang Kristensen, the greatest single collector of the traditional ballads in Scandinavia, and Svend Grundtvig, the greatest single editor. Rural schoolmaster and peasant-born Tang Kristensen, who well understood the worth of his work and of the peasantry he collected from, received condescension and perceived arrogance as well as help from the scholarly representative of the urban cultural elite, and their uncomfortable collaboration can be seen as occurring "on a narrow bridge between the worlds, wrestling over an abyss of class difference and basic misunderstanding" (Rockwell 171, 77–89, 160–61, and *passim*). One might also argue that class has in some way been a factor in choosing Danish ballads to translate: until Erik Dal and Henry Meyer's *Danish Ballads and Folk Songs* one would hardly know, from translators' choices, of the thousands of texts given Tang Kristensen by the peasantry. Instead the translators constructed for their culture a Danish balladry that occupied mainly a manuscript tradition.

A resource like the present one may help reveal paradoxes in these relationships among the learned, the "folk," the consuming middle class, and translation. On one side is an intense concern with purity—the identification of texts unaffected by anything except tradition—and the preservation of those pure texts, sometimes right down to the spelling, in libraries (not in tradition). This is generally linked to a fascination with and an implicit or explicit valuing of "the folk" by editors and translators—and readers, since translators do not work in a cultural vacuum. *Vox populi, vox Dei.*

On the other side is the remarkable dominance of texts constructed by editors in early editions, popular editions, school editions, some scholarly editions, and—notably—the sources chosen by translators. Some of the best known scholarly editors also produce the most influential collections of redactions: Grundtvig (two anthologies), Liestøl, Olrik, Grüner Nielsen. What is "purely" *from* the people is not suitable *for* the people without the mediation of the learned. The paradox is of course compounded when a translator makes his own redactive changes; see the prevalence of "Interpretive" and "Adaptive" translation strategies in the tables. *Vox recensorum, vox Dei.*

Our task is neither to aggrandize nor lament the translating, collecting, editing, class transfer, and paradoxes but to see them correctly and understand them. This begins with understanding our own inherent participation—including the present work—in the process. We then may interrogate the process with the hope of understanding not only ballad scholarship but ourselves. Some will wish to consider how the project might have proceeded more respectfully and freed from reductive admiration.

Certainly to investigate the place of ballad translation in such broad and culturally instinctive patterns will require as complete a bibliographical record as possible, one reason for the earlier emphasis on inclusiveness.

Much of the discussion to this point amounts to an invitation to investigate the translations of the Scandinavian ballads from the perspectives of culture studies and even literary theory as well as in more traditional ways. But it has not required the current paradigm shifts for scholars to see that the translations of the Scandinavian ballads could be studied on many grounds besides texts alone, including intercultural discourse. In 1976 Erik Dal proposed that works of ballad translations deserve study in terms of introductions and commentary; their place in the larger order of translation; the dialect of English chosen as target language; the larger plan of the work (ballads alone, ballads in mixture, etc.); the treatment of verse forms, refrains, and music; relative emphasis among the ballad subgenres; and the role of illustrations ("Oversættelser" 15–26). Certainly anyone who reads Alexander Gray's broad Scots translations must see a cultural as well as narrative and aesthetic affirmation, and anyone who compares the vapid illustrations in Buchanan's *Ballad Stories of the Affections* with Marcel Rasmussen's stark woodcuts in Dal's *Danish Ballads and Folk Songs* will acknowledge that differing meanings are constructed at the metatextual level. Dal also wisely observes that Scandinavians may examine the translation phenomenon with the aim of better understanding themselves ("Oversættelser" 15). As early as 1951 Carl Roos to some degree considered cultural transmission. In "The Translations of the Danish *Folkeviser* seen as Intercultural Communication" I identify the paradox that the English-speaking world has, quantitatively, been surprisingly interested in the Danish ballad but that it has also chosen largely to translate reworked or conflated originals, not genuine tradition. And in a study already noted I examine the images of Scandinavian culture constructed by certain nineteenth-century British translators ("'An Amateur'" 85–90). Some research along these lines will take its place within a larger discourse on the construction of the Scandinavian past and the Anglo-Saxon past; see, for example, Wawn, Shippey, and Frantzen.

DESIDERATA AND PROCEDURES

Given the principles, their implications, and their interactions as discussed above, there is need for a bibliography of ballad translation not only to present information but also to evaluate it. The format developed for this work is called an analytical bibliography: the "analysis" is presented in tables which list every translation found and refer in turn to conventional bibliographies of works including translations and of translators' sources.

The tables are shaped according to twelve desiderata. These reflect both the basic principles as discussed above and various conventional expectations for a work of reference involving Scandinavian ballads. In the present section I discuss what these desiderata are, how (and to what degree) each is satisfied in the tables, specific methodologies, and insights gained in the course of the work. The tables can be used on the basis of the instructions given with them, but those who wish to understand their full implications—and their limitations—will need to consider the discussions here.

1. The guide must be pan-Scandinavian and be keyed to Jonsson, Solheim and Danielson, The Types of the Scandinavian Medieval Ballad.

It has long been understood that any given Scandinavian ballad version may be one form of a supra-national narrative in multiple languages, but until *The Types*, following these connections was a slow, complex process even for specialists, more difficult for non-specialists, and almost impossible for the user of translations. *The Types* (in English) defines 837 ballad narratives and summarizes each; it categorizes each according to narrative content; it indexes each to the national edition; it provides an index to titles; and it provides a bibliography of the most important original sources. In short, it is the indispensable point of cross-reference for any treatment of Scandinavian ballads that goes beyond national boundaries. The work is itself a source of summary translations. The present work is intended to complement *The Types*.

With the two works a user who is interested in any given ballad or translation from any one language can locate available translations of other versions in any of the languages. The combination of works also allows the user (with sufficient patience) to locate all the translations of ballads in certain subject categories: revenant ballads (TSB types A67–72) or ballads in which "attempted seduction leads to marriage" (types D124–28), for example. And to non-readers of

Scandinavian *The Types* can simply make clear the remarkable range of the Scandinavian ballads seen as a regional corpus.

2. *Translations should be keyed to the national scholarly editions and whenever possible to the versions there designated.*

National type numbers and version designations are the common currency of ballad scholarship and discussion. Previous bibliographers of translations, however, have not designated version, without which the user cannot know what access to the tradition the translation is giving.

The seeming neatness in an editor's **A** or **B** version designation can be illusory. Version is an identity judgment, and we have seen that identity is always potentially problematic. The **A** or **B** usually means one discrete variety of a single narrative, but occasionally (especially in *Føroya kvæði. Corpus Carminum Færoensium*) a single number and a single version designation may reflect a complex of two or more related narratives. This reflects the particular nature of the Faroese material.

Version designation in the national editions is not a guarantee of fidelity to tradition. In *Danmarks gamle Folkeviser* Grundtvig reprints Vedel's texts, sometimes as regular versions, even though he often indicts Vedel's editing practices and his texts "conflated from various genuine versions and . . . constructed partly according to the redactor's taste, partly according to his historical knowledge" (3: 347).

When we identify a translation as version **A** or **B** it does not necessarily mean the original is a single "event" (one recording from tradition or a single manuscript text); it may represent two or more sub-versions, conventionally identified by lower-case letters. The sub-versions of *Sveriges Medeltida Ballader* 85A "Axel och Valborg" start around the alphabet a second time, **Aa** to **Af**^{2}. Normally one sub-version becomes the "type," and editorial changes and sub-version deviations will appear in the notes (sixteen pages for SMB 85A!)

An occasional problem with ballad translation is non-standard version designations supplied with the translation or in its source. Christophersen's translations of CCF 166**A** and **B** are designated **D** and **E** in his book, for example, and readers who use Child's many prose translations in *The English and Scottish Popular Ballads* need to be especially cautious on this count. Olrik's *Danske Folkeviser i Udvalg*, one of the most important sources for translators, can be misleading about version; it states, for example, that DgF 133 "Dronning Dagmar i Danmark" is found "only in Vedel" (1: 262), but Olrik's text approximates version **A**, a Vedel source, not **C**, Vedel.

It is not clear whether all recorded texts are created equal in terms of the "distinctness" required to be designated a separate version. It sometimes seems that a text collected on the Jutland heath must stand a bit more apart than must a text from a noblewoman's manuscript to qualify.

To maintain perspective: despite the apparent need to control an enormous material through version designations, they are not an absolute necessity. In Jón Helgason's *Íslenzk fornkvæði*, the most comprehensive Icelandic edition, most ballad texts are *sans* version, although Jón does retain the version designations of his predecessors, Grundtvig and Sigurðsson.

3. The guide should reflect as much translation activity as possible, including venues of all types and at all levels of seeming seriousness.

The rationale for including all material at several apparent margins—and for seeing that much of it is not culturally marginal—has been discussed. The results are the "Translator, Venue, Date" entries, which include kinds of translation activity quite unforeseen at the beginning of the project. Nothing more methodologically innovative than the bibliographical search principle One Thing Leads to Another has evolved under this desideratum. The experience has been sobering and confirms that the academy's uneasy relationship with popular culture extends to the bibliographical. The Cooperative Recreation Services's *Handy Folk Dance Book* was as difficult of access as restricted volumes in rare-book rooms, although it certainly stands in thousands of summer-camp, church-basement and family bookshelves. Neither by initial assumptions nor by the scholarly system I inhabited was I well prepared to pursue the sources this desideratum led to, and a disquieting number of translations appear in the guide more from serendipity and hunches than from subject-heading systems. Knowing that the canon is brimming with ballads about love did not lead me any the sooner to the translation anthologized in Kaines' *Love Poems of All Nations*.

This is an incompletely realized desideratum; a significant number of non-cited translations probably remain in periodicals, folk-song books, children's literature, subject anthologies, and sound recordings.

Of the translation venues other than books and periodicals, not all will be readily usable. The most important resource not cited in the guide is the unpublished "posthumus translations" by Alexander Gray, one of the most important translators of the Danish ballads (Bredsdorff 107).

Percy Grainger's translation of "The Merry Wedding," his own pastiche made from six Faroese ballads, is a special marginal case that raises important questions. There is no fraud; the stitching-up is celebrated. Though the creation of a highly self-conscious and intensely educated mind, the ballad is something like what might (we speculate) be produced by a creative traditional singer: a new, real narrative made from formulas and existing ballad "units." In fact pastiche-making by Faroese is well attested (Chesnutt, "Aspects" 250). This beyond-the-pale pastiche of *ballad* parts might instructively be considered beside some pastiches of *version* parts by a learned editor like Axel Olrik in *Danske Folkeviser i Udvalg*, which have been read by generations of Danish students and in Smith-Dampier's translations by generations of English and American readers as the voice of the Danish folk.

4. *The guide should reflect as much translation activity as possible, including reprintings, partial translations, and prose translations.*

Sound as the principle of inclusiveness is, it has not been made an absolute here. The majority of translations with two stanzas or more have been included. For the smallest fragments, down to a single stanza, the more significant the translator (e.g., for scholarly activity or role in cultural history), the more likely the inclusion. And the more significant the context (e.g., comparative discussion, an important edition), the more likely the inclusion. Translations in Child's *English and Scottish Popular Ballads* would qualify on both counts. Also influential was the supply of other translations; better a piece of a ballad than nothing.

Prose translations and summaries are included here so long as they capture the broad narrative or some significant section. "Prose" conveys no unity on the material so designated, nor an absolute distinction from verse translations. The individual lines in Conroy's translations from Faroese are prosy, but in the aggregate a valid poetic effect is produced; this effect differs from that in the stanzaic prose translations in Hill, *The Tristan Legend*, and from that of the boiled-down prose narratives in Child.

An ideal table would express the relative *impact* of reprintings on the English-speaking world. This has been only partly achieved. The two reprintings of Grundtvig's translation of DgF 537 "De søfarne mænd," for example, give it more relative impact in the table than it probably has had on the world. On the other hand, it has not been feasible to include all the innumerable reprintings of Scott and Longfellow, though this limitation underplays their impact. Thus the tables indicate only the tip of the readership iceberg for translations by these poets and assume some common knowledge of their extreme popularity. (Still, it would make an interesting term project to calculate how many thousands of copies of "The Mother's Ghost" [DgF 89] have gone to the readers of the English-speaking world in a century and a half.) Note also that the popularity of one figure such as Scott can carry translations by another, such as Jamieson ("The Elfin Gray," DgF 52, in *The Lady of the Lake*), down the stream of reprintings.

5. The guide should indicate the presence of integral features: text in the original language, music, refrain.

From first collection through translation what is done with the ballads is usually biased toward the narrative text. Many tunes were not collected, many tunes collected were "corrected" by academics trained in conventional music, and many ballads with tunes have been published in translation without. A similar problem, though less severe, exists for the refrains which pace, punctuate, and counterpoint so many Scandinavian ballads. However, the initial performances of some ballads are in verses without melody or refrain.

The most integral feature of all, original language, may be very important to teachers, anthologists, leaders of "ethnic" activities, and students of translation itself.

This desideratum is realized in the "Language; Music" and "Notes" columns. The indication of text in the original depends somewhat on the proportion of that text to the text translated: the single Danish stanzas at the beginning of Jamieson's full translations in *Illustrations of Northern Antiquities* would not be indicated, while two stanzas of original with four stanzas of translation would be. In rare cases and for undiscernible reasons the text supplied in the original is *not* the text translated; these are signaled in the notes.

"M" in the "Music" column means the presence of readable music in notation. Thus the paradox that sound recordings, in which one hears the text and music components reunited, get no "M." An important limitation of the guide is that there has not been time (nor training) to analyze the genuineness of the music printed with the translation; it may be integral to the original, once integral but now rewritten, borrowed from another text, or composed anew. Thus I take my place with apologies in a flourishing if embarrassed tradition: ballad workers who agree with Bertrand Bronson's arguments that text and tune are integral to each other and who then violate his strictures ("Interdependence").

Translations of ballads with composed music (by Grieg, Grainger, and Sparre Olsen) are not necessarily counterfeits; they may be seen as cases in which the ballad has inspired a significant creation which has its own import.

The omission of refrains in translations is indicated in the "Notes" column. Some originals, of course, have no refrains.

6. *The guide should indicate whether the source version for a translation represents genuine or redacted tradition.*

These indications appear in the "Version" column. Examples of the five kinds of entries that judge genuineness follow:

Ab   Translation of version **A**, sub-version **b**, "genuine."

D (red)   Translation of version **D**, which is a redaction given version status in the national edition.

Red   Translation of a ballad text that has been redacted by collector, by editor(s), or by translator, singly or sequentially, and often unacknowledged.

Red (**F**)   Original translated is a redaction, but close enough to a recognized version, **F**, to preserve many of its distinctive features.

Compos   Translation captures the features common to several or all versions of a ballad type—often a translator's construct rather than a translation from a single text in the original, and often acknowledged. Grades into the conflation variety of redaction.

A basic principle behind this practice is respect for the integrity of the ballad text and the vision of its (re)creator as embodied in oral, manuscript, or broadside tradition.

Redaction is the catch-all term in this work for departures from that integrity. It may involve conflation of material from two or more originals; rewriting of words, lines, stanzas, or the order of components; or additions or deletions of stanzas or larger sections. "Redaction" here is an objective, not a moral judgment, although I acknowledge an aesthetic leaning toward minimal change from original narratives.

Not counted as redactive changes are modernizations in spelling, limited adjustments in word order or phrasing, and almost all of the adjustments made by editors of the national scholarly editions (but see Grundtvig's changes for DgF 95F). Otherwise, the standard is fairly conservative, and in all but the longest source ballads the addition or deletion or fundamental substantive change of even one stanza will usually place that ballad in the "redaction" category.

Admittedly there is a rationale for a more relaxed standard. An editor may drop two stanzas from a version as collected and still have a ballad quite like the singer's. But it will be the editor's ballad, not the singer's, and will hardly satisfy the criterion of respect. Moreover, in practice I have not found a consistent way to assess varying degrees here, beyond the "Red (F)" judgment.

An example of a conflated redaction in an important source is Briem's "Tris-transkvæði" in *Fornir Dansar*, translated by Simpson (257–60). Briem intermixes elements from (at least) versions **A**, **B**, and **D**. A more common redaction is editorial rewriting. A seemingly small rewriting can work major changes in the dynamics of a narrative, as when Peder Syv's addition of a prayer to Christ (DgF 65 "Lindormen" **Ab**) adds an entirely new level of supernatural control to the manuscript version (**Aa**) of a bewitchment ballad. Redaction may be well compounded by the time the translator begins work. An example is DgF 156 "Niels Ebbesen," known in manuscript versions **A**, **B**, **C**, **D**, and **E**. Vedel (1: No. 41) conflates these to form the text he prints in 1591 (DgF **F**). Peder Syv, in his re-issue of and expansion upon Vedel in 1695, adds two stanzas. Abrahamson, Nyerup, and Rahbek's *Udvalgte Danske Viser* (1812–14) No. 94 in turn subtracts a stanza and makes some lesser changes. At their stage of the transmission translators may make their own redactions: Alexander Gray's *Four-and-Forty* No. 21 "Sir Morten of Fogelsang" follows Recke, *Danmarks Fornviser* No. 71 (itself a redaction) for most of his translation but Grüner Nielsen, *Danske Folkeviser* 64–66 (another redaction) for a single stanza and a truncation at the end.

Notably, and significantly, most translations are *not* made from the comprehensive national editions even when those editions are available.

Judging the genuineness of the original the translator has used depends on being able to compare it with a source record. Often this is straightforward, as when *Danmarks gamle Folkeviser* prints a manuscript text and an early redaction from it in Vedel's edition virtually side by side. The translators' own accounts of their sources are often questionable: Prior says the source for the last stanzas in his translation (No. 32) of DgF 101 "Liden Karen" is Geijer and Afzelius No. 3 (Swedish), but his last stanza actually comes from Danish **G**. Too often, especially for ballad types not yet published in *Sveriges Medeltida Ballader* and the new Norwegian national edition, one can only go on general discussions of editorial practices in early and much-translated-from editions. Examples would be Bengt Jonsson's comments on Geijer and Afzelius and on Arwidsson (*Svensk balladtradition* 817–30, 846–54), Erik Dal on Lyngbye and Hammershaimb (*Nordisk folkeviseforskning* 120), Alver on Sophus Bugge, and Richmond ("Editing") and others on Landstad. Even with inferential use of the limited evidence here one often is unsure about genuineness. Thus the prevalence of question marks in some sections of the tables.

A redaction has no tradition, so it is blank in the "Tradition" and "Century" columns.

Editorial changes in ballad texts are usually made clear only in the scholarly editions. Other workers and most translators feel no such obligation, and people who would expect to fail an academic course if they plagiarized a paragraph from an article will feel quite free to include within a ballad conflation or translation half a dozen unattributed stanzas from Jens Madsen's version sung in Nørreby. Great scholarly editors like Grundtvig, Liestol, and Olrik are at pains to prepare editions of *un*genuine, i.e., redacted, ballads for school and home, and Olrik's standard of accountability in his popular edition *Danske Folkeviser i Udvalg* is, simply, much lower than in *Danmarks gamle Folkeviser*. Obviously scholarship is of two minds.

7. The guide should indicate the sociocultural tradition of the source text for the translation.

The terms used in the "Tradition" column: Aristocratic (*adels*), Common-person (*almue*), Cleric-academic (*klerikala*), and Broadside (*flyveblad*), are conventional in ballad scholarship. The compound Aristocratic/Common implies the probability of origin in either of these classes and is a response to a proposed major revision in views of ballad development (Piø). The classification is not parallel: "Broadside" reflects production and distribution, not class.

The first four terms are largely self-explaining. The aristocracy here is mainly the lesser, not the highest aristocracy. "Cleric-academic" (*klerikala*) is proposed by Bengt Jonsson for a limited group of Swedish sources (*Svensk balladtradition*

34). "Common-person" covers everyone else—a remarkable social span. Although this ballad category has a great many versions collected from the peasantry, it is not limited to peasant material; rural cultures have their own hierarchy, and ballads may be collected in urban society.

The tables will show great variation from country to country in this column. If Iceland and Faroe had an aristocracy at the peak time of ballad collecting, that feature is not so coded by editors and collectors. With far the most manuscripts and ballad books from the sixteenth and seventeenth centuries, Denmark has had the most mention of an aristocratic ballad tradition.

The results here rely on existing commentary, assumptions, and scholarship, not a fresh analysis. Useful discussions or summaries in English are in Colbert, Jonsson (*Svensk balladtradition* 855–61), Dal (*Nordisk folkeviseforskning* 426–27), and Piø (327–34). However, readers should know that rarely in Scandinavian ballad scholarship is the issue simply what text came from where. Discussions of sociocultural tradition are often wound into a complex debate on ballad origin and migration and on the waxing or waning of quality as the ballads move among classes.

In his *Nye veje til folkevisen* Iørn Piø insists that the uncritical wholesale attribution of ballad versions found in manuscripts and ballad books to the lesser aristocracy is not defensible, and he revivifies the contention that some of this material must derive from a common-person tradition, sometimes orally performed. His analysis leads him to designate various individual versions in *Danmarks gamle Folkeviser* as representing the "common-person tradition," the "common-person and aristocratic tradition," the "common-person and/or aristocratic tradition," and the "aristocratic tradition," respectively. Hitherto nearly all of these would have been lumped under "aristocratic."

Scholars with an acuity and mastery of the ballad tradition equal to Piø's differ markedly on this facet of his thesis (Jonsson, rev. of *Nye veje* 169–70; Colbert 35–36, 169n). Persuaded of Piø's general position here, but less confident that his methodology can so reliably classify specific versions, I have designated source texts from his "common-person" and "common-person and aristocratic" categories as Aris/Com, indicating the possibility of either origin.

It is important not to essentialize the categories in the "Tradition" column. Ballad types and ballad texts have crossed and re-crossed the boundaries. Meyer's translation of DgF 512 "Nonnens klage" is made from **G**, a version with both broadside and common-person sub-versions. A majority of versions designated common-person tradition are recorded from oral tradition, but certainly not all, and we have seen that manuscripts and ballad books owned in the higher ranks of society may contain ballads collected from other classes. Although terms like "aristocratic tradition" and "broadside tradition" will continue to be used, the *ballads* so identified do not form compact and self-proclaiming categories. We must also beware a tendency to assume we know what it meant to be a "common person" or a baroness in the seventeenth century, let alone how that condition affected one's art. Little of the scholarly discussion allows for the wide variation in world-view that must exist among people within these huge categories.

Nor should the scholarly momentum built up by these terms deflect us from developing other useful classifications—gender "traditions," for example.

What is finally more significant than these sociocultural divisions is that one genre, the ballad, crosses and connects them.

8. The guide should indicate the source work for a translation.

The entry in the "Translator's Source" column is when possible the work actually used, not the ultimate source of a given text. Thus Jamieson translates "Lady Grimild's Wrack" (DgF 5C, *Illustrations* 280–86) from Peder Syv's *Et Hundred udvalde Danske Viser*, which reprints Vedel's 1591 text; the "Translator's Source" column identifies Syv. When Smith-Dampier translates her "Grimild's Revenge" (*Sigurd* 185–94) from this same text as reprinted in *Danmarks gamle Folkeviser*, the column identifies *DgF*. Type numbers and version designations already given in their respective columns are not repeated. Where a translation represents the translator's conflation of more than one source text the multiple sources are sometimes indicated.

Entries are made on the basis of direct comparison of translation and source in the great majority of cases, except that *DgF* reprintings of Vedel's and Syv's texts are assumed to be reliable substitutes. Translators' or other scholars' attributions of source are sometimes followed when a source is inaccessible; sources not seen are so indicated in the bibliography. But neither kind of attribution is always reliable. In his preface Prior has high praise for the scholarly quality of the then-new *Danmarks gamle Folkeviser* and says he translates from Abrahamson, Nyerup, and Rahbek, *Udvalgte Danske Viser* those ballads not yet published in *DgF* (1: iii-iv). But in his translation (No. 32) of DgF 6 "Samson" he uses *both* DgF 6**B** (with some details from **A** and **C**) and ANR 179, and this is typical of his practice for many translations, especially those for the lower type numbers. Even the omnivorous scholarly engine that was Svend Grundtvig misses this translator's redaction when he reports that Prior's number 32 is "from the present edition," i.e., *DgF* (3: 771).

The table does not attempt to give multiple sources for translations which are probably made using both a text in the original language and an intermediate (usually German) translation. George Borrow's probable use of the Danish translations by Lyngbye in his translations from the Faroese has been noted by Dal ("Tyske, franske, og engelske" 88), and one notes that in the "nearly literal" translation of a "Danish Ballad" ("Moderen under Mulde," DgF 89) in "On the State of the Cultivation of the Ancient Literature of the North" (397–98) the translator omits Syv st. 21 just as does Grimm's German translation (No. 30). The practice must be reasonably common, but certainty about such multiple sources is hard won.

The = and ≅ signs in the column reflect cases in which inspection shows that a source text was the same as or similar to that in the standard work indicated but in which inference suggests the text used may have traveled through intermediate editions. Berggreen's *Svenske Folke-Sange og Melodier* is perhaps as likely to be the source for "Peter, the Swineherd" (SMB 177) in Berens, *The Most Beautiful Swedish National Songs* (27) as is *Svenska Fornsånger*, but in the absence of distinguishing evidence the more "standard" *SF* is used in the column for utility's sake.

The principle of clear disclosure of sources for translations would seem self-evident. Students of the translation process, teachers, activity leaders, and others can obviously make direct use of this knowledge, and the practice would seem to give a responsible quality to any work presenting translations.

Thus one of the surprises of this project is that the norm is otherwise, and that clear disclosure tends to be a recent phenomenon. Dal and Meyer's *Danish Ballads and Folk Songs* is exemplary; Simpson and Seemann, Strömbäck, and Jonsson designate sources, as does Karpeles (though her citations for "Svend i Rosensgaard" lead to works which are both, and neither quite, the source for her original).

Attributions of source text in scholarly articles and dissertations are usually clear, and in fact translations sometimes accompany originals published for the first time (e.g., Richmond, "Den utrue egtemann"). Child's many translations are usually sourced.

But among other translators, including the most prominent, there are decidedly varying levels of disclosure. George Borrow's fiction that he learned to read and admire the Danish ballads from a copy of Vedel's *It Hundrede vduaalde Danske*

Viser (1591) that had washed up on the seashore sorts well with his general flamboyance. Actually his huge collection of translations is mainly from the ubiquitous Abrahamson, Nyerup, and Rahbek. As we have seen, Prior, in the largest single collection of translations of Scandinavian ballads, often displays a haziness about source, occasionally almost a smokescreen. Alexander Gray in a way is extremely forthcoming; in an appendix to *Historical Ballads of Denmark* he lists every Danish title (though without DgF type numbers) and the place it is to be found in both Olrik's and Recke's editions of redactions. But only irregularly will the headnote tell us which he used, and it may or may not tell us when Gray conflates sources.

Questions about the significance of this almost generic obscurity are offered in the "Applications" section of this introduction.

9. The guide should provide some systematic description of the strategy followed in the translation.

The "Translation Strategy" column places the translation in one of four classifications. These are defined largely in terms of the relative freedom felt or taken by the translator and in part implement the principle that the guide should help the user understand what access she is being given to the Scandinavian tradition. The judgments are intended to be descriptive, systematic, and to a fair degree objective. They are source-based; the Translation Studies discipline reminds us that other systems are possible. The strategies with their narrative definitions (repeated in "Using the Tables") are as follows:

LITERAL: Follows the original very closely, with such changes as needed to make the translation idiomatic.

CLOSE: Follows the original quite closely, with minor substantive changes, very limited structural changes, and limited "enhancement" or intensification.

INTERPRETIVE: Retains the essential narrative but employs more frequent small and/or some larger changes, and/or tone notably changed by "enhancement."

ADAPTIVE: Changed in substance and/or in structure to the point of changing the essential narrative.

Translation strategy judgments are based on an examination of each translation and its source text (or at least fifty stanzas of each for long ballads). The detailed criteria are as follows:

CRITERIA
(Proportions listed are the maximum for that category)

Feature	LITERAL	CLOSE	INTERP	ADAPT
Additions	—	—	1/20 of st.	more than 1/20 of st.
Deletions	—	1/20 of st.	1/10 of st.	more than 1/10 of st.
Stanza order changes	—	reciprocal, 1/10 of st.	reciprocal, 1/5 of st.	multiple shifts in multiple stanzas
Minor substance changes	—	1/4 of st.	3/4 of st.	any combin. beyond interpretive
Major substance changes	—	1/20 of st.	1/5 of st.	change in basic narrative
Enhancement	—	1/3 of st.	most or all st., moderate degree	most or all st., intense

Placement is largely on a "weakest link" basis; that is, a text is placed in a translation strategy category according to its translation feature with the highest relative incidence. Thus a translation that deletes a tenth of the stanzas of the original will be classified Interpretive even if it has no changes in stanza order, almost no changes in substance, and little enhancement. Cumulative effects are allowed a modest weight, however. Translator's redactions with stanzas from two or more sources are judged against those separate sources when possible.

The features used, the proportions, and the classifications are experimental and obviously arbitrary. There is no consensus system for such applications, nor for that matter on the need for such. The system here is at least the result of several trials.

ILLUSTRATIONS AND COMMENTS

Translation excerpts illustrating the translation strategy criteria are followed by the original lines with, in parentheses, a fairly literal translation of those lines for comparison. *Citations throughout this section are abbreviated to conserve space*; see the appropriate table.

Additions: stanzas largely from the translator's pen. In the present source-based system of strategy definitions this is the most intrusive change.

Deletions: self-defining. Registered mainly at the stanza level but also at the line level when substantial in cumulative effect. Deletions may be significant in various ways. When Smith-Dampier's translation of DgF 337 "Hr. David og hans stesønner," a ballad in which a cruel stepfather puts his adolescent stepsons off to sea in a boat with "mead above and burning coals below," omits any translation of "den ene Broder sovned i den andens Skød" (the one brother slept in the bosom of the other), st. 19, it might possibly stem from doubts as to the origin of the stanza. But that would be a rare departure in her attitude toward Olrik, her source. The omission is more likely to be a bowdlerization based on homophobia. In either event it is an important change.

Stanza order changes: Most common are translator's inversions of two neighboring stanzas or groups of stanzas. Stanzas or groups interchanged over longer distances "count" in the same way. Half-stanzas may be interchanged to form two or more new stanzas with no new lines—actually a change in both order and substance, but counted here.

Minor substance changes: do not singly make notable changes in a narrative, but they are gratuitous and do have an aggregate effect. Examples:

I shot all the king's twelve Jury men,
And *all the twelve I slew*.

Der skjød jeg til den Kongens Lehnsmand,
At Straalen i Hjertet mon staae.

(I shot the king's sheriff,
So that the point stood at his heart.)

"Twas near the feast of *Easter day*

Og det lidte fast mod Pintsedag

—Prior, DgF 318 (ANR), st. 9, 13

(And it drew on to Whitsunday)

Three cross roads are bending	Tríggjar vóru göturnar,
And *one she can descry*,	ein víkur ifrá,
Hervik has gone straight to the barrow	Hervík er gingen á heygin framm
—Kershaw, CCF 16 **D**, st. 27	(Three were the paths,
	One points away;
	Hervik has gone to the barrow)

Major substance changes: The distinction between minor and major changes is a matter of the impact on the narrative, not the "size" of the change. In the following translation of NMB 54 "Draumkvedet," line two is a *minor*, line three a *major* change. By translating *syskjeni* as simply "children" the translator changes the degree of the sin and obscures the echo of the fundamental transgression of Cain—very significant changes in this Christian vision of the after-world:

A serpent and a toad I found;	Kjem eg meg åt podda og ormen,
They *spit fell poison* there.	dei hoggje kvòrare med tanne:
They were the sinful *children* who	de var synduge syskjeni
Had cursed each other here.	som hae kvòrare banna.
—Jorgenson, st. 42	(I found a toad and a serpent,
	Sinking their teeth in each other;
	They were the sinful brothers-and-sisters
	Who had cursed each other.)

In a translation of DgF 271 "Redselille og Medelvold," a story of illicit love, parental rejection, illicit births, and the deaths of the lovers and children, a major change in the rendering of a single line modifies the entire network of societal and emotional factors:

I'm Medelwold's *affianced bride*	Hr. Medelvold haver lokket mig
—Prior, st. 6	(Sir Medelvold has seduced me)

Other changes may be less far-reaching but still major interventions. For example, in Prior's translation of DgF 5**B** "Grimilds hævn" he changes the received name of the principal, Kremoldt, to what it is "supposed to be" on the basis of the international Volsung/Siegfried literature. But it is precisely the variation in features that evolve in international tradition, such as names, that often becomes significant.

Apparent mistranslations are counted as major changes. In "Jomfruen i fugleham" the narrator is a girl:

When that I was a little *boy*	Ieg war meg saa leett ett baarnn
—Cox, DgF 56**A**, st. 1	(I was just a little child)

It has been suggested that mistranslations should be "penalized" more in the schema. This, however, would depart from the descriptive nature of the analysis, which tries to assess narrative import, not punish linguistic or moral error. Indeed, some mistranslations have more the effect of a minor than a major change. And some "mistranslations" are hard to distinguish from translators' choices. (See st. 1, 3 in Borrow's translation of DgF 67 "Ridderen i hjorteham.")

Enhancement is the term employed for decisions made by the translator that do not substitute one narrative content for another (as do major and minor changes), but instead enlarge upon what is there. The ballad tends to be a genre of restraint and understatement; much is evoked that is not said, in terms both of emotional involvement and narrative understanding. Many translators construct texts that are more overtly directive to the reader than are their source texts in these respects, and here would seem to lie one key source of the difference in manner one often feels between translation and source.

Some enhancement is simply explanatory, such as an internal footnote making more clear that a ghost is returning to correct an injustice:

I'm ridin' here for a scrap o' ground	Jeg rider her for en liden Toft,
That was *fausely* sworn to me.	Blev svoren til Fogelsang
— Gray, DgF 92, st.9	(I'm riding here for a little croft
	Was pledged to Fogelsang.)

This kind of enhancement has been called "explicitation" by Lefevere (*Translating Literature* 106–07). Another type is invited by privileging a metrical pattern, here, end-rhyme:

Villemann, in his Magnhild's bower, Played golden checkers *full many an hour.*	Villemann og hass møy so prud dei leika gulltavl i hennar bur.
—Jorgenson, NMB 26, st. 1	(Villemann and his lady fine, They play at the golden chessboard in her bower.)

Some types intensify a perceived mood or create mood gratuitously:

From her *iron-latticed dungeon* little
  Christel she peered out,
And she sees Raven Rune flying
  mournfully about.
	Liten Kerstin hon tittar genom fenstret ut,
	Så fick hon se Rafne-Runé kom
	  flygaande.

—Kenealy, SMB 9, st. 3	(Little Kerstin looked out through the window, She could see the Rune-Raven come flying.)

The demands of a jog-trot rhythm adopted by the translator are probably seen here as well. A similar intensification may be carried by a choice of near-repetition (here with other additions):

She begged so loud, and she begged so long, That at length consent from her God she wrung.	Hun bad ham saa længe, Saa han lod hende gange.
—Borrow, DgF 89, st. 13	(She begged him so long That he let her leave.)

The most important enhancement choice by the translator, however, is probably to make what is *implicit*, called forth based on the common human experience, *explicit*:

He took her up *with little mirth* And laid her body in hallowed earth.	Han tók hennar hvíta hold, grof hann það í vígða mold.
—Batho, ÍF 13**A**, st. 17	(He took her white corpse, He buried it in hallowed earth.)

This strategy certainly asserts more authority over the audience's emotional response than does the strategy of the source.

More showy, though not more significant, is the seeking of intensity or other effects through "enhanced" diction:

Then with one voice the brothers cried:	Det da meldte Brødrene begge tillige:
We've long for *our realms paternal sighed*.	Os længes fast til vort Fædrenerige.
—Borrow, DgF 154, st. 4	(Then said the brothers both besides:
	We ever long for our *fatherland*.)

Diction that is merely stiff or archaizing is not called enhancement, however.

Translators will sometimes employ the reverse of enhancement, though much more rarely. This "counts" the same in the analysis of translation strategy. In the following the translator's understatement gives the groom's haste for the bridal bed more propriety:

And he, from the table rose, and *soon*	Opstod bolde Herr Remold,
was at her side.	Han dvælede ikke længe.
—Prior, DgF 209, st. 10	(Up rose bold Sir Remold,
	He didn't linger long.)

Obviously the neat divisions in the criteria are artificial. In practice distinctions—especially between minor change and enhancement—are often debatable.

This analysis of translation strategy is a lengthy experiment, the success of which will be measured by its utility to various groups of users or its stimulus to further experiments. It finally seemed the most defensible of three problematic options:

1. Present no judgment of translation strategy. This seems objectionable in a work that aims on principle to help users understand the access offered by a translation to its original tradition.

2. Present reactive, inevitably somewhat impressionistic judgments of translation strategy. Various experiments made clear that this would take far too much space and that it "felt" sloppy and was beyond my powers of consistency.

3. Present a criterion-based, partial evaluation of translation strategy that is simplified enough to fit a tabular format.

The term "strategy" may suggest a scope and competence beyond the reality of the system. Thus it is important to emphasize what this experiment may do and what it cannot be.

The evaluation is systematic, with fair comparability for the individual entries.

The entries should give any user to whom a sense of "closeness" to the original is important one measure of that closeness. Leaders developing a program on the Norwegian ethnic heritage will probably not choose adaptive translations, just as they might avoid translations from redacted texts.

The analyses should allow students of narrative to choose translations valid for certain limited uses. They should also facilitate the choice of material to exemplify various translation practices in language courses, courses on translation, and research on the translation process.

The analyses should also alert us to development within a translator's practice and vision: Smith-Dampier's occasional evolution through three stages (DgF 390 "Lave og Jon") or Borrow's early and later translations of DgF 91 "Hedebys gjenganger," for example.

In addition, the analyses of strategy should help us read hospitably. For example, we should expect adaptive and literal translations to reflect very different aims.

This part of the guide is also limited in three important ways.

First, *the translation strategy judgments are descriptive, not value judgments*. Neither a rising nor a descending scale of quality is implied. This is consistent with the Translation Studies affinities of the study (see pp. 45–55). It is also consistent with the limitations of the writer. There may be a handful of people with the thoroughgoing collective command of Danish, Faroese, Icelandic, Norwegian, Swedish, and English that it would take for a truly comprehensive evaluation of all these translations in all their aesthetic as well as other qualities. But none of that group is writing this book.

To confirm that translation strategy is hardly correlated with "success" or quality one may read Halkett's translation of DgF 40 "Harpens Kraft" in Seemann, Strömbäck, and Jonsson, which the analysis makes "Close" but which is stiff and unable to bring across subtleties (e.g., st. 23), then read Conroy's translations from the Faroese, which the analysis makes "Literal" but most of which develop a kind of poetic life. Gray's translations into Scots often make somewhat free with the source, but they have become integral poems as have few others. Finally one might read the translations of "Resan till Österland" in Josef Jonsson and in Edith Thomas. Translators Wirén and Eyre in Jonsson retain the emphasis on romantic longing that is the emotional core of the Swedish original. The translator in Thomas does not. But the adaptation created—the Christian framework, the emphasis on homeland, fatherland, natural beauty—must be given a chance to claim its own validity, and the attempt is as significant culturally as is the conserving translation.

The stance here may be odd and disturbing to those who prefer the more usual model in which a judgmental evaluation of translation "success" is almost always offered, with various other discursive evaluations. To say such an approach is often impressionistic might be unfair, but to call it idiosyncratic would not. What such efforts seem to have most in common is that they do not back the writer into a corner of fixed or even consensus criteria.

All this is partly a question of the scholar's role, perhaps even ego: is the first responsibility (and the most satisfying) to be an arbiter, or to be a student of the translation phenomenon? The second (followed here) assumes that the aesthetic gate-keeping best happens after the translation phenomenon is captured bibliographically and examined descriptively. Rushing to prescriptive judgment may mean that many aspects do not get their due. To avoid misunderstanding let me confirm that not all translations are equally successful as literary works, and W. P. Ker is certainly right in saying that "to bring out, in English, anything like the value of the Danish ballads would require the finest poetical skill." Of course he speaks for ballads in the other languages as well ("On the Danish Ballads" 398).

The second major limitation is that the present analysis of strategy can capture only bits of the complex translation discourse. Left for other studies are stanzaic form, metrics, dialect, diction, and symbolism. (With her single decision not to have the bride in DgF 40 "Harpens Kraft" fear the crossing of Blithe-Bridge, Smith-Dampier vitiates the symbolisms of maturation, gender, and psychic vulnerability in the ballad [Jacobsen and Leavy 30–89; Sørensen 163–65, 182–86].)

The third limitation is that the analysis here is source-text based, an account of departures. Left for others will be other classifications of the translations based on their own character as texts and not as inevitably handicapped descendants of the originals. The most potent translations in our cultural tradition are often not those which have most nearly cloned their sources.

10. The guide should indicate the affinities between the Scandinavian ballads translated and ballads in English.

This desideratum is partly realized in Appendix B, which is based on the concordance of Danish ballads and English cognates in *Danmarks gamle Folkeviser* 12: 112. To give this material much wider application I have indexed it to *The Types of the Scandinavian Medieval Ballad* and arranged the material in the order of TSB type numbers. Appendix B will thus indicate cognates in English for those Faroese, Icelandic, Norwegian, and Swedish ballads having Danish counterparts, but not for others. Time has not allowed for a new analysis of the whole material.

The largely written translation we study here is clearly cognate to the (probably) oral translation of the past, which is reflected in the genetic relationship of the two balladries. If we can successfully interrogate the former we may illuminate the latter, one focus of what Scandinavian scholars call "the ballad question."

11. The guide should meet the standard bibliographical expectations of completeness and accuracy.

This study has worked at including "lost" translations (like Jamieson's version of DgF 265 "Jomfruens harpeslæt," not included in his own table of contents in *Illustrations*) and is offered with some confidence that it includes more than nine-tenths of the corpus. Its presence may stimulate the discovery of the remainder.

The ideal that everything cited in a bibliographical work should have been examined directly has not been met. The inaccessibility or absence in North America of a few works of translation and of several translators' sources has meant a choice between omitting some items or including them on the basis of reports and attributions. The principle of inclusiveness ruled. Works not seen are so indicated, and citations of course are subject to correction.

The principle of consistency is sometimes honored in the breach. The long evolution of the study in concept and its prosecution through brief, intense visits to libraries and inter-library loan have meant that work has not always been done in completely comparable ways. There is neither world enough nor time to replicate some of the steps.

This work began in the conviction that with enough labor and will it could take its place in a series of nearly flawless works begun by Svend Grundtvig and his contemporaries and continued to the present by scholars of encyclopedic knowledge and almost total accuracy.

The next stage was the fall of the elders of the tribe with the discovery that omissions, mistaken attributions, typographical errors, and occasional skipped homework are sprinkled through the iconic works: national editions, popular editions, touchstone bibliographies, exemplary editions of translations. In righteous disillusion I began a file of errors of the mighty.

Fortunately I soon found inaccuracies in my own file of errors—important for the development of a healthier perspective about the study and one's own limitations. This guide is now offered with only the bibliographic claim that it has silently corrected at least as many errors as it introduces.

12. The guide should both facilitate and encourage knowledge in the English-speaking world of a major cultural and artistic resource.

This desideratum is unabashedly evangelical and idiosyncratic, though shared by many who know the Scandinavian ballads well. An important principle in the discipline of Translation Studies is that translation is often a cross-cultural missionary agent.

We cannot experience the ballads even in the original as their creators did in the originating cultures. But the Scandinavian ballads deserve to be heard, read, and interpreted—perhaps as extensions of societal and community values (probably more often asserted than proved), but certainly as concentrated and potent works of art that express key aspects of human development and experience.

One paradoxical conclusion after examining the whole translation corpus is that, despite the enormous translation effort expended, the power of the best ballads has only rarely been captured.

APPLICATIONS

Translating

The present work should allow future translation to be more knowledgeably directed. It makes clear what has so rarely been clear to individual translators: that each effort is part of a much larger translation discourse with both synchronic and diachronic dimensions. Translators like Gray and An Amateur [Prior] have been conscious of their projects in relation to the whole, but this perspective is the exception.

Users will define needs for new translation in their own ways, but the following suggestions are a beginning:

1. Verse translations of virtually any of the Faroese, Icelandic and Norwegian ballads. For that matter, translation from the Swedish has grown very desultory. Only for the Danish ballads are there enough translations so one may target "tactical" translation needs.

2. More balance, i.e., variety in versions of a type. There are too many translations of too few versions of DgF 89 "Moderen under Mulde," for example.

3. More translations of unredacted originals (all languages).

4. More translations of Danish versions from the common-person (*almue*) tradition.

5. More versions "from the back of the book," i.e., later additions to collections. Later-printed versions of DgF 37 "Jomfruen og dværgekongen" and DgF 44 "Hr. Hylleland henter sin jomfru," for example, extend the narrative reach of these types.

6. Complete sets of translated versions of one ballad type, after Christophersen's model.

7. More translations of legendary ballads, an underemphasized subgenre.

8. Experiments with multiple translations and multiple translation models for the same ballad version.

9. Translations of all the ballad types in a language that have cognates in English. For example, still lacking for Danish are translations of DgF 208, 249, 255, 272–74, 305, 446, and 468.

10. Verse translations of ballads now translated only in prose and complete translations of ballads now only partially translated.

11. Additional serious translations of ballads of acknowledged artistic power, e.g., DgF 33 "Germand Gladensvend."

12. Translations to complete our access to pan-Scandinavian patterns, i.e., to provide a translation from each language in which a ballad is found.

13. Translations of important international types still inadequately represented, such as ÍF 38 "Taflkvæði," now translated only in a fragment and at second hand.

14. Translations to complete a thematic "section." Of the rune ballads, for example, DgF 80 "Ungersvends runer" and 81 "Sövnerunerne" still lack verse translations.

15. Translations responding to recent cultural and scholarly focuses, such as gender roles. Has DgF 214 "Lokkesangen" remained untranslated because it is an undeserving ballad or in part because it combines a certain erotic focus with a determined woman's revenge?

16. Translations to reverse the neglect of ballads based in international romance motifs, like DgF 86 "Flores og Margrete," 87 "Karl og Margrete," and 88 "Kong Apollon af Tyre." These have perhaps not seemed "nordic" enough in the past to warrant translation (like the Icelandic sagas derived from continental romances), but their international context does make them important.

Research

A new patterning of information provokes new questions. In addition to its "finding" function this study is intended both to facilitate and to invite research on the translation of the Scandinavian ballads, and ultimately on the translation of other folk genres. An important recent call for broadened international perspectives in folkloristics contains the welcome suggestion for an expansion of the book series Folklore Studies in Translation (Klein 14). Perhaps *studies of folklore in translation* are equally needed. Some possibilities follow; I hope readers will identify many others.

The guide will serve any study of ballad translation which is advantaged by having access to nearly the full corpus. This includes conventional source text-target text comparisons as well as all kinds of studies of the translation process, from its initial choice of material to the model it follows.

Language-based studies, however, are only one possibility. As we have seen, Erik Dal identifies a variety of translation publication attributes, well beyond the translation texts themselves, for investigation ("Oversættelser"). In this Dal parallels and perhaps partly anticipates the discipline of Translation Studies. In the same direction Neil Fraistat has argued convincingly that any book can be seen as a cultural performance that is defined partly by paratext—its physical make-up—as well as "text," and even by its mode of production, advertising, and target audience. A book is an interweaving of "linguistic and bibliographical codes that ultimately constitute each edition's monumentalized discourse" (409–10).

All kinds of historical patterns in translation also ask for examination: cycles of emphasis on certain ballad subjects, for example. Revenant ballads were almost an obsession with translators in the earlier and middle nineteenth century, whereas bewitchment (*bjergtagen*) ballads have been of consistent interest from the beginning. We may wish to understand major shifts in focus over time: early on, the anglophone world translated both Swedish and Danish ballads in considerable numbers, but by the beginning of our century it was translating and reading far more Danish ballads. One may investigate changing norms in accounting for sources, and changing concern for melody and refrain. And one may study the development of a translator.

We need to study the impact of the appearance of *Danmarks gamle Folkeviser, Føroya Kvæði*, and *Íslenzk fornkvæði*, with their "scientific" texts, as potential sources for translators, but also to understand the remarkable persistence and influence of Landstad, of Geijer and Afzelius, and of Abrahamson, Nyerup, and Rahbek as sources despite their redacted texts. There are culture-historical patterns in the venues for translations, such as the heyday of general magazines of literature and culture in the nineteenth century, and almost certainly in changes in the audience for ballad translation. And we should ask how the practices of ballad translation reflect key developments in cultural and intellectual history.

Other large though not specifically historical patterns deserve attention: the re-proportioning, thus distortion, of a national ballad tradition in translation, for example. One who reads the entire corpus of translations from the Norwegian and the Icelandic will find Norwegian balladry made a more comic thing and Icelandic balladry a more sober thing than each is on its home soil. Whence this selection? Some patterns may characterize certain ballads or groups of ballads: why have we insisted (in both original and in translation) on dealing with certain ballads like DgF 38 "Agnete og havmanden" only in redacted forms (Meisling 242–48)?

We need to make and then interpret an important distinction: that between ballad translations offered for their own value and translations offered as illustrations of a program or thesis. Milligan's religious aims and her intention to translate works that "show the differences which spring from diversity of race, temprament, and climate, and yet exhibit that unfailing bond of brotherhood, whereby the Poet-heart everywhere recognizes truth, and love, and the beautiful, and a higher life than ours is here" (v) are far—indeed a whole world-view—distant from the values of a group of nineteenth-century translators connected by a wish to have their ballad translations illustrate a shared racial past of conquest and "rude" vigor (Syndergaard, "'An Amateur'" 85–90).

More largely, and most importantly, we need to identify and understand all the ways in which the English-speaking world has *constructed* Scandinavia by means of its translations of the ballads and the contexts and commentaries in which it has embedded them. We may then connect this understanding with what we know of other constructs in our translations of other literatures such as the Icelandic saga (Wawn).

Finally, we need to investigate the appropriateness of the complex, largely written translation documented here as a model for the complex, largely oral translation that must lie at the heart of international diffusion of ballads—a matter perennially debated by scholars and one at the heart of "the ballad question."

TRANSLATION STUDIES AND BALLAD TRANSLATION

As the nature and results of the present project were becoming fixed I learned of an evolving school in translation scholarship, Translation Studies, whose principles and practice often seemed to accord with my own. The paradigms of this school are most accessibly presented by its advocates in Hermans, "Translation Studies" and in Andre Lefevere's three works *Translation, Rewriting, and the Manipulation of Literary Fame*, "Why Waste Our Time on Rewriting?" and *Translating Literature*. Another work, *The Manipulation of Literature*, edited by Theo Hermans, provides in one book an instructive collection of theoretical statements and practical applications by a group of scholars developing these paradigms in coherent though not lock-step ways. Gentzler's *Contemporary Translation Theories* provides a succinct and useful account of the roots of Translation Studies, its past evolution, its near-identity for a time with the polysystems school of translation (and literary) study, and its possible future evolution as it continues to absorb intellectual impulses, especially those allying it with culture studies (74–143, 181–89; see also Even-Zohar). The recent thinking of this school seems so often consistent with my own that I believe the present guide might serve as an unintended experiment in applying several features of its paradigms, the kind of test-in-use called for by Lefevere ("Why Waste" 220). Certainly Translation Studies expands the present work by supplying a dynamic if retroactive theoretical framework. The guide is, of course, nevertheless designed and intended to support translation scholarship pursued under all theories.

A brief introduction to the Translation Studies paradigm follows, primarily a digestion from the five works noted above. Next the paradigm is applied to the present work, and finally I suggest certain directions for development if the paradigm is fully to suit the translation of folk literature.

The Translation Studies paradigm resists the prevailing normative, source-based, language- and aesthetics-based view of translation scholarship, with its implicit "transcendental and utopian view of translation reproducing the original, the whole original, and nothing but the original" (Hermans, "Translation Studies" 7–9, 13). The mind-set resisted is felt to be idealistic, binary, one-directional, and insufficiently complex, and to produce "an ever-lengthening and ever more complex dance around the 'always already no longer there,'" i.e., the source text

(Bassnett and Lefevere 12). These preoccupations are simply far too limiting and overlook the presence and interplay of all kinds of contextual, intercultural, and indeed translational factors.

The paradigm also resists the marginalization of translation, the assumption that because it is second-hand it must be "generally second-rate" (Hermans, "Translation Studies" 7–8). When this ostensibly marginal activity is performed upon the literature of a source culture also seen as marginal, true intercultural *impact* through translation may be hard to obtain (Vanderauwera). Key reasons offered for this marginalization are the Romantic legacy of seeing literature as "secular scripture"; the Romantic legacy of emphasis on originality and original genius; the Romantic legacy of equating literature with language and language with nationhood and "national genius"; the emphasis by philology on reading in the original; the rise to dominance of university studies of "national languages and literatures"; and the dominance of New Criticism and its privileging of interpretation outside context. Under these massed assumptions have translators become in some sense "blasphemers" (Lefevere, *Translating Literature* 134-37; Hermans, "Translation Studies" 7–8). The marginalization is the more troubling in that, paradoxically, translation is very potent in our culture. For the majority it comprises much of "literature"; it constructs our images of other cultures; it both challenges and aids the evolution of literary systems; it is the venue of "The Western Tradition"; and if we are ever to become free from our Eurocentric, indeed ethnocentric blinders, translation will be our vehicle (Lefevere, *Translating Literature* 6–14, 108–09; Lefevere, "Why Waste" 233–38).

In place of the limitations described above, Translation Studies offers system or polysystem theory: translation is one element within a complex literary system involving a variety of cultural factors and a constant negotiation and struggle among the factors. Nothing occurs "objectively" or in isolation; there is always manipulation toward some end. The study of translation thus must treat cultural factors and the "norms and constraints that govern the production and reception of translation" as well as the source and target utterances themselves (Hermans, "Translation Studies" 10–14; Gentzler 105–08). It is more the study of process than the judgmental application of rules and policing of error. Above all, it must take the functional and contextual, not merely normative and essentialist, view of "the ways in which what is written gets rewritten, in the service of which ideology, which poetics, and with what results" (Lefevere, "Why Waste" 219).

The intellectual roots of the paradigm run to Russian Formalism, with vital contributions from the "Czech school," from Israeli translation scholars, and from a Dutch/Belgian school. It is probably no accident that so much of the development of Translation Studies with its escape from the preoccupation with source text has come from scholars whose world-views were formed in "secondary" language areas and in smaller nations in which translation is a powerful cultural force—"target" languages and cultures, not "source" languages and cultures (Gentzler 74–143, 196–97).

In redressing the imbalance it sees, the new paradigm will inevitably place more emphasis on target text and its function within the literary system and culture than on the source text and on the degree of inevitable "shortfall" of the translation. It also suggests that we discover and analyze the norms of the critic, which are always arbitrary and "brought" to the work rather than inherent in it, whether realized or not (Lambert and van Gorp; Toury, "Rationale" 17). A key strength in Translation Studies from the inception has been its emphasis on the descriptive, its insistence on the empirical realities of translation and translations in the world, as a prerequisite to or even a replacement for normative-aesthetic studies. Accordingly, coherent systems for descriptive and analytical study have appeared (Gentzler 92–93; Toury, "Rationale"; Holmes). Pseudotranslations—non-translated works claiming or understood to be translations—may be as important as real translations once we are able to see them as evidence of the target culture's wishes or restraints, not simply of the writer's perfidy (Toury, "Translation"; Hermans, "Translation Studies" 13).

Within the polysystem, translation practice will be constrained by the receiving culture's ideology, poetics, universe of discourse, and language (Hermans, "Translation Studies" 10–14). Patronage—those people or market forces who commission, accept, or support the publication of translations—in effect establish "the ideological parameters of the acceptable" (Lefevere, *Translating Literature* 116–18; Lefevere, *Translation* 11–25). What is too upsetting to understood norms simply will not appear. Poetics—"the dominant concept of literature in the target culture," the "inventory of literary devices, genres, motifs, symbols, prototypical characters and situations"—can also affect whether a work is translated at all, regardless of its value in the source culture and its poetics (Lefevere, *Translating Literature* 87; Lefevere, "Why Waste" 229). The universe of discourse, "the knowledge, the learning, but also the objects and customs of a certain time" in the source culture and text, will constrain not so much the choice for translation as the process of recreating a work for an inevitably somewhat different universe of discourse in the target culture (Lefevere, "Why Waste" 232–33; Lefevere, *Translating Literature* 87, 114–18). Only at the final level, language, do we come to the conventional domain of the study of translation.

The strategies adopted by the translator may reveal perceived differentials in authority, power, and status between source and target cultures. Edward Fitzgerald's condescending "It is an amusement for me to take what liberties I like with these Persians who (as I think) are not Poets enough to frighten one from such excursions, and who really do want a little Art to shape them" would hardly have been applied to a text and poet representing classical culture (quoted in Lefevere, *Translating Literature* 119).

Important to the Translation Studies paradigm is the concept of *rewriting*, the essential activity of any writing that "claims to represent" another writing (Lefevere, *Translating Literature* 138). Most will agree that translation belongs here, but some may resist accepting "interpretation, criticism, historiography, the putting together of anthologies" as further examples (Lefevere, "Why Waste" 233). But if the key is the claim to *represent*, it is probably irrefutable that these activities qualify. All these rewritings, including translation, are important as the constructors of "literary greatness" and taste in a culture, as reinforcers or subverters of prevailing ideologies or schools, and as guides to the great nonprofessional reading public (Lefevere, "Why Waste" 234–38; Hermans, "Translation Studies" 13–14).

In these functions and others translation ultimately serves as acculturation (Lefevere, *Translating Literature* 11, 127), and indeed Translation Studies seems to be moving toward intersections with the complex of scholarly activity we call culture studies. In an important critique Snell-Hornby calls for students of translation to move their focus from "'text' as a translation unit to 'culture'" (85).

The Translation Studies paradigms have a particular synergy with the present work and probably with the bibliography and study of translations of oral-traditional literature generally. Certainly, if the chief aim of a bibliography of ballad translations were simply to facilitate source text-target text normative analyses, a great deal of the information in the present work, and even more of the labor, would be pointless. Certainly comparisons based on language and aesthetics have an important place, and this guide will provide such studies with several times more resources than they have had. But research that ends with such comparisons has stopped far short of what might be learned under the expanded potential of the new paradigms: insights into the process of acculturation, into our cultures, and thus even into ourselves, as well as into bare texts. Not to utilize this potential is to be complicit in evading the complexity of intercultural communication.

The following section will discuss some of the synergistic relationships between Translation Studies and the present project, most with the potential for interesting research.

Translation Studies is intuitively persuasive in arguing that one cannot evaluate the "success" of a translation event wholly in the abstract without some sense of context, use, and audience expectation. The bare-bones stanzaic translations I sometimes make for my students are appropriate for their needs—to understand the narrative events and the "spareness" of Danish and Swedish ballads—and none of us expects that the translations will provide a more comprehensive poetic experience. I am not a poet, and the students know they get either my creaky translation or none at all. The prose translations (by Sverrir Hólmarsson) provided by Vésteinn Ólason in his *Traditional Ballads of Iceland* carry a similar translational rationale somewhat further. He makes ballad narratives, though not poetry, accessible to a very wide range of readers, including scholars of narrative. Neither of us feels he has failed to protect "the 'legitimate rights' of the original," and Vésteinn in fact deserves great credit for his "translational solution" to the "translational problems" (Toury, "Rationale" 26) of limited energy on the one hand and the daunting task of selecting from a large corpus of ballad types in the original on the other (a standard problem in translating folk literature). By opting for the more-readily produced prose translations, however "inadequate" to some mind-sets, he has been able to make available in English almost the entire corpus of Icelandic ballads, a remarkable benefit to anglophone readers. If we think in polysystem terms of competing and negotiating desiderata (especially utility to the target audience), we can *describe* Vésteinn's solution as one interesting variety of "equivalence" (Lambert and van Gorp 45). He has forestalled no one from undertaking other, poetic translations, and indeed one effect of his prose translations within the target culture might be a missionary one, to stimulate the production of poetic translations.

The marginalized status of translation as seen in the paradigm parallels the perceived marginal status of most folklore, including folk literature, in both the official and the general culture (Bronson, "All This for a Song?"). One overt aim of the present work is to resist a compound marginalizing—of translation, of the ballad, and of the "ballad folk"—in part by simple presence of the work, in part by the expansion of the corpus, and in part by "rewriting" the ballads in this introduction, that is, asserting their worth.

However, with almost any variety of folk literature marginalization becomes a complicated matter. While the marginalization of translation may well be laid at the door of the Romantic movement, folklore stands in a more ambiguous relationship with romanticism. Certainly without the new focus on nationhood and "folk" that was at least coterminous with romanticism, much of the folklore collected in the nineteenth century—including most of our Scandinavian ballads—would hardly have been recovered (Anttonen 21-28). But folk literature, with its multitude of texts sampling a theoretically infinite number of performances for each "work," stands in tension with the Romantic impulse to sacralize Text. Moreover, the Romantic privileging of creative genius is difficult when a given oral-traditional work has a series of usually anonymous creators and when even the recorded performer may be anonymous because collectors, following various cultural codes, did not respect person, class, or occasion enough to record these facts.

The systems viewpoint calls for study of the role of translations in the target culture, among other interactions. My analysis of certain nineteenth-century English translations of the Danish ballads may be seen as an (unknowing) answer to that call, finding that the translations were often used to help project a "warrior past" for England—as well as an enlightened past! ("'An Amateur'" 85–90). But these results depended on first solving the most basic scholarly problem of all: knowledge *of* the translations. Many of the magazine articles in which they were contained were largely unknown to modern scholarship. Thus the principle of inclusion rather than selection in the present guide: "ephemeral" venues for ballad translation contain culturally significant material, quite apart from its aesthetic worth, exactly as the paradigm has it.

According to the systems approach the study of translations can yield other kinds of knowledge about the culture as well. The publication of translations may help in "preserving the self-image of the target culture" and in serving certain ideologies (Lefevere, *Translating Literature* 125; Lefevere, "Why Waste" 219–20), but it may also help *create* certain self-images (Syndergaard, "'An Amateur'" 85–90).

Among the most interesting claims of Translation Studies is that translation practice and empirical translation phenomena may help reveal the self-perceived prestige and centrality of the target or receiving culture. Fitzgerald's dismissive statement toward the poetics and culture of "these Persians" (quoted above) is virtually paradigmatic for the cultural condescension identified by Lefevere, (*Translating Literature* 118–20), and suddenly we realize that it also may explain a proportion of the "adaptive" translating and the use of redacted source texts for the Scandinavian ballads: "these [folk] who . . . are not poets enough . . . really do want a little Art to shape them" (my substitution). We must ask whether the translators' intrusive choices are a matter of vision, or taste, or of condescension for the source singers, the source poetic, and the source culture. The potential for

this kind of analysis is precisely one reason to design a bibliography of translations from folk literature to include the seemingly "bad" translations.

Such design criteria in one sense simply restate the *descriptive* principle of
Translation Studies. The present work seeks to make the descriptive tabular. Some
of the information in the translation tables exemplifies Lambert and van Gorp's
"general macro-structural features" (48–49). Other descriptive information
includes works often thought subliterary, and partial works, even very fragmentary
translations (Lambert and van Gorp 50–51). The utility of these bits was
discussed earlier; in the larger view, once included they become an option opened
to (conceivably wiser) scholars in the future. Fragmentary translations may be as
useful as full ones for a central task under the new paradigm: the study of
"solutions to translational problems" and the identification of an "overall concept
of translation" (Toury, "Rationale" 21–22). (An interesting parallel: the early
cultural decisions to collect and publish folk material were vexed ones because
people resisted on the grounds that this stuff in its empirical reality was trivial,
deteriorated, and obviously not worth the effort.) The suggestion that even pseudo-
translation is a culturally revealing part of the empirical data (Toury, "Rationale"
20–21) is applicable to "Monk" Lewis's smoke-and-mirrors presentation of his
translations of Danish ballads.

My investigation of ballad translation as intercultural communication is one
example of the results one may generate by taking a broadly descriptive look at the
phenomena of translation and identifying the questions that the material itself
seems to generate ("Translations"). That study coheres with the recent interest in
shifting Translation Studies from a focus on texts to a focus on cultures (Snell-
Hornby). It also illustrates the remarkable complexity of the translation of folk
materials, where sources are normally multiple and often redacted.

The Translation Studies concept of "rewritings" has an intuitive affinity for
a traditional genre like the ballad, if only because we understand each re-creation
within a tradition to be a kind of rewriting. Each is the singer's or reciter's claim
to "represent" what he or she knows as "Liti Kjersti" or "Hermundur illi" or
"Riddar Tynne." But there are other more direct rewritings. While each translation
is obviously a rewriting, a surprising number of the *source* texts are editorial rewritings, texts in some way redacted or conflated from the versions as recorded.
These make the culturally interesting implicit claim of better representing tradition
than the products of tradition could do. An important part of the labor in the present guide has gone into determining when source texts are editorial rewritings—
empirical data largely ignored hitherto in translation bibliography. In both the pre-

sent work and my "Translations" I have posed the central cultural question as to why the anglophone world has chosen rewritten sources from which to translate.

Another intermediate layer of rewriting is the German translations of Scandinavian ballads, from which some English translations are made (Lewis, Mangan, An Amateur). A third mode of rewriting is metatextual: the claims in introductions, commentaries, and notes to represent the source culture, the ballad folk, or the nature of the source ballads themselves (Dal, "Oversættelser"; Syndergaard, "'An Amateur'" 85–90). A scholarly preoccupation with the immediate source text-target text transaction ignores a culturally significant phenomenon: the translator often presents these target texts not as self-sufficient works but as illustrations in a construction of ancient Scandinavian culture (Borrow and Bowring, for example).

The Translation Studies emphasis on patronage, all those forces "which help or hinder the writing, reading, and rewriting of literature" (Lefevere, "Why Waste" 227) will reinforce the principle in this bibliography of including the full range of translation venues, including seemingly second-class ones such as textbooks and popular anthologies. The patronage decisions of editors, publishers, and the marketplace have ultimately helped form our taste and indeed our world-view. Essentially ignored or very selectively included in previous bibliographical work on ballad translation, all anthologies and textbooks become significant immediately they are seen in terms of their reach and audience (Syndergaard, "Translations"). Earlier we saw something of the range in such works. The roles of the translated Scandinavian ballads within these larger cultural documents have yet to be studied. Is the paucity of anthologies of translated Norwegian, Icelandic, and Faroese ballads a patronage decision or an availability constraint? If it is the market or a cultural ideology that has found mainly Danish ballad translations to be desirable or useful, why so?

The ballad is largely at arm's length from what Translation Studies would call the dominant (anglophone) culture's poetics at the beginning of the nineteenth century—that is, neoclassical in stance and "poetic" in diction. To some degree the ballad translations of that century and this reflect an evolving poetics and perhaps some acceptance of the source ballads' poetics. For example, George Borrow's translation practice evolves from his unwieldy and ornate poetic diction in *Targum* (1835) to a "tougher" and more restrained language in at least some of his much later published and presumably more revised translations in *Works* (vols. 7–9). The inclusiveness and the empirical features of the present guide invite the study of the poetics dimension.

Other, more problematic phenomena fall under the Translation Studies "poetics" head, above all the ambiguous assessment of the poetic worth of the ballads by translator after translator—a doubleness of mind that runs back at least to Sidney's apologetic praise for "the olde song of Percy and Duglas" in *An Apology for Poetry.*

The very decision to make and publish a translation affirms a powerful worth in the material, and one senses an attraction to and enthusiasm for it, but again and again the translator also feels defensive about its simplicity, "rudeness," and seeming lack of the usual markers of literary meaning. We must be seeing some form of what the Translation Studies paradigm would call a "subversion of the dominant poetics" process here, but it seems much less conscious than the paradigm has envisioned, at least until recently (Gentzler 194–95). Yet another application of the "poetics" viewpoint is to ask why *this* genre is so much more important to the target culture than are some other folk song genres, such as the lyric.

For all its applicability to ballad translation, the Translation Studies paradigm is not yet a perfect match. In the following section I suggest areas for development in the paradigm on the basis of the empirical realities of the Scandinavian ballads and their translations. Such development will almost certainly better suit the paradigm to translation of folk or oral-traditional literature generally.

The descriptive component of the paradigm needs further development to cover the complex and elusive matter of translation *source*—which, as we have seen, is often not acknowledged and often an editorial rewriting. A related problem not true of other translation is the tendency of translators to make their own conflations from various source versions, thus "rewriting" on *both source and target sides* of the process. The conventional assumption of unitary and non-problematic source simply does not hold for the Scandinavian ballad translations. All this suggests introducing into the paradigm an additional question: in what way has the source culture manipulated traditional texts before the target culture begins its operations? The paradigm may also need a slight enlargement to allow for the complexity of attitudes within the target culture itself toward the ballads and translations—a mixture of subversion of the prevailing poetics and yet unease over the alternative poetic.

In three additional senses the Translation Studies paradigm needs to be made more complex to cover the particular realities of this translation corpus. First, it needs to allow for the fact that in this international genre some Scandinavian ballad types already exist in English (or vice versa)—translation rewritings of unknown age and provenance. DgF 83 "Kvindemorderen" has its counterpart in Child 4 "Lady Isabel and the Elf-Knight," DgF 340 "Svend i rosensgaard" in Child 13 "Edward," and so forth. Thus sometimes a translation is not made to introduce a ballad to the target culture but made because it already exists there—a prior translation, in a sense, which guarantees an interest in newer translations. In fact, the Scandinavian and British balladries, in their twenty to thirty very close narrative pairs, offer Translation Studies a corpus of translations in which, despite nearly two centuries of the most varied scholarly labors, *source versions and target versions cannot certainly be determined.* What the discipline might do with this empirical reality is an interesting question.

Second, the paradigm perhaps needs to allow more specifically for the shifts in social class discussed earlier: ballad translating continues the double transfer of cultural performance from both the lesser aristocracy and the lower socioeconomic classes to the middle class. At present Translation Studies seems to concentrate on professional (literati) and non-professional (largely middle class) consumers of literary products.

The final adjustment needed in the paradigm comes at its intersection with the present guide and indeed all bibliographies of translations (not translations of folk genres only). Nowhere does the paradigm emphasize that simply finding the translations of a given sort and bringing them into the international scholarly discourse under bibliographic control may be an extremely hard and in fact novel undertaking. That, however, has been my experience in trying to provide the fullest possible accounting. Translation Studies loses much of the power promised by its empirical and descriptive bases if it is satisfied with less than the full corpus of translation events. The tendency seems to be to select certain translations as empirical events for discussion, but that is not the same as studying the full empirical reality. The smaller and "newer" the receiving society, the more manageable and less problematic it may be to *know* a given translation corpus and to control it bibliographically, so the problem may not have been made central by, for example, scholars from Israel who have led the way in polysystems thinking. But the older, the more numerous, the less canonical, and (paradoxically) often the more popular the material and the translations, the more they tend to slip into the bog of marginality and little notice. The complexities associated with borderline-canonical forms are certainly acknowledged, but one does not observe a heavy emphasis on such material in Translation Studies scholarship.

These adjustments to the paradigm are driven by the peculiar characteristics of the traditional Scandinavian ballads and their translations, but they will apply widely to translation of other folk genres. Determining the precise source, and the proximity to "genuine" tradition, may be as hard for a translation of one of the Grimms' *märchen* as for a Danish ballad: Which edition? What degree of redaction? How "traditional" as originally collected? Maria Tymoczko has initiated a searching discussion of the implications of the unique qualities of oral-traditional material for Translation Studies, and the present comments will make their own contribution. But more voices are needed.

NOTES ON INTRODUCTIONS IN ENGLISH TO THE SCANDINAVIAN BALLADS

Some readers will understandably wish to have a general orientation to the Scandinavian ballads they find recorded here in translation. This balladry is certainly the most numerous one preserved in print, is the most closely connected to Anglo-American balladry, and is arguably the best as human art. Hildeman lamented in 1968 that "there is no extensive modern introduction to the Scandinavian ballad to be found in English" (xvii), and no one has been bold enough to try to fill that lack since. The scope and complexity of the subject, not to mention the lack of consensus and the loose ends, limit the task to those who are most intellectually nervy and who have workhorse constitutions.

Whether for that reason or others, this work cannot fill the need; but it will guide the reader to existing introductions in English in which the synthesizing and descriptive side is not too much outweighed by speculation or polemic.

For some readers this need will be satisfied in the brief but concentrated and authoritative discussions in standard references such as the *Dictionary of the Middle Ages* and *Medieval Scandinavia: An Encyclopedia*. These articles are by recognized authorities, and they provide good bibliographical starting points, at least if the reader is not limited to English. *Medieval Scandinavia* has brief articles on each ballad area; *Dictionary of the Middle Ages* has a general discussion and one on Faroese ballads. However, many smaller libraries may not own these works.

Sven Rossel accomplishes more of Hildeman's "modern introduction" than one could expect in the very small introduction to a small and very useful book, *Scandinavian Ballads*, in the WITS series. The comments combine learning, selectivity, restraint, and scope, within the context of a judicious sampling of ballads in translation, and at a modest price. But twelve pages is after all severely limiting. Library holdings will be scattered. Erik Dal provides an ideal model in the slightly longer introduction to *Danish Ballads and Folk Songs*, but this is limited to the Danish material. Dal is competence itself, and he projects no particular program onto the ballads or the people who produced them. This book is in the collections of both general and academic libraries.

More people, however, have probably met Scandinavian ballads in English in Axel Olrik's *A Book of Danish Ballads* than in any other source. Here E. M. Smith-Dampier translates Olrik's *Danske Folkeviser i Udvalg*—important as the dominant popular and school edition in Denmark and as the work of the second Danish editor of *Danmarks gamle Folkeviser* and the heir of Svend Grundtvig. The introduction requires some caution, as do the texts. It sometimes has a good eye for the potency of the ballads: in the best "we find dread and horror over the involving of the wild forces which so easily bring unhappiness and are so uncontrollable by men" (58). But the introduction can be classist and somewhat over-preoccupied by the historical ballads. In common with a good deal of ballad commentary it posits a universe compounded of the world of the ballads and the real world but admitting the complexity of neither.

The largest introduction to the Danish ballads is in the largest collection, Prior's *Ancient Danish Ballads*. Few will begin with this important but not widely distributed work—and perhaps that is just as well. To his credit Prior is often a conduit to the encyclopedic commentary in *Danmarks gamle Folkeviser*, although he is more likely than Grundtvig to adduce parallels from the romance languages. But there is a frustrating mixture of good judgment (resistance to the tendency to make ballad origins extremely early) and an erratic, even willful quality (his projections of women's roles onto the Middle Ages).

Alexander Gray's collections of translations from the Danish ballads, *Four-and-Forty* and *Historical Ballads of Denmark*, have introductions useful more for Gray's wit, perspective on translating, and trenchant comments on "the historical" than for orientation to the genre.

Scarce, unfortunately, will be the best introduction to the Icelandic ballads in English, Vésteinn Ólason's *The Traditional Ballads of Iceland*. Although the translations are in prose, the reader will have virtually all the Icelandic ballads in English—a unique level of access. The general orientation falls mainly in the introduction. Vésteinn always works from evidence and a wide knowledge of the scholarship.

The other lands have nothing comparable. Mortan Nolsøe, "Ballads and their Cultural Setting in the Faroe Islands" is a useful discussion by a Faroese scholar, though in a scarce journal. Michael Chesnutt's "Aspects of the Faroese Traditional

Ballad in the Nineteenth Century" gives an excellent picture of the context and evolution of the genre. Nora Kershaw's few pages of orientation are preferable to Smith-Dampier's more romanticized discussion in *Sigurd the Dragon-Slayer*. For the ballads in Swedish one can piece together the few pages in Alrik Gustafson's *A History of Swedish Literature* and the English summary in Jonsson's *Svensk balladtradition*, and for the Norwegian ballads one finds still fewer pages in Beyer, *History of Norwegian Literature*.

Other works in English discuss the Scandinavian ballads more largely but with important limitations in approach. Hildeman's essay (cited above) has excellent breadth, but it concentrates more on scholars' work on the ballads than on the ballads themselves. *European Folk Ballads* by Seemann, Strömback, and Jonsson has much in little (two pages) on the Scandinavian ballad area, embedded in a succinct discussion of pan-European ballad traits, and it includes ballads translated from each nordic language. In *European Balladry* William Entwistle has the same ambitious purview but far more discussion. His "Nordic" ballad area runs from Iceland to Hungary to Poland to America[!], but his descriptive discussions are helpful, and they employ the useful discipline of reference to the ballads themselves. Sometimes he can simply be wrong—the ballads of Iceland are "few and insignificant" (206), or interpretively awry—Germand Gladen- svend's feather-cloak in DgF 33 establishes that the "the whole legend is pre- Christian" (220). Entwistle's discussion is dominated by the Danish ballads, and his sources have important limitations (387-88). The two books on European balladry will be available in many academic and some public libraries.

In *Heroic Sagas and Ballads* Stephen Mitchell discusses the Scandinavian ballad as a medieval form and presents briefly but cogently a thesis on the origins and broad development of the heroic ballads and other ballad genres (Chapter 4).

Johannes Steenstrup's *The Medieval Popular Ballad*, translated in 1914 from his important *Vore folkeviser fra middelalderen* (1891), will be reasonably accessible in its augmented paperback reprint of 1968. Like Entwistle's this is an extensive work of uneven value to the newcomer. Again it concerns mainly the Danish ballads (as being the most numerous, first edited, and best[!]), but there is some reference to the other balladries. The declared aim is "to describe what our ballads of the Middle Ages were like originally, and to determine their proper form and subject matter" (1). And read with an eye to the many ballad excerpts and the multi-faceted discussion of "form and subject matter," not to mention refrain, diction, narrative, stance, style, metrics, and ballad world-view, the book can certainly help tell the neophyte what to expect in Scandinavian ballads. Occasionally Steenstrup will point toward their particular power: the ballads of magic "seem . . . to have looked deepest into the human heart" (103). And his emphasis on the spareness and distilled dramatic structuring of the ballads (212-36) would still be endorsed by most critics. But given Steenstrup's polemic, where every descriptive angle is made to serve his preoccupations with origins, "pure" medieval forms, the necessary deterioration of tradition, and the artistic inadequacies of the lower classes, the book siphons attention and energies into issues that have already consumed too much of both.

By now even the neophyte has deduced that an astonishing labor has gone (and continues to go) into collecting, editing, and publishing Scandinavian ballads. The Danish national edition consumed 124 years and the efforts of four main editors and six assistant editors. It would be natural, even if impudent, to ask why: what value to *us* in reading this expropriated verbal art? In what way will these ballads in translation have *meaning* for us? In 1961 Holger Nygard called for us to study the ballads seriously as literary art, but the thinnest chapters in books on ballads still tend to be those on the ballads as literature ("The Critic"). Nevertheless, there is a modest discourse on literary meaning in the Scandinavian ballads, a small part of it in English. The introductions discussed above give some leads. Ull discusses the merman-lover theme, though much here requires caution. Vésteinn Ólason discusses the emotional core of narrative ("St. Olaf"), and Richmond discusses the important motif of the troll ("Ballad Trolls"). Bø proposes that meaning lies in the expression of societal values ("'Margjit og Targjei'"). The 1982 study of ballad narrative by Holzapfel goes beyond technique and into the artistic impact of the works. My study of gender roles in Danish and English ballads applies Villy Sørensen's interpretive schema in which certain ballads express the stresses of transformation of the psyche ("Realizations"). "The Development of the Genres— the Danish Ballad" by Præstgaard Andersen lives up to its title but in the process discusses the generation of meaning.

Readers who are interested in the weighty and sometimes contentious scholarly discussion of the origins, international migrations, forms, collecting and editing, and perceived places in culture of the Scandinavian ballads will begin with Hustvedt's two books. As a bonus the second discusses the formative relationship between Grundtvig's pattern-setting Scandinavian ballad editing and Francis J. Child's monumental *English and Scottish Popular Ballads*. In his *Nordisk folkeviseforskning siden 1800* Erik Dal concentrates on the Scandinavian scholarship. The English summary is substantial enough to be useful. Readers who have more specific interests should begin with the general bibliographies of Holzapfel and Richmond, both of which include scholarship in English.

References

In the interest of conserving space, works cited in the Bibliography of Works Including Translated Ballads or the Bibliography of Translators' Sources are not cited again here.

Abraham, Roger. "Phantoms of Romantic Nationalism in Folkloristics." *Journal of American Folklore* 106 (1993): 3–37.

Alver, Brynjulf. "Merknader til Sophus Bugges folkeviserestitusjonar." *Tradisjon* 1 (1971): 48–52.

Anttonen, Pertti J. "Nationalism, Ethnicity, and the Making of Antiquities as a Strategy in Cultural Representation." *Suomen Antropologi* 19 (1994): 19–42.

Barnes, Michael. *Draumkvæde: An Edition and a Study.* Oslo: Universitetsforlaget, 1974.

Bassnet, Susan and André Lefevere, eds. *Translation, History and Culture.* London: Pinter, 1990.

Benson, Adolph B. "Translations of Swedish Literature." *Swedes in America: 1638–1938.* Ed. Adoph B. Benson and Hedin Naboth. New Haven, CT: Yale UP, for the Swedish American Tercentenary Association, 1938. 237–52.

Beyer, Harald. *A History of Norwegian Literature.* Trans., ed. Einar Haugen. New York: New York UP, for the American-Scandinavian Foundation, 1956.

Brantlinger, Patrick. *Rule of Darkness: British Literature and Imperialism, 1830–1914.* Ithaca: Cornell UP, 1988.

Bredsdorff, Elias. *Danish Literature in English Translation, with a Special Hans Christian Andersen Supplement: A Bibliography.* Copenhagen: Ejnar Munksgaard, 1950.

———. "Sir Alexander Gray, skotsk oversætter af danske folkeviser." *Hvad fatter gjor–: Boghistoriske, litterære og musikalske essays tilegnet Erik Dal.* Herning, Denmark: P. Kristensen, 1982. 92–107.

Bronson, Bertrand Harris. "All This for a Song?" *The Ballad as Song.* Ed. Bertrand Bronson. Berkeley: U California P, 1969. 224–42.

———. "The Interdependence of Ballad Tunes and Texts." *California Folklore Quarterly* 3 (1944): 185–207. Rpt. in *The Critics and the Ballad.* Ed. MacEdward Leach and Tristram P. Coffin. Carbondale, IL: Southern Illinois UP, 1961. 77–102.

———. "On the Union of Words and Music in 'Child' Ballads." *The Ballad as Song.* Ed. Bertrand Bronson. Berkeley: U California P, 1969. 112–139.

Buchan, David. "The Anglophone Comic Ballads." *ARV* 48 (1992): 289–95.

Bø, Olav. "'Margjit og Targjei Risvollo': The Classic Triangle in a Norwegian Medieval Ballad." *Narrative Folksong: New Directions.* Ed. Carol L. Edwards and Kathleen E. B. Manley. Boulder, CO: Westview, 1985. 288–301.

Chesnutt, Michael. "Aspects of the Faroese Traditional Ballad in the Nineteenth Century." *ARV* 48 (1992): 247–59.

——. "Svend Grundtvig: An Essay in Favour of Biography." *Livets gleder: Om forskeren, folkediktningen og maten. En vennebok til Reimund Kvideland.* Ed. Bente Gullveig Alver, et al. Stabekk: Vett & Viten, 1995. 26–34.

Colbert, David. *The Birth of the Ballad: The Scandinavian Medieval Genre.* Stockholm: Svenskt Visarkiv, 1989.

Dal, Erik. *Nordisk folkeviseforskning siden 1800.* København: J. H. Schultz, 1956.

——. "Oversættelser af nordiske folkeviser." *Samlet og spredt om folkeviser.* Odense: Odense Universitetsforlag, 1976. 9–29.

——. "Tyske, franske og engelske oversættelser af færøkvæder." *Fróðskaparrit* 18 (1970): 77–92.

Dictionary of the Middle Ages. Ed. Joseph R. Strayer, et al. 13 vols. New York: Charles Scribner's Sons, 1982–89.

Even-Zohar, Itamar. "The Position of Translated Literature within the Literary Polysystem." *Papers in Historical Poetics.* By Itamar Even-Zohar. Tel-Aviv: Porter Institute for Poetics and Semiotics, 1978. 21–27.

Fraistat, Neil. "Illegitimate Shelley: Radical Piracy and the Textual Edition as Cultural Performance." *PMLA* 109 (1994): 409–23.

Frantzen, Allen J. *Desire for Origins: New Language, Old English, and Teaching the Tradition.* New Brunswick, NJ: Rutgers UP, 1990.

Gentzler, Edwin. *Contemporary Translation Theories.* London: Routledge, 1993.

Grönland, Erling. *Norway in English: Books on Norway and by Norwegians in English 1936–1959. A Bibliography.* Oslo: Norwegian Universities P, 1961.

Grundtvig, Svend. *Prøve paa en ny Udgave af Danmarks gamle Folkeviser.* 2d ed. København: Bianco Luno, 1847.

Gustafson, Alrik. *A History of Swedish Literature.* Minneapolis: U Minnesota P, for the American-Scandinavian Foundation, 1961.

Hermans, Theo, ed. *The Manipulation of Literature: Studies in Literary Translation.* New York: St. Martin's, 1985.

————. "Translation Studies and a New Paradigm." *The Manipulation of Literature: Studies in Literary Translation.* Ed. Theo Hermans. New York: St. Martin's, 1985. 7–15.

Hildeman, Karl-Ivar. "Modern Scandinavian Ballad Research: A Bibliographic Essay." *The Medieval Popular Ballad.* By Johannes C. H. R. Steenstrup. Trans. Edward Godfrey Cox. Seattle: U Washington P, 1968. xi–xxiii. [Not in earlier ed.]

Holzapfel, Otto. *Bibliographie zur mittelalterlichen skandinavischen Volksballade.* Turku: Nordic Institute of Folklore, 1975.

————. "Narrative Technique in the German and Danish Ballads—A Stylistic Sample." *The Ballad as Narrative.* Ed. Flemming G. Andersen, Otto Holzapfel, and Thomas Pettitt. Odense: Odense UP, 1982. 101–52.

Hustvedt, Sigurd B. *Ballad Books and Ballad Men: Raids and Rescues in Britain, America, and the Scandinavian North since 1800.* Cambridge, MA: Harvard UP, 1930.

————. *Ballad Criticism in Scandinavia and Great Britain during the Eighteenth Century.* New York: American-Scandinavian Foundation, 1916.

Jacobsen, Per Schelde and Barbara Fass Leavy. *Ibsen's Forsaken Merman: Folklore in the Late Plays.* New York: New York UP, 1988.

Jonsson, Bengt. Rev. of *Nye veje til folkevisen,* by Iørn Piø. *Sumlen* 1986: 166–70.

————. *Svensk balladtradition. 1. Balladkällor och balladtyper.* Stockholm: Svenskt Visarkiv, 1967.

Jonsson, Bengt R., Svale Solheim, and Eva Danielson, eds., in collaboration with Mortan Nolsøe and W. Edson Richmond. *The Types of the Scandinavian Medieval Ballad: A Descriptive Catalogue.* Oslo: Universitetsforlaget, 1978. Also publ. as Skrifter utgivna av Svenskt Visarkiv 5.

Klein, Barbro. "Folklorists in the United States and the World Beyond." *American Folklore Society Newsletter* 24.1 (Febr. 1995): 12–15.

Lambert, José and Hendrik van Gorp. "On Describing Translations." *The Manipulation of Literature: Studies in Literary Translation.* Ed. Theo Hermans. New York: St. Martin's, 1985. 42–53.

Lansford, Mariella. "German Translations and Criticism of the Danish Medieval Ballad to 1853." Diss. U Illinois, 1980.

Lefevere, André. *Translating Literature: Practice and Theory in a Comparative Literature Context.* New York: Modern Language Association of America, 1992.

62 Introduction

———. *Translation, Rewriting, and the Manipulation of Literary Fame.* London: Routledge, 1992.

———. "Why Waste Our Time on Rewrites? The Trouble with Interpretation and the Role of Rewriting in an Alternative Paradigm." *The Manipulation of Literature: Studies in Literary Translation.* Ed. Theo Hermans. New York: St. Martin's, 1985. 215–43.

Malmin, Marie Helene. "A Bibliography of the Translations and Criticism of Norwegian, Swedish, and Danish Literature in England and America." Diss. U Minnesota, 1929.

Medieval Scandinavia: An Encyclopedia. Ed. Phillip Pulsiano and Kirsten Wolf. New York: Garland, 1993.

Meisling, Peter. *Agnetes latter: En folkevise-monografi.* København: Akademisk Forlag, 1988.

Mitchell, Stephen A. *Heroic Sagas and Ballads.* Ithaca, NY: Cornell UP, 1991.

Ng, Maria and Michael S. Batts. *Scandinavian Literature in English Translation 1928–1977.* Vancouver, CAUTG, 1978.

Nolsøe, Mortan. "Ballads and their Cultural Setting in the Faroe Islands." *ARV* 38 (1982): 155–64.

Den norske Studentersangforenings Koncerttourné gjennem det norske Amerika i mai og juni 1905. Kristiania: Cammermeyer, 1906.

North, John S. "The Rationale—Why Read Victorian Periodicals?" *Victorian Periodicals: A Guide to Research.* Ed. J. Don Vann and Rosemary T. VanArsdel. New York: Modern Language Association of America, 1978. 3–20.

Nygard, Holger O. "The Critic and the Ballad." *Studies in Honor of John C. Hodges and Alwin Thaler.* Ed. Richard Beale Davis and John L. Lievsay. Tennessee Studies in Literature, Special Number. Knoxville, TN: U Tennessee P, 1961. 11–18.

Ólason, Vésteinn. "St. Olaf in Late Medieval Icelandic Poetry." *Narrative Folksong: New Directions.* Ed. Carol L. Edwards and Kathleen E. B. Manley. Boulder, CO: Westview, 1985. 2–17.

Piø, Iørn. *Nye veje til folkevisen.* København: Gyldendal, 1985.

Richmond, W. Edson. *Ballad Scholarship: An Annotated Bibliography.* New York: Garland, 1989.

———. "Ballad Trolls as Narrative Devices." *Folklore on Two Continents.* Ed. Nikolai Burlakoff and Carl Lindahl. Bloomington, IN: Trickster, 1980. 217–22.

————. "The Editing of Ballads for Popular Consumption in Norway." *Sumlen* 1979: 175–83.

Rockwell, Joan. *Evald Tang Kristensen: A Lifelong Adventure in Folklore.* Aalborg Studies in Folk Culture 5. Aalborg and Copenhagen: 1982.

Roos, Carl. "Die dänische Folkevise in der Weltliteratur." *Forschungsprobleme der vergleichenden Literaturgeschichte.* Ed. Kurt Wais. Tübingen: Max Niemeyer, 1951.

Sanders, Andrew. "High Victorian Literature." *An Outline of English Literature.* Ed. Pat Rogers. Oxford: Oxford UP, 1992. 299–346.

Schroeder, Carol. *A Bibliography of Danish Literature in English Translation, 1950–1980: With a Selection of Books about Denmark.* Copenhagen: Det danske Selskab: 1982.

Shippey, T. A. "Goths and Huns: The Rediscovery of the Northern Cultures in the Nineteenth Century." *The Medieval Legacy: A Symposium.* Ed. Andreas Haarder, et al. Odense: Odense UP, 1982. 51–69.

Snell-Hornby, Mary. "Linguistic Transcoding or Cultural Transfer? A Critique of Translation Theory in Germany." *Translation, History and Culture.* Ed. Susan Bassnett and André Lefevere. London: Pinter, 1990. 79–86.

Solberg, Olav. "Jocular Ballads and Carnival Culture." *ARV* 48 (1992): 17–23.

————. "The Norwegian Jocular Medieval Ballad: A Presentation and Some Themes." *Talking Folklore* No. 9 (1990): 34–46.

Syndergaard, Larry. "'An Amateur' and His Translations of the Danish Ballads—Identity and Significance." *Danske Studier* 85 (1990): 80–93.

————. "Realizations of the Feminine Self in Three Traditional Ballads from Scotland and Denmark." *Michigan Academician* 20 (Winter 1988): 85–100.

————. "The Translations of the Danish *Folkeviser* Seen as Intercultural Communication." *Scandinavian Literature in a Transcultural Context: Papers from the XV IASS Conference, University of Washington August 12–18, 1984.* Ed. Sven H. Rossel and Birgitta Steene. Seattle: U Washington, 1984. 222–25.

Sørensen, Villy. "Folkeviser og forlovelser." *Digtere og dæmoner.* København: Gyldendal, 1959. 157–203.

Toury, Gideon. "A Rationale for Descriptive Translation Studies." *The Manipulation of Literature: Studies in Literary Translation.* Ed. Theo Hermans. New York: St. Martin's, 1985. 16–41.

————. "Translation, Literary Translation, and Pseudo-translation." *Comparative Criticism* 6 (1984): 73–85.

Tymoczko, Maria. "Translation in Oral Tradition as a Touchstone for Translation Theory and Practice." *Translation, History and Culture*. Ed. Susan Bassnett and André Lefevere. London: Pinter, 1990. 46–55.

Vanderauwera, Ria. "The Response to Translated Literature. A Sad Example." *The Manipulation of Literature: Studies in Literary Translation*. Ed. Theo Hermans. New York: St. Martin's, 1985. 198–214.

Vann, J. Don and Rosemary T. VanArsdel. *Victorian Periodicals: A Guide to Research*. New York: Modern Language Association of America, 1978.

Wawn, Andrew. "The Spirit of 1892: Sagas, Saga-Steads and Victorian Philology." *Saga-Book of the Viking Society*, 1992: 213–52.

Whisnant, David E. *All That Is Native and Fine: The Politics of Culture in an American Region*. Chapel Hill, NC: U North Carolina P, 1983.

USING THE TABLES OF TRANSLATIONS

This section explains the analytical tables of translations on a column-by-column basis. The methodology of the analysis and some important implications discovered during the work are discussed under "Desiderata and Procedures" in the Introduction. At the beginning of each of the five tables are brief observations on the national ballad editions, resources, and problems specific to the analysis of ballad translations from that language. Abbreviations: N.A.: not applicable; N.I.: no information.

NATIONAL TYPE NUMBER is the basic classification given the original ballad in a comprehensive national edition. The type number prefixes, with their corresponding editions, follow:

DgF (*Danmarks gamle Folkeviser*): Danish
CCF (*Føroya Kvæði. Corpus Carminum Faroensium*): Faroese
ÍF (*Íslenzk fornkvæði. Islandske folkeviser*, ed. Jón Helgason): Icelandic
NMB (*Norske Mellomalderballadar*): Norwegian
SMB (*Sveriges Medeltida Ballader*): Swedish

See the Norwegian section for an important partial exception to the above. SMB type numbers include ballads from both Sweden and Swedish-speaking Finland. When italicized, the prefix serves as the abbreviation for the edition in the tables and elsewhere. National type numbers for ballads not yet published in a comprehensive national edition come from Bengt Jonsson, Svale Solheim, and Eva Danielson's *The Types of the Scandinavian Medieval Ballad* (Oslo, 1978). Some translations included are from ballads or borderline-ballad poems not included in the comprehensive national editions. When these correspond to types in another generally recognized edition, such as H. Grüner Nielsen, *Danske Skæmteviser*, type numbers from those editions are provided.

TSB NUMBER is the number assigned to the ballad in the basic pan-Scandinavian classification and index, *The Types of the Scandinavian Medieval Ballad*. Note that the component parts of a complex ballad given one national type number may sometimes have two or more TSB numbers; that some ballads have been admitted to the national-edition canons but have not subsequently been given TSB numbers because they were judged too recent, too literary, or not narrative enough; and that humorous ballads get somewhat thin coverage in *The Types*.

TITLE gives the title of the original ballad as used or planned in the appropriate national edition. For important exceptions see the Norwegian section.

VERSION translated is identified where possible. Most of the national editions have designated discrete narrative versions of each numbered ballad type, usually with capitals (**A**, **B**, **C**, etc.), but sometimes with Roman numerals. Sub-versions are conventionally given lower-case letters (**Ca**, **Cb**, **Cc**, etc.).

The version column also indicates the genuineness of the text translated by indicating whether it has been reshaped outside its tradition:

Ab: Translation of version **A**, sub-version **b**, "genuine."

Sole: The only version known when it is not designated **A**.

Red: Redaction; the original version translated has been significantly changed from its existence in oral or manuscript or broadside tradition, or combined from two or more versions, sometimes by a translator but more often by the editor(s) of an edition not made to modern scholarly standards. Sometimes acknowledged, often not.

D, red: A redaction given version status (here, **D**) in a comprehensive national edition.

Red (C): The original translated is a redaction, but close enough to a recognized version, **C**, to preserve many of its distinctive features.

Compos: Composite; translation captures the features common to several or all versions of a ballad type—often a translator's construct, and often acknowledged.

TRADITION refers to the more or less conventional classifications, in Scandinavian ballad editing and scholarship, of recorded texts by socioeconomic origin. The column is blank for redactions in that they do not present genuine examples of these traditions.

Aris: Aristocratic (ballads from manuscripts and ballad books of the—often lesser—nobility).

Brds: Broadsides and stall ballads (single sheets commercially produced and cheaply sold).

Cleric: Clerical and academic classes (proposed for some Swedish ballads).

Comm: Common people (urban dwellers and artisans as well as peasants and rural workers; middle as well as lower class; ballads predominantly from oral tradition, but also from ballad books).

Ar/Com: Aristocratic/Common: possible origin in either class.

CENTURY refers to the century in which the source version was recorded, not to the possible origin of its tradition. The column is blank for redactions in that they do not present genuine tradition.

TITLE OF TRANSLATION is usually given without initial article and often without subtitle.

TRANSLATOR, VENUE, DATE provides an abbreviated reference keyed to full citations in the Bibliography of Works Including Translations (pp. 203–30). The translator is listed before the author or editor when they are not the same person and both are known, e.g., "Meyer, in Dal, *DBFS*." (The bibliography, however, is organized conventionally according to author, editor, or title.) The = sign denotes a reprinting; ≅ denotes a reprinting with revisions. Substantially different translations of the same ballad by a translator are entered separately. Listings are in chronological order, except that all reprintings are listed sequentially after the first appearance. Users tracing historical paterns should know that the many translations first published in George Borrow's *Works* in 1923 were done in the early and middle nineteenth century.

TRANSLATOR'S SOURCE gives an abbreviated reference to the full citation in the Bibliography of Translators' Sources (pp. 231–38). Judgment of source is based on direct inspection where possible, in preference to relying on the translators' own unevenly reliable declarations and other received judgments, though all evidence is considered. The = sign or ≅ denotes *a* standard source of substantially the same original ballad, though not necessarily *the* source used, in some cases where confident identification has not been possible.

LANGUAGE; MUSIC

> *L*: The translation is accompanied by a text (though often not complete) in the
> original language.
> *M*: The translation is provided with music, which may or may not be original
> to the source.

TRANSLATION STRATEGY: (See the detailed criteria for this analysis, p. 32) *The
four translation strategy categories below are descriptive, not value judgments.* The analytical criteria do not work for non-stanzaic translations or
translations of other translations, and they work only uneasily for short
fragments.

> *Literal*: Follows original very closely with such changes as needed to make the
> translation idiomatic.
> *Close*: Follows original quite closely, with minor substantive changes, very
> limited structural changes, and limited "enhancement" or intensification.
> *Interp*: Interpretive; retains the essential narrative but employs more frequent
> small and/or some larger changes, and/or tone is notably changed by "en-
> hancement."
> *Adapt*: Adaptive; changed in substance and/or in structure to the point of
> changing the essential narrative.

NOTES indicate translations of incomplete ballads and fragments, prose translations and summaries, translations from other (intermediate) translations, the
omission of an original's refrain in the translation, and miscellaneous points.

TABLE I. TRANSLATIONS FROM THE DANISH

The comprehensive national scholarly edition of the Danish ballads is Grundtvig, Olrik, Grüner Nielsen, Dal, et al, *Danmarks gamle Folkeviser*, in twelve imposing volumes. *DgF* is widely acknowledged as the exemplar and scholarly standard for subsequent ballad editing in Scandinavia, and indeed beyond; it is the direct model for Child's *The English and Scottish Popular Ballads*. (It is perhaps equally significant, in its 124-year history, as an example of shared, intergenerational editorial mission and persistence in scholarly publishing. See the modest but moving final comments of Erik Dal in *DgF* 12: 14.) The concordances in vol. 12, the index volume, give a condensed picture of the relationships among the unparalleled national array of editions of the Danish ballads—scholarly and popular, redacted and "pure"—over four centuries. Many of these appear in the "Translator's Source" column in the table here, though translators have utilized other sources (e.g., Nyerup and Rasmussen, *Udvalg af Danske Viser*) that escape the purview of *DgF* 12. The modern photographic reprint of *DgF* (1966–67) adds brief but trenchant English prefaces to volumes 1–10, and the index volume has brief introductions in English. The English summary in Erik Dal's *Nordisk folkeviseforskning siden 1800* (København: J.H. Schultz, 1956) supplies a brief discussion of the varying conceptions behind the source editions from which most translators have worked.

Occasionally what is a sole version in its "main" appearance in *DgF* becomes version **A** when another version is discovered and printed in "Additions and Corrections" in later volumes.

In the table the non-*DgF* and borderline ballads fall at the end, in this order: first those translated from or corresponding to types in H. Grüner Nielsen, *Danske Skæmteviser*, then those from or corresponding to types in Evald Tang Kristensen, *Et Hundrede gamle danske Skjæmteviser*, then those with neither Grüner Nielsen, Tang Kristensen, nor TSB type numbers.

National Type No.	TSB No.	Title	Version	Tradition	Century	Title of Translation	Translator, Venue, Date	Translator's Source	Lang, Music	Trans. Strategy	Notes
DgF I	E126	Tord af Havsgaard	B, red	—	—	Untitled	Keightley, "Scand. Myth.," 119-20 (1829)	ANR No. 1		Close	8 st. + prose summ.; omits ref.
	E126	Tord af Havsgaard	B, red	—	—	Thor and the Ogre	Amateur [Prior], ODB No. 15 (1856)	Grimm No. 27		NA	From German trans; omits ref.
	E126	Tord af Havsgaard	A	Ar/Com	16	Thor of Asgard	Prior, ADB No. 1 (1860) =Rev. ADB 344 (1860) =Drummond-Davies 14-15 (1861)	DgF		Interp	Omits ref. 11 st. + prose summ. 19 st. + prose summ.
	E126	Tord af Havsgaard	A	Ar/Com	16	Thord of Hafsgaard	Smith-Dampier, MBID 8-11 (1914) ≅Smith-Dampier, DB No. 15 (1920)	DgF		Close Interp	Omits ref. Omits ref.
	E126	Tord af Havsgaard	A	Ar/Com	16	Thor of Havsgaard	Cox, in Steenstrup, MPB 67 (1914)	DgF		Close	3 st. of 23; omits ref
	E126	Tord af Havsgaard	C	Comm	19	Thor of Havsgaard	Cox, in Steenstrup, MPB 68 (1914)	DgF		Interp	2 st. of 25; omits ref.
	E126	Tord af Havsgaard	B, red	—	—	Tord of Hafsborough	Borrow, Works 8:102-05 (1923)	? NR 2: No. 60		Close	Omits ref.
	E126	Tord af Havsgaard	Red	—	—	Tord af Havsgaard	Entwistle, Eur. Ball. 93-94 (1939)	Sv. Grundtvig 1867 No. 1		Interp	2 st. of 28
2	E49	Sivard Snarensvend	Red C	—	—	Death of Sivard Snarensvend	"On the Songs" 4:415-16 (1821)	ANR No. 11		Close	

2	Sivard Snarensvend	Red C	—	End of Sivard Snarenswayne	Borrow, *Works* 7:41-44 (1923) = *Ball. All Nations*, 23-25 (1927)	*AMR* No. 11		Interp	Omits ref.
2	Sivard Snarensvend	Red (A)	—	Siward the Hasty Swain	Prior, *ADB* No. 2 (1860)	*DgF*		Interp	Omits ref.
2	Sivard Snarensvend	A	Ar/Com	17	Cox, in Steenstrup, *MPB* 69 (1914)	*DgF*		Close	2 st. of 16; omits ref.
2	Sivard Snarensvend	Red	—	Sivord Snarensvend	Smith-Dampier, *SD-S* 197-99 (1934)	Grundtvig 1882 I: No. 3.		Interp.	
3	Sivard og Brynild	A	Arist	16	Siward and Brynild	Prior, *ADB* No. 3 (1860)	*DgF*		Interp	Omits ref.
3	Sivard og Brynild	A	Arist	16	Sivard	Ker, *Epic* 128-29 (1908)	*DgF*		N. A.	Prose
3	Sivard og Brynild	A	Arist	16	Sivard and Brynild	Cox, in Steenstrup, *MPB* 129 (1914)	*DgF*		Close	Omits ref.
3	Sivard og Brynild	D, red	—	Tale of Brynild	Borrow, *Works* 7:69-74 (1923) = *Ball. All Nations* 28-33 (1927)	ANR No. 17		Interp	Omits ref.
3	Sivard og Brynild	Red (A)	—	Sivord and Brynhild	Smith-Dampier, *SD-S* 201-07 (1934)	Grundtvig 1867 No. 2		Adapt	
3	Sivard og Brynild	B	Arist	17	Sivord and Brynild	Halkett, in Seemann No. 12 (1967)	*DgF*	L	Close	
4	Frændehævn	C, red	—	Sir Luomor	Prior, *ADB* No. 4 (1860)	*DgF*		Interp	
4	Frændehævn	C, red	—	Proud Signild	Borrow, *Works* 7:387-93 (1923) = *Ball. All Nations* 94-99 (1927)	ANR No. 129		Interp	Omits ref.
4	Frændehævn	Red	—	Kinship's Vengeance	Smith-Dampier, *SD-S* 177-83 (1934)	Grundtvig 1882 I: No. 6		Adapt	Misleading attribution

National Type No.	TSB No.	Title	Version	Tradition	Century	Title of Translation	Translator, Venue, Date	Translator's Source	Lang. Music	Trans. Strategy	Notes
5	E56	Grimilds hævn	C, red	—	—	Lady Grimild's Wrack	Jamieson, *INM* 280-86 (1814) =Long fellow, *PPE* 65-67 (1847)	Syv (Vedel 1: No. 7)		Close	
5	E56	Grimilds hævn	Red (**B**)			Lady Grimild's Wrack	Jamieson, *INM* 279 (1814)	ANR No. 15		Close	3 st. of 37
5	E56	Grimilds hævn	Red (**Ab**)	—	—	Grimhild's Revenge. A.	Prior, *ADB* No. 5, 1:38-45 (1860)	*DgF*, ANR No. 16		Interp	
5	E56	Grimilds hævn	**Bb**, red	—	—	Grimhild's Revenge. B.	Prior, *ADB* No. 5, 1:46-52 (1860)	ANR No. 15		Interp	
5	E56	Grimilds hævn	Red (**C**)	—	—	Grimhild's Revenge. C.	Prior, *ADB* No. 5, 1:53-62 (1860)	*DgF*, ANR No. 14		Interp	
5	E56	Grimilds hævn	Red (**C**)	—	—	Grimhild's Vengeance. 1.	Borrow, *Works* 7:51-56 (1923)	ANR No. 14		Close	
5	E56	Grimilds hævn	**Bb**, Red	—	—	Grimhild's Vengeance. 2.	Borrow, *Works* 7:57-61 (1923)	ANR No. 15		Interp	
5	E56	Grimilds hævn	Red (**Ab**)	—	—	Grimhild's Vengeance. 3.	Borrow, *Works* 7:62-68 (1923)	ANR No. 16		Close	
5	E56	Grimilds hævn	**A**	Ar/Com	16	Grimhild's Revenge	Cox, in Steenstrup 102-09 (1914)	*DgF*	L	Close	5 st. of 43
5	E56	Grimilds hævn	**C**, red	—	—	Grimhild's Revenge	Smith-Dampier, *SD-S* 185-94 (1934)	*DgF*		Interp	
6	D61	Samson	**Bc**, red	—	—	The Guardsman	Amateur [Prior], *ODB* No. 32 (1856)	Grimm No. 11		N.A.	From German tr. Omits ref.
6	D61	Samson	Red (**Bc**)	—	—	Samson	Prior, *ADB* No. 6 (1860) =Coppée 3:374-75 (1886)	*DgF*, ANR No. 179		Adapt	Omits ref.

7	EII9	Kong Diderik og hans kæmper	Red (B⊃)	—		The Ettin Langshanks	Jamieson, *INA* 295-305 (1814) =Longfellow, *PPE* 67-69 (1847)	Syy (Vedel I:No. 4)	Close	
7	EI0	Kong Diderik og hans kæmper	H, red	—		The Tournament	"On the Songs," 4:414 (1821)	Syy (Vedel I: No. 5)	Interp	9 st. of 67
7	EII9	Kong Diderik og hans kæmper	Red (Bb)	—		Vidrik Verlandson	Borrow, *Rom. Ball.* 98-110 (1826) =Stoddard 204-11 (1883) = *Works* 9:339-47 (1923)	ANR No. 3	Interp	Omits ref.
7	EI0	Kong Diderik og hans kæmper	Red (H)	—		The Tournament	Borrow, *Rom. Ball.* 82-97 (1826) = *Works* 9:328-38 (1923)	ANR No. 1	Interp	Omits ref.
7	EII9	Kong Diderik og hans kæmper	Red (Bb)	—		Vidrik Verlandsson's Battle with Langben the Giant	Howitt, *LRNE* 1:313-20 (1852)	ANR No. 3	Close	
7	EII9	Kong Diderik og hans kæmper	Red (Bb)	—		Vidrick Verlandson and Giant Langbane	Prior, *ADB* No. 7 (1860)	ANR No. 3	Interp	Omits ref.
7	EI0	Kong Diderik og hans kæmper	F	17	Arist	The Tournament	Prior, *ADB* No. 8 (1860)	*DgF*	Interp	Omits ref.
7	EI0	Kong Diderik og hans kæmper	Red	—		Oh, Seventy-Seven Twice-Told Were They	Smith-Dampier, *DB.* No. 12 (1920) ≅ *BDB* I: No. 4 (1939)	Olrik I: No. 4	Close / Close	
7	EI0	Kong Diderik og hans kæmper	Red (D)	—		Sigurd and Hamling	Karpeles, *FS Eur.* No. 1 (1956)	*DgF*	L M Adapt	8 st. of 43
8	E7	Kong Diderik i Birtingsland	Red (b)	—		King Diderik's Warriors' Expedition to Birtingland	Stokes, "Dan. Ball.," Rev. 215 (1858)	? ANR No. 2	Close	3 st. of 52; omits ref.
8	E7	Kong Diderik i Birtingsland	a	16	Ar/Com	King Diderik in Birtingsland	Prior, *ADB* No. 9 (1860) ≅ Steenstrup, *MPB* 29 (1914)	*DgF*	Interp	Omits ref. 3 st. of 46; incl.ref.

National Type No.	TSB No.	Title	Version	Tradition	Century	Title of Translation	Translator, Venue, Date	Translator's Source	Lang./Music	Trans. Strategy	Notes
8	E7	Kong Diderik i Birtingsland	Red (**b**)	—	—	Expedition to Birting's Land	Borrow, *Works* 7:1-8 (1923) = *Ball. All Nations* 1-8 (1927)	ANR No. 2		Interp	Omits ref.
8	E7	Kong Diderik i Birtingsland	Red (**b**)	—	—	Untitled	Entwistle, *Eur. Ball.* 100, 110, 212 (1939)	ANR No. 2		Close	4 st. of 52; Parallel transls.
9	E158	Kong Diderik og løven	G, red	—	—	Battle of King Tidrich and the Lion with the Linden-Worm	?Jamieson, *IWA* 225-30 (1814)	Syv (Vedel 1: No. 13)		Interp	Omits ref.
9	E158	Kong Diderik og løven	G, red	—	—	King Diderik and the Dragon	Prior, *ADB* No. 10 (1860)	*DgF* or ANR 5		Interp	Omits ref.
9	E158	Kong Diderik og løven	G, red	—	—	King Diderik and the Lion's Fight with the Dragon	Borrow, *Works* 7:14-19 (1923) = *Ball. All Nations* 9-14 (1927)	ANR No. 5		Interp	Omits ref.
10	E37	Ulv van Jærn	F, red	—	—	Untitled	Stokes, "Dan. Ball.," Rev. 6:215 (1858)	Syv No. 9 or NR 2: No. 67		Close	Omits ref.
10	E37	Ulv van Jærn	Red (**G**)	—	—	Vidrick Verlandson and Wolf of Yern	Prior, *ADB* No. 11 (1860)	ANR No. 9		Interp	Omits ref.
10	E37	Ulv van Jærn	Red (**G**)	—	—	Ulf van Yern	Borrow, *Works* 7:33-40 (1923)	ANR No. 9		Interp	Omits ref.
11	E132	Orm Ungersvend og Bermer-Rise	D, red	—	—	Berner the Giant, and Orm Ungersvend	"On the Songs" 4:415 (1821)	Vedel 1: No. 15		Interp	16 st. of 51

No	Code	Danish title	Version	Ar/Com	No	Version title	Source	ANR/DgF	L	Interp	Notes
11	E132	Orm Ungersvend og Bermer-Rise	D, red	—	—	Birting. A Fragment	Borrow, *Targum* 59-61 (1835) = *Works* 16:59-61 (1924)	ANR No. 7		Interp	16 st. of 51; omits ref.
11	E132	Orm Ungersvend og Bermer-Rise	D, red	—	—	Giant of Bern and Orm Ungerswayne	Borrow, *Works* 7:25-32 (1923) = *Ball. All Nations* 15-22 (1927)	ANR No. 7		Close	Some *Targum* lines; omits ref.
11	E132	Orm Ungersvend og Bermer-Rise	A	Ar/Com	16	Young Orm and the Bermer-Giant	Child, *ESPB* 2:49-50 (1885)	*DgF*		N. A.	Prose summ.
11	E132	Orm Ungersvend og Bermer-Rise	A	Ar/Com	16	Childe Orm and the Berm Giant	Prior, *ADB* No. 12 (1860)	*DgF*		Interp	Omits ref.
12	A32	Raadengaard og ørnen	A	Arist	16	Rodengard and the Eagle	Prior, *ADB* No. 13 (1860)	*DgF*		Close	Omits ref.
13	D231	Ravngaard og Memering	A	Arist	16	Ravngard and Memering	Prior, *ADB* No. 14 (1860) = M. Leach, *Ball. Bk.* 190-96 (1955)	*DgF*		Interp	
13	D231	Ravengaard og Memering	A	Arist	16	Ravengaard og Memering	Child, *ESPB* 2:34-35 (1885)	*DgF*		N. A.	Prose summ.
13	D231	Ravengaard og Memering	Compos	—	—	Ravengaard og Memering	Child, *ESPB* 2:35 (1885)	*DgF*		N. A.	Prose summ.; oral versions
13	D231	Ravengaard og Memering	A	Arist	16	Untitled	Christophersen 178-87 (1952)	*DgF*	L	Literal	Omits ref.
13	D231	Ravengaard og Memering	B	Comm	19	Untitled	Christophersen 186-91 (1952)	*DgF*	L	Literal	Omits ref.
13	D231	Ravengaard og Memering	C	Comm	19	Untitled	Christophersen 190-95 (1952)	*DgF*	L	Literal	Omits ref.
13	D231	Ravengaard og Memering	G	Comm	19	Untitled	Christophersen 196-99 (1952)	*DgF*	L	Literal	Omits ref.
13	D231	Ravengaard og Memering	H	Comm	19	Untitled	Christophersen 198-203 (1952)	*DgF*	L	Literal	Omits ref.

National Type No.	TSB No.	Title	Version	Tradition	Century	Title of Translation	Translator, Venue, Date	Translator's Source	Lang; Music	Trans. Strategy	Notes
13	D231	Ravengaard og Memering	I	Comm	19	Untitled	Christophersen 202-07 (1952)	*DgF*	L	Literal	Omits ref.
13	D231	Ravengaard og Memering	K, red	—	—	Untitled	Christophersen 206-13 (1952)	*DgF*	L	Literal	Compos. of oral vers.; omits ref.
13	D231	Ravengaard og Memering	L	Comm	19	Untitled	Christophersen 212-15 (1952)	*DgF*	L	Literal	Omits ref.
13	D231	Ravengaard og Memering	M	Comm	19	Untitled	Christophersen 216-21 (1952)	*DgF*	L	Literal	Omits ref.
13	D231	Ravengaard og Memering	N	Comm	19	Untitled	Christophersen 220-21 (1952)	*DgF*	L	Literal	3 st.; omits ref.
13	D231	Ravengaard og Memering	O	Comm	20	Untitled	Christophersen 220-21 (1952)	*DgF*	L	Literal	1 st.; omits ref.
14	E61	Memering	Ab	Arist	16	Hero Mimmering	Amateur [Prior], *ODB* No. 34 (1856)	Grimm No. XIII		N. A.	=**b** in *DgF*l; From German trans.
14	E61	Memering	Aa	Ar/Com	16	Memering	Prior, *ADB* No. 15 (1860)	*DgF*		Interp	=**a** in *DgF*l
14	E61	Memering	Ab	Arist	16	Mimmering Tan	Borrow, *Works* 7:45-46 (1923) =*Ball. All Nations* 26-27 (1927)	ANR No. 12		Close	=**b** in *DgF*l
14	E61	Memering	Aa	Ar/Com	16	Memering	Cox, in Steenstrup, *MPB* 92 (1914)	*DgF*		Close	=**a** in *DgF*l
14	E61	Memering	Aa	Ar/Com	16	Mimering	Gray, *FaF* No. 19 (1954)	Recke No. 22		Interp	=**a** in *DgF*l; omits ref.
15	E19	Den skallede Munk	a	Brds	17	The Bald-head Monk	Prior, *ADB* No. 16 (1860)	*DgF*		Interp	

15	EI9	Den skallede Munk	The Bald Monk	17	Brds	a	Cox, in Steenstrup, *MPB* 119-20 (1914)	*DgF*	Close	3 st. of 28
15	EI9	Den skallede Munk	The Stalwart Monk	17	Brds	a	Borrow, *Works* 7:98-102 (1923) = *Ball. All Nations* 41-44 (1927)	ANR No. 22	Interp	
15	EI9	Den skallede Munk	The Bald-Pated Monk	—	—	Red	Gray, *FaF* No. 35 (1954)	Recke No. 20	Interp	
16	EI2	Greve Genselin	Sir Guncelin	—	—	**Cb**, red	Jamieson, *INA* 310-16 (1814) = Longfellow, *PPE* 70-71 (1847)	Syv (Vedel 1: No. 6)	Interp	
16	EI2	Greve Genselin	Sir Genselin	16	Arist	**A**	Prior, *ADB* No. 17 (1860)	*DgF*	Close	
16	EI2	Greve Genselin	Sir Guncelin's Wedding	—	—	**Ct**, red	Borrow, *Works* 8:96-101 (1923)	NR 2: No. 58 or Grimm XIV	Interp	Omits ref.
16	EI2	Greve Genselin	Untitled	—	—	Red	Cox, in Steenstrup, *MPB* 15 (1914)	?*DgF*		3 st.; omits ref.
17	EI7	Kong Diderik og Holger Danske	Stark Tiderich and Olger Danske	—	—	**Bb**, red	Jamieson, *INA* 267-74 (1814) = Longfellow, *PPE* 64-65 (1847)	Syv (Vedel 1: No. 12)	Close	
17	EI7	Kong Diderik og Holger Danske	Diderik og Olger Danske	—	—	**Bb**, red	Stokes, "Dan. Ball.," Rev 6:214 (1858)	ANR No. 4	Interp	10 st. of 29; omits ref.
17	EI7	Kong Diderik og Holger Danske	Stout Diderik and Olger the Dane	16	Ar/Com	**B**	Prior, *ADB* No. 18 (1860)	*DgF*	Interp	
17	EI7	Kong Diderik og Holger Danske	Holger Danske and Stærk Diderik	—	—	Red	Bushby, "Holger Danske" (1861) = *Poems* 357-60 (1876)	N. Grundtvig 1847 84	Interp	
17	EI7	Kong Diderik og Holger Danske	Diderik and Olger the Dane	—	—	**Bb**, red	Borrow, *Works* 7:9-13 (1923)	ANR No. 4	Interp	Omits ref.

National Type No.	TSB No.	Title	Version	Tradition	Century	Title of Translation	Translator, Venue, Date	Translator's Source	Lang. Music	Trans. Strategy	Notes
17	E17	Kong Diderik og Holger Danske	Red	—	—	Holger Danske and Stout Didrik	Smith-Dampier, *DB* No. 13 (1920) ≃ *BDB* I: No. 5 (1939)	Olrik I: No. 5		Interp	
18	E52	Svend Vonved	Red (D)	—	—	Child Bonved	"On the Songs" 4:416-17 (1821)	ANR No. 10		Interp	21 st. of 71; omits ref.
18	E52	Svend Vonved	Red (D)	—	—	Svend Vonved	Borrow, *Rom. Ball* 61-81 (1826) = *Works* 9:314-27 (1923)	ANR No. 10		Adapt	
18	E52	Svend Vonved	Red (D)	—	—	Swayne Vonved	Stokes, "Dan. Ball." 651-53 (1852)	ANR No. 10		Interp	44 st. of 71
18	E52	Svend Vonved	A	Arist	17	Childe Norman's Riddle Rhymes	Prior, *ADB* No. 19 (1860)	*DgF*		Interp	
18	E52	Svend Vonved	A	Arist	17	Svend Normand	Meyer, in Dal, *DBFS* No. 20 (1967)	*DgF*		Close	
18	E52	Svend Vonved	A	Arist	17	Svend Vonved	Colbert, "Danish B. B." 10 (1978)	*DgF*		Literal	4 st. of 92; omits ref.
19	E90	Angelfyr og Helmer Kamp	Red (B)	—	—	Angelfyr and Helmer Kamp	Prior, *ADB* No. 20 (1860)	*DgF*		Adapt	Omits ref.
19	E90	Angelfyr og Helmer Kamp	A	Arist	17	Angelfyr and Helmer the Warrior	Kershaw 186-91 (1921)	*DgF*		Close	
19	E90	Angelfyr og Helmer Kamp	B	Ar/Com	16	Angelfyr and Helmer the Warrior	Kershaw 186-92 (1921)	*DgF*		Close	7 st. of 18; omits ref.
19	E90	Angelfyr og Helmer Kamp	D, red	—	—	Alf of Odderskier	Borrow, *Works* 7:75-78 (1923)	ANR No. 18		Interp	Omits ref.

19	E90	Angelfyr og Helmer Kamp	Red	—	—	Alf of Odderskerry	Smith-Dampier, *BDB* I: No. 2 (1939)	Olrik I: No. 2	Interp	
19	E90	Angelfyr og Helmer Kamp	A	Arist	17	Angelfyr and Helmer Kamp	Meyer, in Dal, *DBfS* No. 21 (1967)	*DgF*	Close	
20	D430	Hagbard og Signe	Fed	—	—	Hafbur and Signe	Stokes, "Dan. Ball." 656-58 (1852)	Winther 192f.	Interp	Omits ref.
20	D430	Hagbard og Signe	Rad	—	—	Hafbur and Signe	Borrow, *Works* 7:353-66 (1923)	ANR No. III	Interp	Omits ref.
20	D430	Hagbard og Signe	I, red	—	—	Hafbur and Signild	Amateur [Prior], *ODB* No. 7 (1856)	Grimm No. 9	N.A.	From German tr.; omits ref.
20	D430	Hagbard og Signe	Red (1)	—	—	Habor and Signild. A.	Prior, *ADB* No. 21A (1860)	*DgF*	Interp	Omits ref.
20	D430	Hagbard og Signe	Ba	Arist	17	Habor and Sinnelille. B.	Prior, *ADB* No. 21B (1860)	*DgF*	Interp	Omits ref.
20	D430	Hagbard og Signe	Red	—	—	Hafbur and Signy	Morris, *Poems* 152-66 (1891) = *Poems/Love* 175-90 (1896) = *Collected Works* 9:213-24 (1911)	ANR No. III	Interp	
20	D430	Hagbard og Signe	Red	—	—	Havbor and Signelil	Smith-Dampier, *DB* No. 10 (1920) ≅ *BDB* I: No. I (1939)	Olrik I: No. I	Interp	
20	D430	Hagbard og Signe	Ba	Arist	17	Havbor and Signe	Meyer, in Dal, *DBfS* No. 22 (1967)	*DgF*	Close	
21	D388	Longobarderne	A	Arist	16	The Lombards	Prior, *ADB* No. 22 (1860)	*DgF*	Interp	Omits ref.
22	D401	Regnfred og Kragelil	A, ?red	—	—	Royal Herd Girl	Amateur [Prior], *ODB* No. 4 (1856)	Grimm No. VI	N.A.	From German tr.; omits ref.
22	D401	Regnfred og Kragelil	A, ?red	—	—	Regnar and Kragelille	Prior, *ADB* No. 23 (1860)	*DgF*	Interp	Omits ref.
22	D401	Regnfred og Kragelil	A, ?red	—	—	Kragelil	Borrow, *Works* 8:106-08 (1923) = *Ball. All Nations* 121-23 (1927)	? NR 2: No. 63	Interp	Omits ref.

National Type No.	TSB No.	Title	Version	Tradition	Century	Title of Translation	Translator, Venue, Date	Translator's Source	Lang. Music	Trans. Strategy	Notes
23	D403	Karl og Kragelil	Red (A)	—	—	Karl and Kragelille	Prior, *ADB* No. 24 (1860)	ANR No. 205		Interp	Omits ref.
24	E156	Ormekampen	a	Arist	17	The Fight with the Worm	Prior, *ADB* No. 25 (1860)	*DgF*		Close	Omits ref.
24	E156	Ormekampen	a	Arist	17	Combat with the Worm	Cox, in Steenstrup, *MPB* 47 (1914)	*DgF*		Close	4 st. of 19
25	E48	Hævnersværdet	sole	Arist	16	Avenging Sword	Stokes, "Dan. Ball." Rev. 214 (1858)	*DgF*		Interp	22 st. of 38; omits ref.
25	E48	Hævnersværdet	sole	Arist	16	Sword of Vengeance	Prior, *ADB* No. 26 (1860)	*DgF*		Interp	Omits ref.
25	E48	Hævnersværdet	Red(sole)	—	—	Avenging Sword	Smith-Dampier, *BfD* 10-13 (1910)	Olrik I: No. 16		Adapt	
25	E48	Hævnersværdet	Red(sole)	—	—	Avenging Sword	Smith-Dampier, *DB* No. 16 (1920) ≅ *BDB* No. 16 (1939) = Rossel, *Scand. Ball.* No. 28 (1982)	Olrik I: No. 16		Interp	Parts from *BfD*
25	E48	Hævnersværdet	sole	Arist	16	Avenger's Sword	Entwistle, *Eur. Ball.* 217 (1939)	*DgF*		Close	3 st. of 38; omits ref.
26	E68	Liden Grimmer og Hjelmer Kamp	**Bd**, red	—	—	Sir Grimmer	Amateur [Prior]No. 33 (1856)	Grimm No. 74		N.A.	From German tr.; omits ref.
26	E68	Liden Grimmer og Hjelmer Kamp	**A**	Arist	16	Grimmer. A.	Prior, *ADB* No. 27A (1860)	*DgF*		Adapt	Omits ref.
26	E68	Liden Grimmer og Hjelmer Kamp	Red (**Bd**)	—	—	Grimmer. B.	Prior, *ADB* No. 27B (1860)	ANR No. 13		Interp	Omits ref.

26	E68	Liden Grimmer og Hjelmer Kamp	A	Arist	16	Liden Grimmer og Helmer Kamp	Child, *ESPB* 2:57 (1885)	*DgF*		N.A.	Prose summ.
26	E48	Liden Grimmer og Hjelmer Kamp	Red (**Bd**)	—	—	Grimmer and Kamper	Borrow, *Works* 7:47-50 (1923)	ANR No. 13		Close	Omits ref.
27	E138	Rigen Rambolt og Aller hin stærke	**Bb**, red	—	—	Ribolt's Fight with the Dragon and Aller	Borrow, *Works* 7:79-83 (1923)	ANR No. 19		Interp	
28	E139	Ungen Ranild	sole	Arist	17	Childe Ranild	Prior, *ADB* No. 28 (1860)	*DgF*		Close	
28	E139	Ungen Ranild	—	Brds	18	Ramund	Borrow, *Works* 8:90-95 (1923)	ANR No. 222		Interp	From tr. of Swedish brds.
30	E133	Holger Danske og Burmand	**D**, red	—	—	Olger the Dane	Amateur [Prior] No. 26 (1856)	Grimm No. 79		N.A.	From German tr.; omits ref.
30	E133	Holger Danske og Burmand	Red	—	—	Olger the Dane	Prior, *ADB* No. 29 (1860)	*DgF*		Interp	Omits ref.
30	E133	Holger Danske og Burmand	**D**, red	—	—	Olger the Dane and Burmand	Borrow, *Works* 7:20-24 (1923)	ANR No. 6		Interp	Omits ref.
31	E115	Svend Felding	**A**	Arist	16	Swain Felding	Prior, *ADB* No. 30 (1860)	*DgF*		Interp	
31	E115	Svend Felding	**C**, red	—	—	Swayne Felding	Borrow, *Works* 7:84-90 (1923) = *Ball. All Nations* 34-40 (1927)	ANR No. 20		Close	
31	E115	Svend Felding	**A**	Arist	16	Ballad on Svend Felding	Cox, in Steenstrup, *MPB* 126, 205-07 (1914)	*DgF*	L	Close	7 st. of 35 + prose summ.
31	E115	Svend Felding	**A**	Arist	16	Svend Felding	Meyer, in Dal, *DBFS* No. 23 (1967)	*DgF*		Close	

National Type No.	TSB No.	Title	Version	Tradition	Century	Title of Translation	Translator, Venue, Date	Translator's Source	Lang/Music	Trans. Strategy	Notes
32	D301	Svend Felding og Dronning Jutte	B	Ar/Com	16	Swain Felding and Queen Judith	Prior, *ADB* No. 31 (1860)	*DgF*		Interp	Omits ref.
32	D301	Svend Felding og Dronning Jutte	Bb, red	—	—	Swayne Felding's Dispute with Queen Judte	Borrow, *Works* 7:91-97 (1923)	ANR 21		Close	Omits ref.
32	D301	Svend Felding og Dronning Jutte	A	Arist	16	Svend Felding	Cox, in Steenstrup, *MPB* 154, 208 (1914)	*DgF*	L	Close	Omits ref.
33	A74	Germand Gladensvend	F, red	—	—	Germand Gladensvend	Stokes, "Second Batch" 87-88 (1855)	ANR No. 25		Interp	Omits ref.
33	A74	Germand Gladensvend	F, red	—	—	Germand Gladenswayne	Borrow, *Works* 7:112-19 (1923)	ANR No. 25		Close	Omits ref.
33	A74	Germand Gladensvend	F, red	—	—	German Gladenswain	Prior, *ADB* No. 80 (1860) =Rossel, *Scand. Ball.* No. 1 (1982)	ANR No. 25		Interp	Omits ref.
33	A74	Germand Gladensvend	Red (C)	—	—	Germand Gladensvend	Smith-Dampier, *BDB* I: No. 6 (1939)	Olrik I: No. 6		Interp	
33	A74	Germand Gladensvend	C	Arist	16	Germand Gladensvend	Jacobsen 38 (1988)	*DgF*		Literal	2 st. + prose partial summ.; omits ref.
34	A62	Hr. Tønne af Alsø	Red (B)	—	—	Sir Tonné	Prior, *ADB* No. 102 (1860) =Drummond-Davies 21-26 (1861)	ANR No. 45 & *DgF*		Interp	Omits ref.
34	A62	Hr. Tønne af Alsø	Red (B)	—	—	How Sir Tonne Won His Bride	Buchanan, *BSB* 84-96 (1866)	ANR No. 45		Adapt.	
34	A62	Hr. Tønne af Alsø	Red (B)	—	—	Ermeline	Borrow, *Works* 7:178-89 (1923)	ANR No. 45		Interp	Omits ref.

#	Code	Danish Title				English Title	Source	Coll.	Type	Notes
35	A61	Peder Gudmandsøn og dværgene	A	Arist	17	Peter Gudmanson and the Dwarfs	Prior, *ADB* No. 130 (1860)	*DgF*	Interp	Omits ref.
35	A61	Peder Gudmandsøn og dværgene	A	Arist	17	Peder Gudmanson and the Dwarfs	Cox, in Steenstrup, *MPB*73 (1914)	*DgF*	Interp	Omits ref.
37	A54	Jomfruen og dværgekongen	E	Comm	19	The Lady and the Dwarf-King	Prior, *ADB* No. 155 (1860) =M. Leach, *Ball. Bk.* 147-48 (1955)	*DgF*	Interp	
37	A54	Jomfruen og dværgekongen	A	Arist	16	Jomfruen og Dværgekongen	Child, *ESPB* 1:361-622 (1882)	*DgF*	N.A.	Prose summ.
37	A54	Jomfruen og dværgekongen	Compos	—	—	Maiden and the Dwarf King	Jacobsen 54-56 (1988)	*DgF*	N.A.	Prose
38	A47	Agnete og havmanden	**Ak**, red	—	—	Deceived Merman	Borrow, "Deceived M." (1825)	ANR No. 50	Adapt	Omits ref.
38	A47	Agnete og havmanden	**Ak**, red	—	—	Deceived Merman	Borrow, *Rom. Ball.* 120-23 (1826) = *Works* 9:353-55 (1923) =*Ball. All Nations* 157-59 (1927) =Hull 76-77 (1940)	ANR No. 50	Adapt	Re-uses some st.; omits ref. Fragment
38	A47	Agnete og havmanden	**Ak**, red	—	—	Agnes and the Merman	[Bushby], "Ballads" 130: 481-82 (1864)	*DgF*	Interp	Omits ref.
38	A47	Agnete og havmanden	**Ak**, red	—	—	Agnes and the Merman	Prior, *ADB* No. 153 (1860)	ANR No. 50	Interp	
38	A47	Agnete og havmanden	C	Comm	19	Agnes and the Hill-King	Prior, *ADB* No. 154 (1860)	*DgF*	Close	
38	A47	Agnete og havmanden	C	Comm	19	Agnes and the Hill-Man	Morris, *Poems* 146-48 (1891) =Poems/Love 169-70 (1896) =*Coll. Works* 9:208-09 (1911) =J. Stephens, Beck & Snow 1024 (1937) =Woods 653-54 (1930)	*DgF*	Close	

National Type No.	TSB No.	Title	Version	Tradition	Century	Title of Translation	Translator, Venue, Date	Translator's Source	Lang; Music	Trans. Strategy	Notes
38	A47	Agnete og havmanden	Red	—	—	Agnete and the Merman	Bratli 8 (1911) =Haraldsted 32-36 (1939)	Heiberg redact	L L	Adapt	Concert version Danish text differs
38	A47	Agnete og havmanden	Red	—	—	Agnes and the Merman	Smith-Dampier, *NKB* 48-51 (1912)	Olrik I: No. 11		Interp	
38	A47	Agnete og havmanden	Red	—	—	Agnes and the Merman	Smith-Dampier, *DB* No. 19 (1920) ≅ *BDB* I: No. 11 (1939)	Olrik I: No. 11		Interp Close	Re-uses some st.
38	A47	Agnete og havmanden	Red	—	—	Agnete and the Merman	Cox, in Steenstrup, *MPB* 223-24 (1914) =Hull 71 (1940)	S. Grundtvig 1867 No. 9		Close	10 st. of 50; omits ref. 5 st. of 50
38	A47	Agnete og havmanden	Non-*DgF*	Comm	20	Agnete	Hull 73 (1940)	Informant		N.A.	4 st. from Danish immigrant
38	A47	Agnete og havmanden	Red	—	—	Agnete and the Merman	Gray, *FaF* No. 1 (1954)	Olrik I: No. 11		Interp	
38	A47	Agnete og havmanden	Compos	—	—	Agnete and the Merman	Jacobsen 56-57 (1988)	*DgF*		N.A.	Prose
39	A48	Nøkkens svig	C	Arist	17	The Water-King	M. Lewis, *Monk* 289-93 (1796) ="Water King" 59:197 (1797) =*Tales of Wonder* 1:56-60 (1801) =Carrick, *Charms* No. 19 (ca. 1810) =Reburn, letter (1882) =Gardner-Medwin, "Miss Reburn" 95 (1976) =Hull 69 (1940)	Herder, *Volksl.* 2.2: No. 26		N.A.	From German tr.; omits ref. 4 st. of 20; Iowa 4 st. of 20; Iowa 4 st. of 20

39	A48	Nøkkens svig	C	Arist	17	The Water-Man	M. Lewis, *Tales* 1:60-61 (1801)	Herder 2.2: No. 26		N.A.	From German tr.; omits ref.
39	A48	Nøkkens svig	C	Arist	17	The Mer-Man, and Marstig's Daughter	Jamieson, *PBS* 1:208-18 (1806) = Longfellow, *PPE* T9 (1847) ≅ [Bushby], "Ballads" 130:487-88 (1864) ≅ Browne & Moffat 163 (1901)	Syv No. 91		Interp	Omits ref.
							≅ Bantock 100-03 (1911)				8 st. + prose summ.
						Marstig's Daughter	=Van Doren, *Anthol.* 405-06 (1928)		M	Adapt	Mistitled 6 st.
						Marstig's Daughter	=Van Doren & Lapolla, *Anthol. High sch. ed.* 405-06 (1929)		L M	Adapt	Da. text *DgF* 146 Many other printings ↓ ↓ ↓ ↓
							=Van Doren, *Anthol.* rev. 978 (1935)				
							=Van Doren & Lapolla, *World's* 405-06 (1928)				
39	A48	Nøkkens svig	C	Arist	17	Marsk stig's Daughters. 2.	Amateur [Prior], *ODB* No. 22 (1856)	Grimm No. 89.2		N.A.	From German tr.; omits ref.
39	A48	Nøkkens svig	A	Arist	16	Water-Sprite's Treachery	Prior, *ADB* No. 140 (1860)	*DgF*		Interp	Omits ref.
39	A48	Nøkkens svig	C	Arist	17	Mar stig's Daughter and the Merman	Prior, *ADB* No. 141 (1860)	*DgF*		Interp	Omits ref.
39	A48	Nøkkens svig	C	Arist	17	The Merman	Borrow, *Rom. Ball.* 117-19 (1826) = *Works* 9:351-52 (1923) =Warner, *Library* 41:16949 (1902)	ANR No. 49		Adapt	Omits ref.
39	A48	Nøkkens svig	C	Arist	17	Treacherous Merman	Borrow, *Works* 7:196-97 (1923) = *Ball. All Nations* 72-73 (1927)	ANR No. 49		Interp	Omits ref.; some lines *Rom. Ball.*

National Type No.	TSB No.	Title	Version	Tradition	Century	Title of Translation	Translator, Venue, Date	Translator's Source	Lang./Music	Trans. Strategy	Notes
39	A48	Nøkkens svig	Red	—	—	Knavish Merman	Smith-Dampier, *BFD* 21-23 (1910) ≅ *DB* No. 18 (1920) ≅ *BDB* 2: No. 4 (1939)	Olrik 2: No. 4		Interp	
39	A48	Nøkkens svig	Red	—	—	The Fause Kelpie	Gray, *FaF* No. 3 (1954)	Olrik 2: No. 4		Interp	
39	A48	Nøkkens svig	Compos	—	—	Deceit of the Nix	Jacobsen 57-59 (1988)	*DgF*		N.A.	Prose
40	A50	Harpens kraft	**Eb**, red	—	—	Power of the Harp	Prior, *ADB* No. 79 (1860)	ANR No. 53		Interp	
40	A50	Harpens kraft	**Eb**, red	—	—	Power of the Harp	Borrow, *Works* 7:208-11 (1923) = *Ball. All Nations* 77-79 (1927)	ANR No. 53		Interp	
40	A50	Harpens kraft	Red **(A)**	—	—	Mighty Harp	Smith-Dampier, *BDB* 1: No. 8 (1939)	Olrik 1: No. 8		Interp	
40	A50	Harpens kraft	Red **(A)**	—	—	The Harp's Power	Entwistle, *Eur. Ball.* 222-23 (1939)	DgF		Interp	
40	A50	Harpens kraft	Red **(A)**	—	—	Power of the Harp	Gray, *FaF* No. 2 (1954)	Olrik 1: No. 8		Close	
40	A50	Harpens kraft	**G**	Comm	19	Power of Music	Meyer, in Abrahamsen/Dal 10-11 (1965) ≅ Dal, *DBFS* No. 1 (1967) = Rossel, *Scand. Ball.* No. 2 (1982)	*DgF*		Close	Misattributed
40	A50	Harpens kraft	**B**	Ar/Com	16	Might of the Harp	Halkett, in Seeman 22-27 (1967)	*DgF*	L M	Interp	
40	A50	Harpens kraft	**B**	Ar/Com	16	Harpens Kraft	Colbert, "Danish" 10 (1978)	*DgF*		Literal	Omits ref.
40	A50	Harpens kraft	Comp	—	—	Power of the Harp	Jacobsen 59-60 (1988)	*DgF*		N.A.	Prose

41	E148	Rosmer	Ab, red		—	Untitled	Jamieson, *PBS* 1:215-16 (1806) =Rev. *Pop. Ball. S.* col. 476 (1806) ≃ *PBS* 2:202-09 (1806) =Child, *ESB* 1:424-28 (1857) =Child, *ESB* 1:253-57 (1860)	Syv (Vedel 2: No. 6)	Close Interp	5 st. of 30 + prose summ.; omits ref. Full. Omits ref.
41	E148	Rosmer	Bb, red		—	Third Ballad of Rosmer Hafmand	Jamieson, *INA* 416-19 (1814)	Syv (Vedel 2: No. 8)	Interp	
41	E148	Rosmer	C, red		—	Second Ballad of Rosmer Hafmand	Jamieson, *INA* 411-15 (1814) =Longfellow, *PPE* 77-78 (1847)	Syv (Vedel 2: No. 7)	Interp	
41	E148	Rosmer	Ab, red		—	Rosmer the Merman	Amateur [Prior], *ODB* No. 23 (1856)	Grimm No. 49	N.A.	From German tr.; omits ref.
41	E148	Rosmer	Ab, red		—	Rosmer. A.	Prior, *ADB* No. 108 A (1860)	ANR No. 31	Interp	Omits ref.
41	E148	Rosmer	C, red		—	Rosmer. B.	Prior, *ADB* No. 108 B (1860)	ANR No. 32, *DgF*	Interp	Omits ref.
41	E148	Rosmer	Ab, rec		—	Rosmer Mereman	Borrow, *Works* 7:133-37 (1923)	ANR No. 31	Interp	Omits ref.
41	E148	Rosmer	C, red		—	Rosmer	Borrow, *Works* 7:138-41 (1923)	ANR No. 32	Interp	Omits ref.
41	E148	Rosmer	Compos		—	Rosmer	Jacobsen 60-61 (1988)	*DgF*	N.A.	Prose
42	AI2	Havfruens spaadom	B, red		—	Queen and the Mermaid	Prior, *ADB* No. 61 (1860)	ANR No. 69	Interp	
42	AI2	Havfruens spaadom	B, red		—	Mermaid's Prophecy	Borrow, *Works* 7:268-71 (1923)	ANR No. 69	Interp	
42	AI2	Havfruens spaadom	A	Arist	16	Mermaid's Spaeing	Smith-Dampier, *BDB* 1: No. 10 (1939)	Olrik 1: No. 10	Interp	

National Type No.	TSB No.	Title	Version	Tradition	Century	Title of Translation	Translator, Venue, Date	Translator's Source	Lang. Music	Trans. Strategy	Notes
42	A12	Havfruens spaadom	A	Arist	16	Mermaid as Spaewife	Gray, *FaF* No. 4 (1954)	Olrik 1: No. 10		Interp	
43	A52	Hr. Luno og havfruen	sole	Arist	16	Sir Luno and the Mermaid	Prior, *ADB* No. 138 (1860)	*DgF*		Interp	
43	A52	Hr. Luno og havfruen	sole	Arist	16	Sir Luno and the Mermaid	Smith-Dampier, *BDB* 2: No. 2 (1939) =Warnock & Anderson 520-21 (1959)	Olrik 2: No. 2		Close	
44	E140	Hr. Hylleland henter sin jomfru	A	Arist	16	How Sir Hylleland Wins his Bride	Prior, *ADB* No. 133 (1860)	*DgF*		Interp	
44	E140	Hr. Hylleland henter sin jomfru	Red (A)	—	—	Hylleland Brings Home his Bride	Gray, *FaF* No. 27 (1954)	Recke No. 42		Interp	
45	A49	Hr. Bosmer i elvehjem	A	Arist	16	Sir Bosmer in Elfland	Prior, *ADB* No. 151 (1860)	*DgF*		Interp	
45	A49	Hr. Bosmer i elvehjem	Red	—	—	Sir Bosmer in Elfland	Smith-Dampier, *BDB* 2: No. 5 (1939)	Olrik 2: No. 6		Interp	
45	A49	Hr. Bosmer i elvehjem	Red	—	—	Sir Bosmer in Elfland	Gray, *FaF* No. 5 (1954)	Olrik 2: No. 6		Interp	
46	A65	Elvehøj	**Bd**, red	—	—	Elver's Hoh	M. Lewis, *Tales* 1: 31-33 (1801)	Herder 1.2: No. 14		N.A.	From German tr.; omits ref.
46	A65	Elvehøj	**Bd**, red	—	—	Elvershöh	F.,J., "Elvershöh" (1817)	Herder 1.2: No. 14		N.A.	From German tr.; omits ref.

46	A65	Elvehøj	Bd, red		—	Elfer Hill	Jamieson, *PBS* 1:225-28 (1806) = Longfellow, *PPE* 79 (1847)	Vedel 2: No. 9		Close	Omits ref.
							= Van Doren, *Anthol.* rev. ed. 979-81 (1935)				Omits ref.
							= Holst 114-15 (1941)				Omits ref.
46	A65	Elvehøj	Bd, red		—	Elvir Hill	Borrow, *Rom. Ball.* 111-14 (1826) = *Works* 9:348-49 (1923)	ANR No. 34		Adapt	Omits ref.
							= Holst 116-17 (1941)				Omits ref.
46	A65	Elvehøj	Bd, red		—	Elfhill-Side	Robinson, "Popular" 288-89 (1836)	ANR No. 34		Interp	Omits ref.
46	A65	Elvehøj	Bd, red		—	The Elf Hill	Amateur, [Prior], *ODB* No. 12 (1856)	Grimm No. 33		N.A.	From German tr.; omits ref.
46	A65	Elvehøj	A	Arist	16	Elfin Hill. A.	Prior, *ADB* No. 136 A (1860)	*DgF*		Interp	Omits ref.
46	A65	Elvehøj	Red (B)		—	Elfin Hill. B.	Prior, *ADB* No. 136 B (1860)	*DgF* & ANR 34		Interp	Omits ref.
46	A65	Elvehøj	Bd, red		—	Elver's Height	Baker, in Loewe 2:32-38 (1903)	Herder I.2: No. 14	M	N.A.	From German tr.; omits ref.
46	A65	Elvehøj	Rec		—	Oluf's Ballad	Forestier, in Stub 13-17 (1907)	Unknown	M	Adapt	4 st. Literary
46	A65	Elvehøj	Bd, red		—	Lord Ronald and the Fairies	Gray, *Songs* 64-65 (1920)	Herder I.2: No. 14		N.A.	From German tr.; omits ref.
46	A65	Elvehøj	Red (Ca)		—	The Elf Hill	Meyer, in Dal, *DBFS* No. 3 (1967)	*DgF*		Close	
47	A63	Elveskud	Red (B)		—	Erl-King's Daughter	M. Lewis, "Erl-Kings" 371-72 (1796) ≅ *Tales* 1:53-55 (1801)	Herder 2.2: No. 27		N.A.	From German tr.; omits ref.

National Type No.	TSB No.	Title	Version	Tradition	Century	Title of Translation	Translator, Venue, Date	Translator's Source	Lang. Music	Trans. Strategy	Notes
47	A63	Elveskud	Red (B)	—	—	Erl-King's Daughter	L, D.H. 153-54 (1830)	Herder 2.2: No. 27		N.A.	From German tr.; omits ref.
47	A63	Elveskud	Red (B)	—	—	Erl-King's Daughter	Mangan, "Stray L" 631-32 (1840) =Anth. Germ. 2:53-56 (1845) =Poems 215-18 (1894) =Longfellow, PoP8:151-53 (1876)	Herder 2.2: No. 27		N.A.	From German tr.; omits ref.
47	A63	Elveskud	B	?Arist	17	Sir Oluf and the Elf-King's Daughter	Jamieson, PBS1:219-24 (1806) =Grimm, Drei Alts. L 14-16 (1813) =Child ESB1:403-06 (1857) =Child, ESB1:298-301 (1860) =Wilson, PPS2:38-39 (1877)	Syv No. 87		Adapt	Omits ref.
47	A63	Elveskud	B	?Arist	17	Sir Olave	Amateur [Prior], ODB No. 11 (1856)	Grimm No. 8		N.A.	From German tr.; omits ref.
47	A63	Elveskud	A	Arist	16	Sir Olave. A.	Prior, ADB No. 81 A (1860)	DgF		Interp	
47	A63	Elveskud	Red (B)	—	—	Sir Olave. B.	Prior, ADB No. 81 B (1860)	DgF, ANR 35		Adapt	
47	A63	Elveskud	Red (B)	—	—	Elf Dance	Buchanan, BSA52-55 (1866)	ANR No. 35		Adapt	
47	A63	Elveskud	A	Arist	16	Elveskud	Child, ESPB1:375-76 (1882)	DgF		N.A.	Prose summ.
47	A63	Elveskud	Red (B)	—	—	Sir Olaf	Borrow, Works7:142-44 (1923)	ANR No. 35		Close	

47	A63	Elveskud	Red	—	—	Elfin Shaft	Smith-Dampier, *DB* No. 17 (1920) ≅ Smith-Dampier, et al, "Group" 767–68 (1924) ≅ *BDB*1: No. 7 (1939)	Olrik 1: No. 7		Close	
47	A63	Elveskud	B	?Arist	17	Elf-Shot	Meyer, in Dal, *DBfS* No. 2 (1967)	*DgF*		Close	
47	A63	Elveskud	Red	—	—	Elfin Sorcery	Meyer, in Billeskov Jansen & Mitchell 1:15-19 (1972)	Olrik 1: No. 7	L	Close	
48	A59	Hr. Magnus og bjærgtrolden	Red	—	—	Sir Magnus and the Elf-Maid	Prior, *ADB* No. 156 (1860) =M. Leach, *Ball. Bk.* 129-31 (1955)	*DgF*		Interp	
49	A439	Malfred og Magnus	A	Arist	17	Malfred and Mogens	Prior, *ADB* No. 82 (1860)	*DgF*		Interp	Omits ref.
50	B12	Hellig-Olavs væddefart	A, red	—		King Oluf the Saint	Borrow, in Borrow-Bowring 59-61 (1830) =Longfellow, *PPE* 79-81 (1847) =Longfellow, *PoP* 3:177-81 (1876) ≅ *Works* 7:228-32 (1923)	ANR No. 57		Interp	
50	B12	Hellig-Olavs væddefart	A, red	—		Saint Olave's Voyage	Amateur [Prior], *ODB* No. 21 (1856)	Grimm No. 1		N.A.	From German tr.
50	B12	Hellig-Olavs væddefart	A, red	—		Saint Olave's Voyage	Prior, *ADB* No. 33 (1860) =Rev. *ADB* 345 (1860)	*DgF*		Interp	16 st. of 51
50	B12	Hellig-Olavs væddefart	Red	—		King Oluf and His Brother	Smith-Dampier, *BDB*2: No. 6 (1939)	Olrik 2: No. 7		Interp	
50	B12	Hellig-Olavs væddefart	B	Ar/Com	16	St. Olav's Race	Meyer, in Dal, *DBfS* No. 8 (1967)	*DgF*		Close	
50	B12	Hellig-Olavs væddefart	C	Arist	17	Hellig Olavs væddefart	Jacobsen 40 (1988)	*DgF*		Literal	2 st. of 17 + prose summ.

National Type No.	TSB No.	Title	Version	Tradition	Century	Title of Translation	Translator, Venue, Date	Translator's Source	Lang; Music	Trans. Strategy	Notes
51	E116	Hellig-Olav og troldene	sole, red	—	—	Saint Oluf	Borrow, *Rom. Ball.* 53-57 (1826) = *Works* 9: 308-11 (1923)	ANR No. 58		Adapt	Omits ref.
51	E116	Hellig-Olav og troldene	sole, red	—	—	Saint Olave at Hornelen	Prior, *ADB* No. 34 (1860)	ANR No. 58		Interp	Omits ref.
51	E116	Hellig-Olav og troldene	Red	—	—	King Olaf and the Trolls	Smith-Dampier, *BfD* 3-6 (1910)	Olrik I: No. 9		Adapt	
51	E116	Hellig-Olav og troldene	Red	—	—	Saint Olaf and the Trolls	Smith-Dampier, *BDB* I: No. 9 (1939)	Olrik I: No. 9		Close	Uses some *BfD*
52	A14	Trolden og bondens hustru	D, red	—	—	Alice Brand	Scott, *Lady* 158-64 (1810) = *Poetical W.* 243-44 (1914)	Syv (Vedel 2: No. 1)		Adapt	Literary adapt. Innumerable eds.
52	A14	Trolden og bondens hustru	D, red	—	—	Elfin Gray	Jamieson, in Scott, "Lady" 367-75 (1810) =Scott, *Poetical W.* 296-98 (1914)	Syv (Vedel 2: No. 1)		Interp	Many later eds.; some lack trans.
52	A14	Trolden og bondens hustru	D, red	—	—	The Elf	Amateur [Prior], *ODB* No. 1 (1856)	Grimm No. 68		N.A.	From German tr.; omits ref.
52	A14	Trolden og bondens hustru	D, red	—	—	Elf and the Farmer's Wife. A.	Prior, *ADB* No. 124 A (1860)	*DgF*		Interp	Omits ref.
52	A14	Trolden og bondens hustru	Red (A)	—	—	Elf and the Farmer's Wife. B.	Prior, *ADB* No. 124 B (1860)	*DgF*		Interp	Omits ref.
52	A14	Trolden og bondens hustru	B	Arist	17	Elf and the Farmer's Wife. C.	Prior, *ADB* No. 124 C (1860)	*DgF*		Close	Omits ref.
52	A14	Trolden og bondens hustru	D, red	—	—	Wee, Wee Gnome	Buchanan, *BSA* 21-27 (1866)	ANR No. 23		Adapt	
52	A14	Trolden og bondens hustru	D, red	—	—	Ellen of Villenskov	Borrow, *Works* 7:103-08 (1923)	ANR No. 23		Interp	Omits ref.

52	A14	Trolden og bondens hustru	B	Arist	16	Troll and the House-wife	Cox, in Steenstrup, *MPB* 155-56, 191-92 (1914)	*DgF*	L	Close	3 st. of 14; omits ref.
52	A14	Trolden og bondens hustru	C	Arist	17	Troll and the House-wife	Cox, in Steenstrup, *MPB* 155-56, 191-92 (1914)	*DgF*	L	Adapt	5 st. of 23; omits ref.
52	A14	Trolden og bondens hustru	A	Ar/Com	16	Troll and the Farmer's Wife	Jacobsen 36 (1988)	*DgF*		Literal	3 st. of 13 + prose summ.
54	A20	Varulven	Red	—	—	Untitled	[Bushby], "Ballads" 131:47-48 (1864)	*DgF*		Interp	16 st. + prose summ.
55	A19	Jomfruen i ulveham	A	Arist	16	Maiden Transformed to a Wer-wolf	Prior, *ADB* No. 115 (1860)	*DgF*		Interp	Omits ref.
56	A16	Jomfruen i fugleham	Red	—	—	Maid as a Hind and a Hawk	Prior, *ADB* No. 117 (1860)	*DgF*		Interp	Omits ref.
56	A16	Jomfruen i fugleham	E	?Arist	16	Transformed Damsel	Borrow, *Works* 7:145-46 (1923) = *Ball. All Nations* 56-57 (1927)	ANR No. 36		Interp	Omits ref.
56	A16	Jomfruen i fugleham	Red (Be)	—	—	Transformed Damsel	Borrow, *Works* 7:147-49 (1923) = *Ball. All Nations* 58-60 (1927)	ANR No. 37		Close	Omits ref.
56	A16	Jomfruen i fugleham	Red (F)	—	—	Cruel Step-Dame	Borrow, *Works* 7:150-52 (1923)	ANR No. 38		Interp	Omits ref.
56	A16	Jomfruen i fugleham	Red	—	—	Enchanted Maiden Maiden in Bird's Plumage	Smith-Dampier, *DB* No. 20 (1920) ≅ *BDB* 1: No. 13 (1939)	Olrik I: No. 13		Interp	
56	A16	Jomfruen i fugleham	A	Arist	16	Maiden Transformed into a Bird	Cox, in Steenstrup, *MPB* 53-54 (1914)	*DgF*		Adapt	4 st. of 23; omits ref.

National Type No.	TSB No.	Title	Version	Tradition	Century	Title of Translation	Translator, Venue, Date	Translator's Source	Lang/Music	Trans. Strategy	Notes
56	A16	Jomfruen i fugleham	C	Arist	16	Maiden Transformed into a Bird	Cox, in Steenstrup, *MPB* 175 (1914)	*DgF*		Interp	4 st. of 19; omits ref.
56	A16	Jomfruen i fugleham	Red	—	—	Maid as Hind and Hawk	Gray, *FaF* No. 23 (1954)	Olrik I: No. 13		Interp	
56	A16	Jomfruen i fugleham	C	Arist	16	Feathered Maiden	Meyer, in Dal, *DBFS* No. 5 (1967) =Rossel, *Scand. Ball.* No. 4 (1982)	*DgF*		Close	
57	—	Nattergalen	sole	Brds	18	The Nightingale	Stokes, "Second Batch" 94-95 (1855)	ANR No. 39		Adapt	
57	—	Nattergalen	sole	Brds	18	The Nightingale	Prior, *ADB* No. 116 (1860) =Drummond-Davies 17-19 (1861)	*DgF*		Interp	14 of 26 st. + prose summ.
57	—	Nattergalen	sole	Brds	18	Nightingale, or the Transformed Damsel	Borrow, *Works* 7:153-56 (1923)	ANR No. 39		Interp	
57	—	Nattergalen	sole	Brds	18	Nattergalen	Child, *ESPB* 1:336-37 (1882)	*DgF*		N.A.	Prose summ.
57	—	Nattergalen	sole	Brds	18	The Nightingale	Wood, in Lund, *SBFS* 4-5 (1947)	ANR No. 39	L M	Adapt	4 st. of 26
57	—	Nattergalen	sole	Brds	18	The Nightingale	Grainger, *Night.* 2 (1931) =*DFMS: Power* L2 (n.d.) =I. Lewis, *Source* G. 249 (1991)	Own collecting	L M	N.I.	3 st. + prose summ.
58	A27	Jomfruen i hindeham				Untitled	Ker, "On Dan. B." 1:368 (1904) =*Coll. Ess.* 2:78 (1925)				See Swedish, SMB 10

58	A27	Jomfruen i hindeham				Maiden Hind	Smith-Dampier, *BDB* 1: No. 12 (1939) =Creekmore, *Little Tr.* 506)1952 =Creekmore, *Lyrics* 227-28 (1959) =Abrahamsen/Dal 12-13 (1965)			See Swedish, SMB 10
58	A27	Jomfruen i hindeham				Girl in Hind's Skin	Gray, *FaF* No. 24 (1954)			See Swedish, SMB10
59	A28	Jomfruen i ormeham	sole	Arist	16	Maiden in the Shape of a Snake	Prior, *ADB* No. 119 (1860)	*DgF*	Interp	Omits ref.
59	A28	Jomfruen i ormeham	sole	Arist	16	Jomfruen i Ormeham	Child, *ESPB* 1:307 (1882)	*DgF*	N.A.	Prose summ.
59	A28	Jomfruen i ormeham	Red	—	—	Serpent Bride	Smith-Dampier, *BDB* 2: No. 9 (1939)	Olrik 2: No. 10	Interp	
59	A28	Jomfruen i ormeham	Red	—	—	Maid Disguised as a Serpent	Gray, *FaF* No. 25 (1954)	Olrik 2: No. 10	Interp	
60	A17	Valravnen	**F, red**	—	—	Night Raven	Amateur [Prior], *ODB* No. 9 (1856)	Grimm No. 31	N.A.	From German tr.; omits ref.
60	A17	Valravnen	**F, rec**	—	—	The Raven	Prior, *ADB* No. 88 (1860)	*DgF*	Interp	Omits ref.
60	A17	Valravnen	**F, red**	—	—	The Verner Raven	Borrow, *Works* 7:120-24 (1923)	ANR No. 26	Close	Omits ref.
60	A17	Valravnen	Red	—	—	Wood-Raven	Smith-Dampier, *BfD* 24-27 (1910)	Olrik 2: No. 12	Interp	
60	A17	Valravnen	**A**	Arist	16	The Valraven	Cox, in Steenstrup, *MPB* 29-30 (1914)	*DgF*	Interp	2 st. of 25
60	A17	Valravnen	Red	—	—	Wood-Raven	Smith-Dampier, *BDB* 2: No. 11 (1939)	Olrik 2: No. 12	Interp	Uses some *BfD*
61	A35	Ravn fører runer	sole	Arist	17	Raven Rune-bearer	Prior, *ADB* No. 93 (1860)	*DgF*	Interp	Omits ref.
61	A35	Ravn fører runer	Red	—	—	Corbie as Rune-Bearer	Gray, *FaF* No. 29 (1954)	Recke No. 59	Interp	

National Type No.	TSB No.	Title	Version	Tradition	Century	Title of Translation	Translator, Venue, Date	Translator's Source	Lang; Music	Trans. Strategy	Notes
62	A26	Blak og Ravn hin brune	Red (A)	—	—	Mournful Marriage	Stokes, "Dan. Ball." 654-55 (1852)	Winding 65-71		Interp	
62	A26	Blak og Ravn hin brune	Red (A)	—	—	Unfortunate Marriage	Borrow, Works 7:202-07 (1923)	ANR No. 52		Interp	Omits ref.
63	A25	Bedeblak	sole	Arist	18	Bedeblack	Prior, ADB No. 125 (1860)	DgF		Interp	
63	A25	Bedeblak	Red	—	—	Bedeblak	Gray, Fa/ No. 26 (1954)	Recke No. 53		Interp	
64	A23	Dalby-bjørn	B, red	—	—	Dalby Bear	Amateur [Prior], ODB No. 16 (1856)	Grimm No. 75		N.A.	From German tr.; omits ref.
64	A23	Dalby-bjørn	B, red	—	—	Dalby Bear	Prior, ADB No. 83 (1860)	DgF		Interp	
64	A23	Dalby-bjørn	B, red	—	—	Dalby Bear	Borrow, Works 7:109-11 (1923) = Ball. All Nations 45-47 (1927)	ANR No. 24		Close	Omits ref.
64	A23	Dalby-bjørn	B, red	—	—	Dalby Bear	Cox, in Steenstrup, MPB 180 (1914)	DgF		Close	4 st. of 28; omits ref.
64	A23	Dalby-bjørn	Red (A)	—	—	Bear of Dalby	Smith-Dampier, BDB 2: No. 10 (1939)	Olrik 2: No. 11		Close	
65	A29	Lindormen	Ab, red	—	—	Lindworm	Prior, ADB No. 118 (1860)	DgF		Interp	Omits ref.
65	A29	Lindormen	Ab, red	—	—	Serpent Knight	Borrow, Works 7:57-58 (1923) = Ball. All Nations 61-62 (1927)	ANR No. 40		Close	Omits ref.
65	A29	Lindormen	A	Arist	16	The Dragon	Smith-Dampier, BDB 2: No. 13 (1939)	Olrik 2: No. 14		Interp	
66	A30	Jomfruen i linden	A	Arist	16	Maid in the Linden Tree	Prior, ADB No. 120 (1860)	DgF		Interp	

			C	Arist				DgF			
66	A30	Jomfruen i linden	C	Arist	17	Maid in the Linden Tree	Cox, in Steenstrup, *MPB* 185 (1914)	*DgF*		Close	4 st. Of 36; omits ref.
67	A43	Ridderen i hjorteham	Red (B)	—	—	Knight Disguised as a Hart	Prior, *ADB* No. 159 (1860)	*DgF*		Interp	
67	A43	Ridderen i hjorteham	E	?Arist	17	Knight in the Deer's Shape	Borrow, *Works* 7:159-62 (1923)	ANR No. 41		Interp	Omits ref.
67	A43	Ridderen i hjorteham	Red	—	—	Knight in Deer's Skin	Gray, *FaF* No. 37 (1954)	Recke No. 51		Interp	
67	A43	Ridderen i hjorteham	A	Arist	15	Knight in Deerskin	Meyer, in Dal, *DBFS* No. 74k (1967)	*DgF*	L	Interp	7 st. fragm.
68	A44	Ridderen i fugleham	C	Arist	17	Knight in Bird-Dress	Prior, *ADB* No. 131 (1860) =Drummond-Davies 75 (1861)	*DgF*		Interp	17 st. + prose summ.
68	A44	Ridderen i fugleham	A	Arist	16	Ridderen i Fugleham	Child, *ESPB* 5:39 (1894)	*DgF*		N.A.	Prose summ.
68	A44	Ridderen i fugleham	B	Arist	17	Ridderen i Fugleham	Child, *ESPB* 5:39 (1894)	*DgF*		N.A.	Prose summ.
68	A44	Ridderen i fugleham	C	Arist	18	Ridderen i Fugleham	Child, *ESPB* 5:39 (1894)	*DgF*		N.A.	Prose summ.
68	A44	Ridderen i fugleham	Red	—	—	Knight in the Feather-Fell	Smith-Dampier, *BDB* 2: No. 12 (1939)	Olrik 2: No. 13		Close	
69	A46	Kæmperne paa Dovrefjeld	c, red	—	—	Heroes of Dovrefjeld	Borrow, *Rom. Ball.* 58-60 (1826) = *Works* 9:312-13 (1923)	ANR No. 48		Adapt	Omits ref.
69	A46	Kæmperne paa Dovrefjeld	c, red	—	—	Untitled	Stokes, "Sec. Batch" 91 (1855)	ANR No. 48		Close	
69	A46	Kæmperne paa Dovrefjeld	c, red	—	—	Twelve Wizards	Amateur [Prior], *ODB* No. 6 (1856)	Grimm No. 29		N.A.	From German tr.; omits ref.
69	A46	Kæmperne paa Dovrefjeld	c, red	—	—	Twelve Wizards	Prior, *ADB* No. 87 (1860)	ANR No. 48		Interp	Omits ref.

National Type No.	TSB No.	Title	Version	Tradition	Century	Title of Translation	Translator, Venue, Date	Translator's Source	Lang. Music	Trans. Strategy	Notes
70	A45	Ungen Svendal	E	Comm	19	Young Swennendal	Prior, *ADB* No. 84 (1860) =Rev. *ADB* 345 (1861) =Rossel, *Scand. Ball.* No. 5 (1982)	*DgF*		Interp	Omits ref.
70	A45	Ungen Svendal	Bc, red	—	—	Young Swaigder	Borrow, *Works* 7:163-69 (1923) = *Ball. All Nations* 63-68 (1927)	ANR No. 42		Close	Omits ref.
70	A45	Ungen Svendal	A	Arist	16	Child Sveidal	Ker, *Epic* 126 (1897)	*DgF*		Close	2 st. of 42; omits ref.
70	A45	Ungen Svendal	Red	—	—	Young Sveidal	Cox, in Steenstrup, *MPB* 228 (1914)	*DgF*		Close	3 st.; omits ref.
70	A45	Ungen Svendal	Red	—	—	Young Svejdal	Smith-Dampier, *DB* No. 14 (1920) ≈ *BDB* 1: No. 14 (1939)	Olrik I: No. 14		Interp	
72	D47	Unge Hr. Tor og Jomfru Tore	A	Arist	16	Sir Thor and Lady Silvermor	Prior, *ADB* No. 122 (1860)	*DgF*		Interp	
72	D47	Unge Hr. Tor og Jomfru Tore	D, red	—	—	Finnish Arts	Borrow, *Works* 7: 212-23 (1923)	ANR No. 54		Interp	Omits ref.
72	D47	Unge Hr. Tor og Jomfru Tore	A	Arist	16	Young Sir Thor and Lady Thore	Cox, in Steenstrup, *MPB* 143-44 (1914)	*DgF*	L	Interp	
73	A10	Ridderens runeslag	B, red	—	—	Fair Mettelille	Prior, *ADB* No. 105 (1860)	ANR No. 117		Interp	
73	A10	Ridderens runeslag	B, red	—	—	Maid Mettelil	Buchanan, *BSA* 45-50 (1866)	ANR No. 117		Adapt	
73	A10	Ridderens runeslag	B, red	—	—	Damsel Mette	Borrow, *Works* 7-367-71 (1923)	ANR No. 117		Interp	Omits ref.

73	A10	Ridderens runeslag	A	Arist	16	Untitled	Cox, in Steenstrup, *MPB* 172 (1914)	*DgF*		Close	3 st. of 39; omits ref.
73	A10	Ridderens runeslag	Red	—	—	Sir Oluf and His Gilded Horn	Smith-Dampier, *BDB* 2: No. 8 (1939)	Olrik 2: No. 9		Interp	
73	A10	Ridderens runeslag	Red	—	—	Sir Oluf and His Magic Lute	Grey, *FaF* No. 30 (1954)	Olrik 2: No. 9 & Recke No. 148		Interp	Omits ref.
73	A10	Ridderens runeslag	A	Arist	16	Knight's Runes	Meyer, in Dal, *DBfS* No. 4 (1967)	*DgF*		Close	
73	A10	Ridderens runeslag	A	Arist	16	Sir Peter and Sir Oluf	Arengo Jones in Seeman 58-65 (1967)	*DgF*	L	Adapt	
74	A8	Tidemand og Blidelil	B	Arist	17	Sir Tideman and Blidelill	Prior, *ADB* No. 149 (1860)	*DgF*		Adapt	
75	A9	Det tvungne samtykke	Red	—	—	Compulsory Marriage	Prior, *ADB* No. 173 (1860)	*DgF*		Interp	Omits ref.
75	A9	Det tvungne samtykke	Ae	Arist	17	Forced Consent	Borrow, *Works* 8:42-44 (1923)	ANR No. 149		Interp	Omits ref.
76	A4	Ridder Stigs bryllup	Red (A)	—	—	Knight Stig's Wedding	Prior, *ADB* No. 85 (1860)	ANR No. 46		Interp	Omits ref.
76	A4	Ridder Stigs bryllup	Red (A)	—	—	Child Stig and Child Findal	Borrow, *Works* 7:190-95 (1923)	ANR No. 46		Interp	Omits ref.
76	A4	Ridder Stigs bryllup	B	Arist	17	Sir Stig's Wedding	Cox, in Steenstrup, *MPB* 43 (1914)	*DgF*		Interp	2 st. of 44; omits ref.
76	A4	Ridder Stigs bryllup	F	Arist	17	Knight Stig's Wedding	Cox, in Steenstrup, *MPB* 13 (1914)	*DgF*		Interp	2 st. of 22; omits ref.
76	A4	Ridder Stigs bryllup	Red	—	—	Sir Stig and His Runes	Smith-Dampier, *BDB* 2: No. 14 (1939)	Olrik 2: No. 15		Close	
76	A4	Ridder Stigs bryllup	Red	—	—	Sir Stig's Runes	Gray, *FaF* No. 28 (1954)	Olrik 2: No. 15		Interp	38 of 61 st.

National Type No.	TSB No.	Title	Version	Tradition	Century	Title of Translation	Translator, Venue, Date	Translator's Source	Lang. Music	Trans. Strategy	Notes
76	A4	Ridder Stigs bryllup	C	Arist	17	Ridder Stig's Bryllup	Richmond, "Stig I." 36-37 (1958)	*DgF*		N.A.	Prose summ.
78	A2	Hr. Peder og Mettelille	Red (**Bb**)	—	—	Sir Peter and Mettelille	Prior, *ADB* No. 86 (1860)	ANR No. 47		Interp	Omits ref.
79	A3	Kongesønnens Runner	A	Arist	17	Retorted Rune	Prior, *ADB* No. 107 (1860)	*DgF*		Interp	Omits ref.
81	A11	Sövnerunerne	A	Comm	19	Sövnerunerne	Child, *ESPB* I:391 (1882)	*DgF*		N.A.	Prose summ.
82	A41	Ribold og Guldborg	G, red	—	—	Ribolt and Guldborg	Jamieson, *IMM* 317-34 (1814) =Longfellow, *PPE* 71-73 (1847)	Syv No. 88		Interp	
82	A41	Ribold og Guldborg	G, red	—	—	Fatal Appeal	Amateur [Prior], *ODB* No. 31 (1856)	Grimm No. 3		N.A.	From German tr.; omits ref.
82	A41	Ribold og Guldborg	G, red	—	—	Ribolt and Guldborg	Prior, *ADB* No. 94A (1860)	ANR No. 148		Interp	Omits ref.
82	A41	Ribold og Guldborg	T	?Comm	—	Rederbrand and Guldborg	Prior, *ADB* No. 94B (1860)	*DgF*		Interp	Omits ref.
82	A41	Ribold og Guldborg	Compos	—	—	Ribold and Guldborg	Child, *ESPB* I:89 (1882)	*DgF*		N.A.	Prose summ.
82	A41	Ribold og Guldborg	G, red	—	—	Sir Ribolt	Borrow, *Works* 8:36-41 (1923) = *Ball. All Nations* 104-09 (1927)	ANR No. 148		Interp	Omits ref.
82	A41	Ribold og Guldborg	Red	—	—	Ribold og Guldborg	Smith-Dampier, *BDB* 2: No. 1 (1939)	Olrik 2: No. 1		Interp	Danish-Icel. composite
82	A41	Ribold og Guldborg	Red	—	—	Ribold and Guldborg	Gray, *FaF* No. 12 (1954)	Olrik 2: No. 1		Interp	Danish-Icel. composite

82	A41	Ribold og Guldborg	A	Arist	16	Ribold og Guldborg	Gardner-Medwin, "Paradise" 306-07 (1963)	DgF	L	Close	7 st. of 41
82	A41	Ribold og Guldborg	C	Arist	17	Ribold og Guldborg	Gardner-Medwin, "Paradise" 309-10 (1963)	DgF	L	Close	9 st. of 54
83	A42	Hildebrand og Hilde	Red(Ea)	—	—	Hellalyle and Hildebrand	Stokes, "Sec. Batch" 89 (1855)	ANR No. 154		Interp	
83	A42	Hildebrand og Hilde	F, red	—	—	Hillelild	Amateur [Prior], ODB No. 2 (1856)	Grimm No. 16		N.A.	From German tr.; omits ref.
83	A42	Hildebrand og Hilde	A	Arist	16	Hildebrande and Hille	Prior, ADB No. 94C (1860)	DgF		Interp	Omits ref.
83	A42	Hildebrand og Hilde	Red(Ba)	—	—	Hillelille and Hildebrand	Prior, ADB No.94D (1860)	ANR No. 154		Interp	
83	A42	Hildebrand og Hilde	F, rel	—	—	Hillelille in Her Chamber	Prior, ADB No.94E (1860)	DgF		Interp	Omits ref.
83	A42	Hildebrand og Hilde	H	Comm	19	Hyldebrand and Hyldestil	Prior, ADB No.94F (1860)	DgF		Interp	Omits ref.
83	A42	Hildebrand og Hilde	Red(Ba)	—	—	Helga and Hildebrand	Buchanan, BSA 16-20 (1866)	ANR No. 154		Adapt	
83	A42	Hildebrand og Hilde	Compcs	—	—	Hildebrand and Hilde	Child, ESPB 1:89-90 (1882)	DgF		N.A.	Prose summ.
83	A42	Hildebrand og Hilde	Red(Ba)	—	—	Hildebrand and Helleil	Morris, Poems 141-44 (1891) =Poems/Love 162-65 (1896) =Coll. Works 9:203-05 (1911)	ANR No. 154		Close	
83	A42	Hildebrand og Hilde	Red	—	—	Untitled	Ker, "On Dan. B." 1:365 (1904) =Coll. Ess. 2:74 (1925)	Olrik I: No. 15		Literal	Prose
83	A42	Hildebrand og Hilde	A	Arist	16	Hildebrand and Hilde	Cox, in Steenstrup, MPB 50 (1914)	DgF		Close	4 st. of 42; omits ref.

National Type No.	TSB No.	Title	Version	Tradition	Cen-tury	Title of Translation	Translator, Venue, Date	Translator's Source	Lang. Music	Trans. Strategy	Notes
83	A42	Hildebrand og Hilde	C	Arist	17	Hildebrand and Hilde	Cox, in Steenstrup 93 (1914)	DgF		Interp	2 st. of 34
83	A42	Hildebrand og Hilde	Red	—	—	Griefs of Hillelille	Smith-Dampier, BDB I: No 15 (1939)	Olrik I: No. 15		Interp	
83	A42	Hildebrand og Hilde	Red	—	—	Sorrows of Hillelille	Gray, FaF No. 13 (1954)	Olrik I: No. 15		Interp	
84	A40	Hustru og mands moder	H	?Arist	17	Sir Stig and Lady Torelild	Jamieson, IMA 344-47 (1814)	Syv No. 90		Interp	
84	A40	Hustru og mands moder	H	?Arist	17	Wicked Mother-in-law	Prior, ADB No. 89 (1860)	ANR No. 43		Interp	
84	A40	Hustru og mands moder	A*	Comm	19	Hustru og Mands Moder	Child, ESPB I:82-83 (1882)	DgF		N.A.	Prose summ
84	A40	Hustru og mands moder	Compos	—	—	Hustru og Mands Moder	Child, ESPB I:83 (1882)	DgF		N.A.	2 st. + prose summ
84	A40	Hustru og mands moder	H	?Arist	17	Wicked Stepmother	Borrow, Works 7:170-74 (1923)	ANR No. 43		Interp	
84	A40	Hustru og mands moder	F	Arist	17	Wicked Stepmother	Borrow, Works 7:175-77 (1923) = Ball. All Nations 69-71 (1927)	ANR No. 44		Close	
85	A40	Hustru og slegfred	sole	Arist	16	Hustru og Slegfred	Child, ESPB I:83 (1882)	DgF		N.A.	Prose summ.
89	A68	Moderen under mulde	B	?Arist	17	Ghaist's Warning	Jamieson, in Scott, "Lady" 376-81 (1810) = Scott, Poetical W. 298-99 (1914) = Robinson, "Popular" 285 (1836)	Syv No. 78	L	Interp	Many later eds.; some lack trans.
89	A68	Moderen under mulde	B	?Arist	17	Untitled	"On the State" 397-98 (1820)	Syv No. 78		Interp	Cp. Grimm No. 30
89	A68	Moderen under mulde	B	?Arist	17	Ghost's Warning	Amateur [Prior], ODB No. 5 (1856)	Grimm No. 30		N.A.	From German tr.; omits ref.

89	A68	Moderen under mulde	Red (B)	—	—	Return of the Dead	Milligan 229-33 (1856)	Oehlenschläger *GdF* 82-85	Close	
89	A68	Moderen under mulde	Red	—	—	Buried Mother	Prior, *ADB* No. 35 (1860) =Drummond-Davies 11-12 (1861)	ANR No. 28	Interp	Omits ref. 16 st. + prose summ.
89	A68	Moderen under mulde	Red	—	—	Mother's Ghost	Longfellow, *Aftermath* (1873) =*Tales* (1873) =*Comp. P. Wks.* 282-83 (1893) =*Works* 4:248-51 (1966)	ANR No. 28	Close / Close	Not seen. *Many* later eds.
89	A68	Moderen under mulde	Red	—	—	Swayne Dyring	Stokes, "Dan. Ball." 653-54 (1852) ≅"Dan. Ball. II," Rev. 47 (1861)	Winding 31-34	Interp	
89	A68	Moderen under mulde	Lit	—	—	Cruel Stepmother	Unidentified, in Reburn (1882) =Gardner-Medwin, "Miss Reburn" 97-98 (1976)	N.I.	Adapt / N.A.	From unident. literary adapt. 1 st + prose summ.
89	A68	Moderen under mulde	Red	—	—	Mother under the Mould	Morris, Coll. *Works* 24:352-55 (1915)	ANR No. 28	Close	
89	A68	Moderen under mulde	Red	—	—	Return of the Dead	Borrow, *Works* 7:127-32 (1923) =*Ball. All Nations* 50-55 (1927)	ANR No. 28	Interp	
89	A68	Moderen under mulde	B	?Arist	17	Mither's Ghaist	Gray, *Arrows* No. 50 (1932)	Loewe 10-20	N.A.	From German tr. of Jamieson tr.
89	A68	Moderen under mulde	A	Arist	16	Buried Mother	Cox, in Steenstrup, *MPB* 188-89, 220 (1914)	*DgF*	Close	10 st. of 46; omits ref.
89	A68	Moderen under mulde	Red (A)	—	—	Mother under the Mould	Smith-Dampier, *BDB* 2: No. 7 (1939)	Olrik 2: no. 8	Interp	

National Type No.	TSB No.	Title	Version	Tradition	Century	Title of Translation	Translator, Venue, Date	Translator's Source	Lang. Music	Trans. Strategy	Notes
89	A68	Moderen under mulde	Øa	Comm	19	Buried Mother	Meyer, in Dal, *DBFS* No. 6 (1967)	*DgF*		Close	
90	A67	Fæstemanden i graven	Red	—	—	Untitled	"On the Songs" 3:152-53 (1821)	ANR No. 29		Interp	Omits ref.; Misattributed
90	A67	Fæstemanden i graven	Red	—	—	Aager and Eliza	Borrow, *Rom. Ball.* 47-52 (1826) = *Works* 9:304-07 (1923)	ANR No. 29		Interp	Omits ref.
90	A67	Fæstemanden i graven	Red	—	—	Aager and Eliza	Borrow, in Borrow-Bowring 62-63 (1830) = Longfellow, *PPE* 81-82 (1847) = Kaines, *Love* P8-11 (1870) = Creekmore, *Lyrics* 229-31 (1959)	ANR No. 29		Interp	Omits ref.; some from *Rom. Ball.*
90	A67	Fæstemanden i graven	B	Arist	17	Sir Aage and Lady Elsey	Amateur [Prior], *ODB* No. 14 (1856) = Rev. *ODB* 250 (1856)	Grimm No. 2		N.A.	From German tr.
90	A67	Fæstemanden i graven	Red	—	—	Aage og Else	Stokes, "Dan. Ball.," *Rev.* 215 (1858)	ANR No. 29		Interp	
90	A67	Fæstemanden i graven	A	Arist	17	Sir Ogey and Lady Elsey. A.	Prior, *ADB* No. III A (1860) = Drummond-Davies 27-29 (1861) = M. Leach, *Ball. Bk.* 258-62 (1955) = Rossel, *Scand. Ball.* No. 6 (1982)	*DgF*		Interp	Omits ref.
90	A67	Fæstemanden i graven	Red	—	—	Sir Ogey andlady Elsey. B.	Prior, *ADB* No. III B (1860)	ANR No. 29		Interp	
90	A67	Fæstemanden i graven	Red	—	—	Sir Aagé and Elsé	[Bushby], "Ballads" 131:42-43 (1864)	ANR No. 29		Interp	

90	A67	Fæstemanden i graven	Rel	—	—	Sir Aage and Maid Else	Kenealy, *Poems* 404-07 (1864) =*Poetical W* 3:328-31 (1879)	ANR No. 29	Interp	
90	A67	Fæstemanden i graven	Red	—	—	Aage and Elsie	Buchanan, "Old Ball. D." 693-95 (1865) =*Master-S.* 240-43 (1874) ≅ *BSA* 112-116 (1866)	ANR No. 29	Adapt	
90	A67	Fæstemanden i graven	A	Arist	17	Fæstemanden i Graven	Child, *ESPB* 2:228 (1885)	*DgF*	N.A.	Prose summ
90	A67	Fæstemanden i graven	Red	—	—	"It was the Knight Sir Aage"	Butler 143-45 (1874)	Oehlenschläger, *Axel*	Interp	Lit. adapt. in play
90	A67	Fæstemanden i graven	Red	—	—	Knight Aagen and Maiden Else	Morris, *Poems* 148-51 (1891) =*Poems/Love* 171-74 (1896) ≅ *Coll. Works* 9:210-12 (1911)	ANR No. 29	Interp	
90	A67	Fæstemanden i graven	Red (A)	—	—	Aage and Else	M. Thomas 266-70 (1902)	*DgF*, Olrik I: No. 3	Interp	
90	A67	Fæstemanden i graven	Red	—	—	Untitled	Kolle 117-19 (1906)	Oehlenschläger, *Axel*	Interp	Lit. adapt. in play
90	A67	Fæstemanden i graven	Red	—	—	Untitled	Freeland 93-95 (n.d.)	Oehlenschläger, *Axel*	Interp	Lit. adapt. in play
90	A67	Fæstemanden i graven	Red	—	—	Rime of the Dead Lover Aage and Else	Smith-Dampier, *BfD* 38-42 (1910) ≅ *DB* No. 27 (1920) ≅ *BDB* 1: No. 3 (1939) =Warnock & Anderson 514-15 (1959)	Olrik, I: No. 3	Interp	

National Type No.	TSB No.	Title	Version	Tradition	Century	Title of Translation	Translator, Venue, Date	Translator's Source	Lang. Music	Trans. Strategy	Notes
90	A67	Fæstemanden i graven	A	Arist	17	Betrothed in the Grave	Cox, in Steenstrup, *MPB* 31, 129-30, 190-91 (1914)	*DgF*	L	Close	8 st. of 34
90	A67	Fæstemanden i graven	B	Arist	17	Betrothed in the Grave	Cox, in Steenstrup, MPB 229 (1914)	*DgF*		Interp	3 st. of 13
90	A67	Fæstemanden i graven	Red	—	—	Aage and Else	Gray, *FaF* No. 20 (1954)	Recke No. 4		Adapt	Omits ref.
90	A67	Fæstemanden i graven	A	Arist	17	Aage og Else	With 565-66 (1965)	*DgF*	L	Close	8 st. + prose summ
90	A67	Fæstemanden i graven	A	Arist	17	Fæstemanden i Graven	Colbert, "Danish" 13 (1978)	*DgF*		Literal	1 st. of 34 + 2 Smith Dampier st.
91	A69	Hedebys gjenganger	a	?Arist	16	Heddybee-Spectre	Borrow, *Rom. Ball.* 37-39 (1826) = *Works* 9:297-98 (1923)	ANR No. 27		Adapt	Omits ref.
91	A69	Hedebys gjenganger	a	?Arist	16	Hedeby's Ghost	Howitt, *LRNE* 309-11 (1852)	ANR No. 27		Interp	
91	A69	Hedebys gjenganger	a	?Arist	16	Hedeby's Ghost	Amateur [Prior], *ODB* No. 36 (1856)	Grimm No. 73		N.A.	From German tr.; omits ref.
91	A69	Hedebys gjenganger	a	?Arist	16	Hedeby's Ghost	Prior, *ADB* No. 129 (1860)	*DgF*		Interp	6 st. + prose summ
91	A69	Hedebys gjenganger	a	?Arist	16	Ghost of Hedeby	[Bushby], "Ballads" 131:41 (1864)	?ANR No. 27		Interp	Revises Prior; omits ref.
91	A69	Hedebys gjenganger	a	?Arist	16	Hedeby's Ghost	Cox, in Steenstrup, *MPB* 59 (1914)	*DgF*		Interp	4 st. of 16; omits ref.

91	A69	Hedebys gienganger	a	?Arist	16	Heddeby Spectre	Borrow, *Works* 7:125-26 (1923) = *Ball. All. Nations* 48-49 (1927)	ANR No. 27	Close	
91	A69	Hedebys gienganger	Red (a)	—	—	Ghost of Hedeby	Gray, *FaF* No. 22 (1954)	Recke No. 70	Interp	
92	A70	Hr. Morten af Fuglsang	Red (A)	—	—	Sir Morten of Fogelsang	Howitt, *LRNE* 307-09 (1852)	ANR No. 30	Interp	
92	A70	Hr. Morten af Fuglsang	A	Arist	17	Sir Morten of Fogelsong	Prior, *ADB* No. 38 (1860) =Coppée 321-22 (1886)	*DgF*	Interp	
92	A70	Hr. Morten af Fuglsang	Red (A)	—	—	Sir Morten of Fogelsang	[Bushby], "Ballads" 131:44 (1864)	?ANR No. 30	Close	2 st. + prose summ
92	A70	Hr. Morten af Fuglsang	Red (A)	—	—	Sir Morten of Fogelsong	Buchanan, *BSA* 97-100 (1866)	ANR No. 30	Interp	
92	A70	Hr. Morten af Fuglsang	Red (A)	—	—	Dead Rides Sir Morten	Smith-Dampier, "Dead Rides" (1928) ≅ "Sir Morten" 199-200 (1932)	GrN, *DF* 64-66	Interp	
92	A70	Hr. Morten af Fuglsang	Red (A)			Sir Morten of Fogelsang	Gray, *FaF* No. 21 (1954)	Recke No. 71 & GrN, *DF* 64-66	Interp	
93	B15	Dødningens bistand	Red	—	—	Saint Gertrude	Prior, *ADB* No. 41 (1860)	*DgF*	Interp	Some Faroese lines
94	B27	Livsvandet	A	?Arist	?17	Maryby Well	Amateur [Prior], *ODB* No. 25 (1856)	Grimm No. 5	N.A.	From German tr.; omits ref.
94	B27	Livsvandet	A	?Arist	?17	Maribo Well	Prior, *ADB* No. 39 (1860)	*DgF*	Interp	
94	B27	Livsvandet	A	?Arist	17	Fountain of Maribo	Borrow, *Works* 7:198-201 (1923) = *Ball. All. Nations* 74-76 (1927)	ANR No. 51	Close	

National Type No.	TSB No.	Title	Version	Tradition	Century	Title of Translation	Translator, Venue, Date	Translator's Source	Lang. / Music	Trans. Strategy	Notes
95	A38	Den talende strengeleg	A	Comm	19	Cruel Sister. A.	Prior, *ADB* No. 37A (1860) =H. Leach, *Angevin Br.* 365-66 (1921) =M. Leach, *Ball. Bk.* 77-78 (1955)	*DgF*		Interp	
95	A38	Den talende strengeleg	E	Comm	19	Cruel Sister. B.	Prior, *ADB* No. 37B (1860)	*DgF*		Interp	
95	A38	Den talende strengeleg	F, red	—	—	Untitled	Prior, *ADB* 1:383-84 (1860)	*DgF*		Adapt	6 st. of 25; omits ref.
95	A38	Den talende strengeleg	aa	Comm	20	Two Sisters	Grainger, *Night.*, unpag. (1931) =*DFMS: Power L2* (1950) =T. Lewis, *Source G250* (1991)	Own collect.	L M	Close	Oral from NFS Grundtvig 1847 redact.
95	A38	Den talende strengeleg	F, red	—	—	Talking Harp	Meyer, in Dal, *DBfS* No. 7 (1967)	*DgF*		Close	
96	B8	Jesusbarnet, Stefan og Herodes	A	Comm	18	St. Stephen, and Herod	Prior, *ADB* No. 40 (1860)	*DgF*		Interp	
96	B8	Jesusbarnet, Stefan og Herodes	A	Comm	18	Untitled	Child, *ESPB* 1:233-34 (1882) =Strömbäck 136 (1968)	*DgF*		Close	6 st. + prose summ
96	B8	Jesusbarnet, Stefan og Herodes	A	Comm	18	Boyhood of Jesus, Stephan, and Herod	Cox, in Steenstrup, *MPB* 99-100 (1914)	*DgF*		Interp	4 st. of 11
96	B8	Jesusbarnet, Stefan og Herodes	A	Comm	18	Infant Jesus, Stephen and Herod	Meyer, in Dal, *DBfS* No. 9 (1967)	*DgF*		Interp	
97	B4	Jesus og Jomfru Maria	A	Comm	18	Jesus and the Virgin Mary. A.	Prior, *ADB* No. 43 A (1860)	*DgF*		Interp	

97	B4	Jesus og Jomfru Maria	B	Brds	18	Jesus and the Virgin Mary. B.	Prior, *ADB* No. 43 B (1860)	*DgF*		Interp	
98	B16	Maria Magdalena	Red	—	—	Mary Magdalene	Prior, *ADB* No. 44 (1860)	*DgF*		Interp	
99	B6	Den blinde mand ved Jesu Kors	sole	Brds	18	Jesus and the Virgin Mary. C.	Prior, *ADB* No. 43 C (1860)	*DgF*		Interp	
100	B7	Den hellige Jakob	A	Brds	18	Saint James and the Vision of Hell	Prior, *ADB* No. 45 (1860)	*DgF*		Interp	
101	B14	Liden Karen-St. Katharina	Red	—	—	Little Katey	Prior, *ADB* No. 32 (1860)			N.A.	From Danish-Swedish combin.
103	B10	St. Jørgen og dragen	Fed	—	—	St. George and the Dragon	Prior, *ADB* No. 49 (1860)	*DgF*		Interp	
104	B22	Engelens budskab	Red	—	—	Angel's Errand	Prior, *ADB* No. 46 (1860)	*DgF*		Adapt	Omits ref.
105	B32	Den rige mands sjæl	sole	Brds	18	Rich Man's Soul. B.	Prior, *ADB* No. 47B (1860)	*DgF*		Interp	
105	B32	Den rige mands sjæl	sole	Brds	18	Untitled	Stokes, "Dan. Ball. II," Rev. 47 (1861)	*DgF*		Close	
106	B33	Sjælen for Himmerigs dør	sole	Brds	18	Soul at Heaven's Door	Cox, in Steenstrup, *MPB* 145 (1914)	*DgF*	L	Literal	
107	B24	Barnesjælen	A	Comm	19	Soul of the Child	Meyer, in Dal, *DBFS* No. 10 (1967)	*DgF*		Close	
108	B29	Ildprøven	Red	—	—	Ordeal by Fire	Prior, *ADB* No. 50 (1860)	?*DgF*		Interp	
108	B29	Ildprøven	Da	Arist	17	Innocence Defamed	Borrow, *Works* 8:45-47 (1923) = *Ball. All Nations* 110-12 (1927)	Sandvig 1: No. 8		Adapt	Omits ref.
109	B20	Møen paa baalet				Maid on the Pyre					See Faroese section
109	B20	Møen paa baalet	Red	—	—	Ole and Christine	M. Louise Baum, in Gilbert 83 (1910)	N.I.	M	Adapt	Song-dance

National Type No.	TSB No.	Title	Version	Tradition	Century	Title of Translation	Translator, Venue, Date	Translator's Source	Lang. Music	Trans. Strategy	Notes
110	D328	Den myrdede hustru	A	Comm	19	Murdered Wife	Prior, ADB No. 52 (1860)	DgF		Interp	
111	B28	Helbredelsen	A	Arist	16	Miraculous Cure	Prior, ADB No. 48 (1860)	DgF		Interp	Omits ref.
112	D299	Helligbrøden	Red (G)	—	—	Sabbath Breaking	Prior, ADB No. 36 (1860)	ANR No. 147		Interp	Omits ref.
112	D299	Helligbrøden	Red (G)	—	—	Sir Jonas and Sir Nielus	Borrow, Works 8:32-35 (1923)	ANR No. 147		Interp	Omits ref.
114	D393	Henrik af Brunsvig	Red	—	—	Henry of Brunswick	Prior, ADB No. 53 (1860)	DgF		Interp	
114	D393	Henrik af Brunsvig	B	Arist	17	Henry of Brunswick	Child, ESPB 1:195 (1882)	DgF		N.A.	Prose summ
114	D393	Henrik af Brunsvig	A	Arist	16	Henry of Brunswick	Cox, in Steenstrup, MPB 120-21(1914)	DgF	L	Close	5 st. of 44
116	CI	Erik Emuns drab	Red	—	—	Erik Emun and Swarthy Plog	Prior, ADB No. 54 (1860)	DgF & ANR No. 60		Interp	
116	CI	Erik Emuns drab	Red	—	—	Erick Emun and Sir Plog	Borrow, Works 7:238-40 (1923) =Ball. All Nations 80-82 (1927)	ANR No. 60		Close	
117	D365	Ridder Stigs fald	sole	Arist	16	Knight Stig's Death	Prior, ADB 2:345-47 (1860)	DgF		Close	Omits ref.
117	D365	Ridder Stigs fald	Red (a)	—	—	Death of Knight Stig	Smith-Dampier, BDB 1: No. 19 (1939)	Olrik I: No. 19		Close	
117	D365	Ridder Stigs fald	Red (a)	—	—	Death of Sir Stig	Gray, HBD No. 1 (1958)	Olrik I: No. 19		Interp	Omits ref.
117	D365	Ridder Stigs fald	sole	Arist	16	Ridder Stigs Fald	Richmond, "Stig I." 38 (1958)	DgF		N.A.	Prose summ

121	D258	Valdemar og Tove	D	?Arist	17	Tove-lille	Prior, *ADB* No. 66 (1860)	*DgF* or ANR 95	Interp	
121	D258	Valdemar og Tove		—		Valdemar og Tove (A)	Smith-Dampier, *DB* No. 1 (1920) = *BDB* I: No. 17 (1939)			See Icel., *IFkv* 53
121	D258	Valdemar og Tove	Red	—		Valdemar og Tove (B)	Smith-Dampier, *DB* No. 2 (1920) ≈ *BDB* I: No. 18 (1939) = H. Leach, *Pageant* 292-95 (1946)	Olrik I: No. 18	Close	
121	D258	Valdemar og Tove		—		Valdemar and Tove, A	Gray, *HBD* No. 2 (1958)			
121	D258	Valdemar og Tove	Red	—		Valdemar and Tove, B	Gray, *HBD* No. 3 (1958)	Olrik I: No. 18	Interp	See Icel., *IFkv* 53
121	D258	Valdemar og Tove	A	Arist	17	Valdemar and Tovelil	Meyer, in Dal, *DBfS* No. 11 (1967) = Rossel, *Scand. Ball.* No. 12 (1982)	*DgF*	Close	
125	D105	Hin rige Valravn	Red	—		Valraven and the Danish King	Smith-Dampier, *BDB* I: No. 46 (1939)	Olrik I: No. 46	Interp	
126	D346	Kong Valdemar og hans søster	Red (E)	—		King Waldmar and His Sister	Stokes, "Sec. Batch" 91-94 (1855)	ANR No. 62 & Syv No. 41	Interp	
126	D346	Kong Valdemar og hans søster	E, red	—		Sir Buris and the Fair Christine	Amateur [Prior], *ODB* No. 17 (1856)	Grimm No. 83	N.A.	From German tr.; omits ref.
126	D346	Kong Valdemar og hans søster	Red (E)	—		Sir Buris and Christine	Prior, *ADB* No. 57 (1860)	*DgF* & ANR 62	Interp	Omits ref.
126	D346	Kong Valdemar og hans søster	Red (E)	—		King Valdemar and His Sister	Borrow, *Works* 7: 241-54 (1923)	ANR No. 62	Interp	Omits ref.

National Type No.	TSB No.	Title	Version	Tradition	Century	Title of Translation	Translator, Venue, Date	Translator's Source	Lang. Music	Trans. Strategy	Notes
127	D347	Kong Valdemar og hans søsterdatter	B, red	—	—	Ingerlille	Amateur [Prior], *ODB* No. 18 (1856)	Grimm No. 84		N.A.	From German tr.
127	D347	Kong Valdemar og hans søsterdatter	B, red	—	—	Ingerlille	Prior, *ADB* No. 58 (1860)	ANR No. 65		Interp	
128	D232	Liden Kirsten og Dronning Sofie	G	?Arist	17	Fair Exile	Amateur, Prior, *ODB* No. 13 (1856)	Grimm No. 56		N.A.	From German tr.; omits ref.
128	D232	Liden Kirsten og Dronning Sofie	G	?Arist	17	Fair Christel and the Heathen King	Prior, *ADB* No. 150 (1860)	*DgF*		Interp	
129	D257	Stolt Signild og Dronning Sofie	Red (sole)	—	—	Wassel Dance	Jamieson, *IMA* 389-92 (1814) =Longfellow, *PPET* 5-76 (1847)	Syv No. 27		Close	
129	D257	Stolt Signild og Dronning Sofie	Red (sole)	—	—	The Wake	Amateur [Prior], *ODB* No. 20 (1856)	Grimm No. 46		N.A.	From German tr.; omits ref.
129	D257	Stolt Signild og Dronning Sofie	Red (sole)	—	—	The Wake	Prior, *ADB* No. 56 (1860)	*DgF* & ANR No. 64		Interp	
129	D257	Stolt Signild og Dronning Sofie	Red (sole)	—	—	Signe at the Wake	Buchanan, *BSA* 171-74 (1866)	ANR No. 64		Interp	
129	D257	Stolt Signild og Dronning Sofie	Red (sole)	—	—	King's Wake	Borrow, *Works* 7:255-58 (1923) =Ball. All Nations 83-85 (1927)	ANR No. 64		Interp	Omits ref.

No.	ID	Danish title	Code	Arist	No.	English title	Reference	Source	M/L	Treatment	Notes
129	D257	Stolt Signild og Dronning Sofie	sole	Arist	16	Proud Signild and Queen Sophie	Cox, in Steenstrup, *MPB* 18, 31 (1914)	*DgF*		Interp	5 st. of 38
129	D257	Stolt Signild og Dronning Sofie	Red (sole)	—	—	Proud Signild and Queen Sophia	Gray, *FaF* No. 15 (1954)	Recke No. 315		Interp	Omits ref.
131	D16	Esbern Snare	E	?Arist	17	Sir Asbiorn Snaré	Prior, *ADB* No. 69 (1860)	*DgF*		Interp	
131	D16	Esbern Snare	Red	—	—	Wooing of Esbern Snare	Fausböll, in Smith-Dampier et al 765-66 (1924)	Olrik I: No. 20		Close	
131	D16	Esbern Snare	Compos	—	—	Wooing of Esbern Snare	Brix 762 (1924)	?*DgF*		N.A.	Prose summ.
131	D16	Esbern Snare	Red	—	—	Esbern Snare	Smith-Dampier, *BDB* I: No. 20 (1939)	Olrik I: No. 20		Close	
131	D16	Esbern Snare	Red	—	—	Osborn Snare's Courtship	Trask, in Deutsch 1942 48-49 = Deutsch 1967 26-27	N.I.	M / L	Adapt	8 st. + prose summ / Omits ref.
131	D16	Esbern Snare	Red	—	—	Sir Cauline and Sir Guy	Gray, *FaF* No. 34 (1954)	Olrik I: No. 20		Interp	
132	C3	Dronning Dagmar og Junker Strange	B	Arist	17	King Waldmar's Suit to Queen Dagmar / Dagmar and Strange	Prior, *ADB* No. 59 (1860) / =Smith-Dampier et al 768 (1924)	*DgF*		Interp	Omits ref. / 7 st. + prose summ
132	C3	Dronning Dagmar og Junker Strange	Red (C?)	—	—	King Waldemar's Wooing	Borrow, *Works* 7: 259-64 (1923)	ANR No. 67		Interp	
132	C3	Dronning Dagmar og Junker Strange	Red	—	—	Queen Dagmar and Sir Strange	Gray, *HBD* No. 5 (1958)	Recke No. 81		Close	
133	C4	Dronning Dagmar i Danmark	A	Ar/Com	16	Queen Dagmar in Denmark	Prior, *ADB* No. 60 (1860)	*DgF*		Interp	

National Type No.	TSB No.	Title	Version	Tradition	Cen-tury	Title of Translation	Translator, Venue, Date	Translator's Source	Lang. Music	Trans. Strategy	Notes
133	C4	Dronning Dagmar i Danmark	B, red	—	—	Queen Dagmar's Arrival in Denmark	Borrow, *Works* 7:265-67 (1923)	ANR No. 68		Interp	Omits ref.
133	C4	Dronning Dagmar i Danmark	A	Ar/Com	16	Queen Dagmar's Bridal / Bridal of Queen Dagmar	Smith-Dampier, *DB* No. 3 (1920) = *BDB* I: No. 22 (1939)	Olrik I: No. 22		Close Interp	
133	C4	Dronning Dagmar i Danmark	A	Ar/Com	16	Marriage of Queen Dagmar	Gray, *HBD* No. 6 (1958)	Olrik I: No. 22		Interp	
135	C6	Dronning Dagmars død	Red (A)	—	—	Queen Dagmar's Death	Prior, *ADB* No. 62 (1860)	*DgF*		Interp	Omits ref.
135	C6	Dronning Dagmars død	Red	—	—	Death of Queen Dagmar	Smith-Dampier, "Death" (1914)	Olrik I: No. 23		Close	Revises 1914
135	C6	Dronning Dagmars død	Red	—	—	Queen Dagmar's Death	Smith-Dampier, *DB* No. 4 (1920)	Olrik I: No. 23		Close	Revises 1920
135	C6	Dronning Dagmars død	Red			Death of Queen Dagmar	Smith-Dampier, *BDB* I: No. 23 (1939)	Olrik I: No. 23		Close	
135	C6	Dronning Dagmars død	C, red	—	—	Dagmar	Borrow, *Works* 7:272 (1923) = *Ball. All Nations* 86 (1927)	ANR No. 70		Interp	6 st. of 39; omits ref.
135	C6	Dronning Dagmars død	Red	—	—	Death of Queen Dagmar	Gray, *HBD* No. 7 (1958)	Olrik I: No. 23		Interp	
135	C6	Dronning Dagmars død	A	Ar/Com	16	Queen Dagmar's Death	Meyer, in Abrahamsen/Dal 22-25 (1967) =Dal, *DBFS* No. 12 (1967) =Rossel, *Scand. Ball.* No. 13 (1982) =Balslev-Clausen No. 68 (1988)	*DgF*	M	Close	
136	C5	Kong Sverker den unge	A	Ar/Com	16	King Swerker the Younger	Prior, *ADB* No. 70 (1860)	*DgF*		Interp	Omits ref.

136	C5	Kong Sverker den unge	A	Ar/Com	16	Untitled	Stokes, "Dan. Ball. II", Rev. 48 (1861)	*DgF*		Literal	5 st. of 11; omits ref.
136	C5	Kong Sverker den unge	Red	—	—	Battle of Lena	Smith-Dampier, *BDB* I: No. 21 (1939)	Olrik I: No. 21		Interp	
136	C5	Kong Sverker den unge	Rec	—	—	Battle of Lena	Gray, *HBD* No. 4 (1958)	Olrik I: No. 21		Close	
139	C7	Dronning Bengerd	Red	—	—	Queen Bengerd	Smith-Dampier, *DB* No. 5 (1920) ≅ *BDB* I: No. 24 (1939)	Olrik I: No. 24		Interp	
139	C7	Dronning Bengerd	B, Red	—	—	Queen Berngerd	Borrow, *Works* 7:273-76 (1923)	ANR No. 71		Interp	
139	C7	Dronning Bengerd	Red	—	—	Queen Bengerd	Gray, *HBD* No. 8 (1958)	Olrik I: No. 24		Interp	
142	C11	Kong Hakon Hakonsøns død	B, rec	—	—	King Hacon's Death	Borrow, *Works* 7:233-37 (1923)	ANR No. 59		Interp	Omits ref.
143	D353	Tule Vognsøn og Svend Graa	A	?Arist	16	Thule Vognson and Gray Swain	Prior, *ADB* No. 71 (1860)	*DgF*		Close	Omits ref.
144	D366	Hr. Jon og Fru Bodil	F, red	—	—	Lady Bodild	Prior, *ADB* No. 144 (1860)	?*DgF*		Interp	Omits ref.
144	D366	Hr. Jon og Fru Bodil	A	Arist	16	Hr. Jon og Fru Bodil	Ker, "On Dan. B." 5:400-01 (1908) = *Coll. Ess.* 2:114 (1925)	*DgF*		N.A.	Prose summ
145	C14	Marsk Stig	A	Arist	16	Mar Stig	Prior, *ADB* No. 72 (1860)	*DgF*		Interp	Omits ref.
145	C14	Marsk Stig	A	Arist	16	Marsk Stig	Cox, in Steenstrup, *MPB* 225-26 (1914)	*DgF*		Close	5 st. of 108; omits ref.
145	C14	Marsk Stig	F	Ar/Com	16	Marsk Stig	Cox, in Steenstrup, *MPB* 77 (1914)	*DgF*		Close	3 st. of 14; omits ref.

National Type No.	TSB No.	Title	Version	Tradition	Century	Title of Translation	Translator, Venue, Date	Translator's Source	Lang. Music	Trans. Strategy	Notes
145	C14	Marsk Stig	Red (A)	—	—	Long Ballad of Marsk Stig	Smith-Dampier, *DB* No. 8 (1920) ≅ *BDB* 1: No. 28 (1939)	Olrik I: No. 28		Interp	28 st. of 105 Full version
145	C14	Marsk Stig	Red	—	—	Marst Stig and His Lady	Smith-Dampier *DB* No. 7 (1920) ≅ *BDB* 1: No. 27 (1939)	Olrik I: No. 27		Interp	
145	C14	Marsk Stig	Red	—	—	King-Slaying in Finderup	Smith-Dampier *DB* No. 6 (1920) ≅ *BDB* 1: No. 25 (1939)	Olrik I: No. 25		Interp	
145	C14	Marsk Stig	Red	—	—	Marsk Stig Made an Outlaw	Smith-Dampier, *BDB* 1: No. 26 (1939)	Olrik I: No. 26		Interp	
145	C14	Marsk Stig	L, red	—	—	Marsk Stig. Part I	Borrow, *Works* 7:280–85 (1923)	ANR No. 75		Interp	Omits ref.
145	C14	Marsk Stig	M, red	—	—	Marsk Stig. Part II	Borrow, *Works* 7: 286–91 (1923)	ANR No. 76		Interp	Omits ref.
145	C14	Marsk Stig	N, red	—	—	Marsk Stig. Part III	Borrow, *Works* 7:292–98 (1923)	ANR No. 77		Interp	Omits ref.
145	C14	Marsk Stig	O, red	—	—	Marsk Stig. Part IV	Borrow, *Works* 7:299–303 (1923)	ANR No. 78		Interp	Omits ref.
145	C14	Marsk Stig	Red (A)	—	—	Long Ballad of Marsk Stig	Gray, *HBD* No. 13 (1958)	Olrik I: No. 28		Interp	
145	C14	Marsk Stig	Red	—	—	Murder of the King at Finderup	Gray, *HBD* No. 10 (1958)	Olrik I: No. 25		Interp	
145	C14	Marsk Stig	Red	—	—	Outlawry of Marsk Stig	Gray, *HBD* No. 11 (1958)	Olrik I: No. 26		Interp	
145	C14	Marsk Stig	Red	—	—	Marstig and His Wife	Gray, *HBD* No. 12 (1958)	Olrik I: No. 27		Interp	

145	C14	Marsk Stig	C	Ar/Com	16	Marsti and His Wife	Meyer, in Dal, *DBFS* No. 13 (1967) =Rossel, *Scand. Ball.* No. 14 (1982)	*DgF*		Close	
145	C14	Marsk Stig	I	Ar/Com	16	The Banishment	Meyer, in Dal, *DBFS* No. 15 (1967) =Rossel, *Scand. Ball.* No. 16 (1982)	*DgF*		Interp	
145	C14	Marsk Stig	G	Ar/Com	16	King's Murder	Meyer, in Dal, *DBFS* No. 14 (1967) =Rossel, *Scand. Ball.* No. 15 (1982)	*DgF*		Interp	Ms. anomalous
145	C14	Marsk Stig	K	Ar/Com	16	Outlaws	Meyer, in Dal, *DBFS* No. 16 (1967) =Rossel, *Scand. Ball.* No. 17 (1982)	*DgF*		Close	
146	D435	Marsk Stig's døttre	M, red	—	—	English Maidens	Stokes, "Dan. Ball." 65ln (1852)	Winding 9		Interp	3 st. + prose summ
146	D435	Marsk Stig's døttre	C, red	—	—	Marsk Stig's Daughters. I.	Amateur[Prior], *ODB* No. 22 (1856)	Grimm No. 89		N.A.	From German tr.
146	D435	Marsk Stig's døttre	C, red	—	—	Marsk Stig's Daughters. 5	Prior, *ADB* No. 73 (1860)	ANR No. 79		Interp	
146	D435	Marsk Stig's døttre	Red	—	—	Two King's Daughters	Gilbert, in Gilbert 81 (1910)	N.I.	M	N.A.	5 st. fragment
146	D435	Marsk Stig's døttre	A	Arist	16	Marsk Stig's Daughters	Cox, in Steenstrup, *MPB* 31, 203 (1914)	*DgF*		Close	6 st. of 50
146	D435	Marsk Stig's døttre	B	Arist	17	Marsk Stig's Daughters	Cox, in Steenstrup, *MPB* 94 (1914)	*DgF*		Close	3 st. of 25
146	D435	Marsk Stig's døttre	Red (C)	—	—	Marsk Stig's Daughters	A. Mathewson, in Botsford, *FSMP* 2:188-90 (1922) =Botsford, *CFS* 2:54-56 (1931)	Berggreen *FSM* 1860 I: No. 57	L M	Interp	11 st. of 34
146	D435	Marsk Stig's døttre	C, red	—	—	Marsk Stig's Daughters	Borrow, *Works* 7:304-06 (1923)	ANR No. 79		Adapt	Omits ref.
146	D435	Marsk Stig's døttre	Red (B)	—	—	Marsk Stig's Daughters	Smith-Dampier, *BDB* 2: No. 18 (1939)	Olrik 2: No. 19		Adapt	

National Type No.	TSB No.	Title	Version	Tradition	Century	Title of Translation	Translator, Venue, Date	Translator's Source	Lang. Music	Trans. Strategy	Notes
146	D435	Marsk Stig's døttre	Red	—	—	Marsk Stig's Daughters	Krone, in Krone & Ostlund, SMD 34-35 (1941)	?Berggreen FSM 1860 I: No. 57	M	Adapt	6 st. of 34
147	D363	Indtagelsen af Riberhus	D, red	—	—	Mar Stig No. 6	Prior, ADB No. 74 (1860)	ANR No. 80		Interp	
147	D363	Indtagelsen af Riberhus	D, red	—	—	Songs of Ranild. 1.	Borrow, Works 7:307-09 (1923)	ANR No. 80		Close	
147	D363	Indtagelsen af Riberhus	D, red	—	—	Untitled	Lorentzen 612-13 (1930)	ANR No. 80		Close	5 st. of 20
147	D363	Indtagelsen af Riberhus	Red	—	—	Untitled	Entwistle, Eur. Ball. 31 (1939)	N.I.		Adapt	4 st.
147	D363	Indtagelsen af Riberhus	D, red	—	—	Untitled	Entwistle, Eur. Ball. 110 (1939)	ANR No. 80		Close	3 st. of 20; omits ref.
148	C19	Rane Jonsens giftermaal	Red (C)	—	—	Mar Stig. No. 7	Prior, ADB No. 75 (1860)	ANR No. 81		Interp	
148	C19	Rane Jonsens giftermaal	B	Ar/Com	16	Wooing of Ranil Jonson Wedding of Rane Jonson	Smith-Dampier, BfD 31-33 (1910) ≅ BDB 2: No. 17 (1939)	?Olrik 2: No. 18		Interp	
148	C19	Rane Jonsens giftermaal	Red (C)	—	—	Songs of Ranild. 2.	Borrow, Works 7:310-11 (1923)	ANR No. 81		Interp	
148	C19	Rane Jonsens giftermaal	Red (B)	—	—	Ranil's Wedding	Gray, FaF No.17 (1954)	Recke No. 99 & Olrik 2: No.18		Interp	
149	C20	Ranild Jonsens endeligt	D, red	—	—	Mar Stig	Prior, ADB No. 76 (1860)	ANR No. 82		Interp	
149	C20	Ranild Jonsens endeligt	D, red	—	—	Songs of Ranild. 3.	Borrow, Works 7:312-14 (1923)	ANR No. 82		Interp	
150	C12	Mindre-Alfs vikingstog	sole, ?red	—	—	Sir Alf the Freebooter. I.	Borrow, Works 7:328-29 (1923)	ANR No. 90		Close	

151	C17	Mindre-Alfs endeligt	B, red	—	Sir Alf the Freebooter. 2.	Borrow, *Works* 7:330-33 (1923)	ANR No. 91	Interp	Omits ref.
152	DI76	Røverne for norden Skov	Red	—	Robbers at Nordenshaw	Howitt, *LRNE* 303-07 (1852)	ANR No. 93	Interp	
152	DI76	Røverne for norden Skov	Red	—	Robbers at Nordenwood	Prior, *ADB* No. 64 (1860)	ANR No. 93	Interp	Omits ref.
154	C24	Kong Birger og hans brødre	Red (C)	—	King Byrge and His Brothers	Borrow, *Works* 7:315-20 (1923)	ANR No. 85	Interp	Omits ref.
155	C10	Kong Birgers søster Bengta	Red (A)	—	Sir Laurens Steals a Bride	Smith-Dampier, *BDB* 2: No. 16 (1939)	Olrik 2: No. 17	Interp	
155	C10	Kong Birgers søster Bengta	Red (A)	—	Squire Lavers	Gray, *HBD* No. 9 (1958)	Olrik 2: No. 17	Interp	
156	C25	Niels Ebbesen	Red (F)	—	Niels Ebbesön	Prior, *ADB* No. 63 (1860)	ANR No. 94	Interp	
156	C25	Niels Ebbesen	E	Ar/Com	16	Niels Ebbesön	Cox, in Steenstrup, *MPB* 218 (1914)	*DgF*	Literal	2 st. of 25
156	C25	Niels Ebbesen	F, red	—	Niels Ebbesön	Cox, in Steenstrup 151-52, 227 (1914)	*DgF*	L Close	2 st. of 83
156	C25	Niels Ebbesen	Red	—	Niels Ebbesön	Smith-Dampier, *DB* 48-61 (1920) ≅ *BDB* 1: No. 29 (1939) = Warnock & Anderson 515-18 (1959)	Olrik 1: No. 29	Interp	
156	C25	Niels Ebbesen	Red (F)	—	Re-modeled Conclusion of Niels Ebbeson. Revised Conclusion. Niels Ebbeson B	Smith-Dampier, *DB* 62-64 (1920) ≅ *BDB* 1: No. 30 (1939)	Olrik 1: No. 29 p. 202-04	Interp Interp	
156	C25	Niels Ebbesen	Red (F)	—	Niels Ebbesen	Borrow, *Works* 7:340-52 (1923)	ANR No. 94	Interp	
156	C25	Niels Ebbesen	Red	—	Niels Ebbesen	Gray, *HBD* No. 15 (1958)	Olrik 1: No. 29	Interp	
156	C25	Niels Ebbesen	F, red	—	Niels Ebbesen	Meyer, in Dal, *DBFS* No. 17 (1967)	*DgF*	Close	

National Type No.	TSB No.	Title	Version	Tradition	Century	Title of Translation	Translator, Venue, Date	Translator's Source	Lang/Music	Trans. Strategy	Notes
158	C26	Herr Bugges død	C	Arist	16	Sir Bugge's Death	Cox, in Steenstrup 161, 202 (1914)	*DgF*	L	Close	2 st. of 33
164	D313	Niels Paaskesøn og Lave Brok	sole	Arist	17	Niels Paaskesön and Lave Brok	Cox, in Steenstrup, *MPB* 48 (1914)	*DgF*		Close	4 st. of 13
172	C39	Christian den Anden i Sverrig	A	Arist	16	King Christian of Denmark in Sweden	Cox, in Steenstrup, *MPB* 41-42, 192-93 (1914)	*DgF*		Close	7 st. of 30; omits ref.
173	—	Christian den Anden og adelen	a	Arist	16	Ballad of the Eagle	Smith-Dampier, *BDB* 1: No. 31 (1939)	Olrik 1: No. 31		Interp	
173	—	Christian den Anden og adelen	b	Arist	17	Eagle Song	Meyer, in Dal, *DBFS* No. 18 (1967)	*DgF*		Close	
175	D436	Frederik den Anden i Ditmærsken	K	Comm	19	Frederic II in the Ditmarsh	Meyer, in Dal, *DBFS* No. 19 (1967)	*DgF*		Interp	
178	D233	Folke Lovmandsøn og Dronning Helvig	Red	—	—	Folker Lowmanson	Prior, *ADB* No. 65 (1860)	ANR No. 96		Interp	Omits ref.
182	C18	Karl Algotsøn	I	Comm	18	Carol Algotson	Meyer, in Dal, *DBFS* No. 28 (1967)	*DgF*		Close	
183	D411	Kvindemorderen	Compos	—	—	Kvindemorderen	Child, *ESPB* 1:27 (1882)	*DgF*		N.A.	Prose
183	D411	Kvindemorderen	Red	—	—	Wulfstan and Venelil	Smith-Dampier, *BDB* 2: No. 3 (1939)	Olrik 2: No. 3		Interp	
183	D411	Kvindemorderen	Ic	Comm		Rimmer and Gold-Castle	Grainger, *Two Danish F.* (1951)	Own recording	M	Close	4 st. of 30 + prose summ

National Type No.	TSB No.	Title	Version	Tradition	Century	Title of Translation	Translator, Venue, Date	Translator's Source	Lang./Music	Trans. Strategy	Notes
222	D4	Jomfruen paa tinge	Red (A)	—	—	Heiress in Parliament-Ha'	Gray, *HBD* No. 14 (1958)	Olrik I: No. 40		Interp	
224	D145	Væddemaalet	Red (Ka)	—	—	Ingefred Torlufs Daughter	Prior, *ADB* No. 104 (1860)	ANR No. 118		Interp	Omits ref.
224	D145	Væddemaalet	Compos	—	—	Væddemaalet	Child, *ESPB* 5:25 (1894)	*DgF*		N.A.	Prose summ
226	D126	Hertug Henrik	F	Arist	17	Window Courtship	Amateur [Prior], No. 27 (1856)	Grimm No. 24		N.A.	From German tr.; omits ref.
226	D126	Hertug Henrik	Red (F)	—	—	Duke Henry and the Maiden Malfred	Prior, *ADB* No. 128 (1860)	ANR No. 189		Interp	Omits ref.
228	D15	Svar som Tiltale	Red (Aa)	—	—	Speech and Rejoinder	Howitt, *LRME* 300-01 (1852)	ANR No. 211		Interp	
228	D15	Svar som Tiltale	Red (Aa)	—	—	Lady's Rejoinder	Prior, *ADB* No. 167 (1860)	ANR No. 211		Interp	
228	D15	Svar som Tiltale	Red (B)	—	—	An Ower-True Tale	Smith-Dampier, *BfD* 28-30 (1910)	Olrik I: No. 41		Interp	
228	D15	Svar som Tiltale	Red (B)	—	—	Tit for Tat	Smith-Dampier, *BDB* I: No. 41 (1939)	Olrik I: No. 41		Interp	Some from *BfD*
230	D150	I Rosenslund	Red (C)	—	—	Baffled Suitor	Prior, *ADB* No. 126 (1860)	ANR No. 122		Interp	
230	D156	I Rosenslund	A	Arist	17	I Rosenslund	Child, *ESPB* 2:482 (1886)	*DgF*		N.A.	Prose summ.
231	D97	Den dyre kaabe	Compos	—	—	Den dyre Kaabe	Child, *ESPB* 2:482 (1886)	*DgF*		N.A.	Prose

209	D241	Stolt Ellins havn	Red (b)	—	—	Proud Eline	Prior, *ADB* No. 139 (1860)	ANR No. 132		Interp	Omits ref.
209	D241	Stolt Ellins havn	b, red	—	—	Proud Elin's Revenge	Cox, in Steenstrup 45, 167, 195 (1914)	?*DgF*	L	Close	9 st of 28
210	D245	Herr Peders slegfred	Red (B)	—	—	Sir Peter and Christine	Prior, *ADB* No. 160 (1860)	ANR No. 157		Interp	
210	D245	Herr Peders slegfred	Red (B)	—	—	Sir Peter	Borrow, *Works* 8:57-59 (1923)	ANR No. 157		Interp	Omits ref. First 24 of 36 st.
210	D245	Herr Peders slegfred	Red	—	—	Sir Peter's Leman	Smith-Dampier, *BDB* 1: No. 45 (1939) =M. Leach, *Ball. Bk.* 245-46 (1955)	Olrik 1: No. 45		Interp	Section from Swedish
217	D122	To brude om en brudgom	Red	—	—	Two Brides and One Groom	Smith-Dampier, *BDB* 2: No. 29 (1939)	Olrik 2: No. 30		Interp	
218	D72	Stolt Ellensborg	Red	—	—	Proud Ellensborg	Smith-Dampier, *BDB* 2: No. 26 (1939)	Olrik 2: No. 27		Interp	
218	D72	Stolt Ellensborg	Aa	Arist	17	Proud Ellensborg	Holzapfel 141-45 (1982)	*DgF*	L	Literal	
220	D423	Stolt Elselille	E	?Arist	17	Fair Elspey	Amateur [Prior], *ODB* No. 37 (1856)	Grimm No. 55		N.A.	From German tr.; omits ref.
220	D423	Stolt Elselille	Red (E)	—	—	Fair Elsey	Prior, *ADB* No. 114 (1860)	ANR No. 180		Interp	
220	D423	Stolt Elselille	A	Arist	17	Proud Elselille	Cox, in Steenstrup, *MPB* 12 (1914)	*DgF*		Close	5 st. of 144; omits ref.
222	D4	Jomfruen paa tinge	Red (A)	—	—	Maiden at the Thing / Maiden at the Ting / Maiden at the Thing	Smith-Dampier, *DB* No. 22 (1920) =Smith-Dampier, et. al. 764-68 (1924) ≅ *BDB* 1: No. 40 (1939)	Olrik 1: No. 40		Interp	Heavily revised
222	D4	Jomfruen paa tinge	Compos	—	—	Maiden at the Ting	Brix 762 (1924)	?*DgF*		N.A.	Prose summ.

National Type No.	TSB No.	Title	Version	Tradition	Century	Title of Translation	Translator, Venue, Date	Translator's Source	Lang; Music	Trans. Strategy	Notes
193	D354	Døtre hævne fader	**B**, red	—	—	Two Sisters	Buchanan, *BSA* 28-31 (1866) = *B., W., "Scan. Ball.."* 289-90 (1867)	ANR No. 171		Adapt	
193	D354	Døtre hævne fader	Red **(A)**	—	—	Avenging Daughters	Smith-Dampier, *BfD* 14-16 (1910) ≅ *BDB* 1: No. 34 (1939) =Creekmore, *Little Tr.* 507-08 (1952) =Creekmore, *Lyrics* 226-27 (1959)	Olrik I: No. 34		Interp	Large revision
193	D354	Døtre hævne fader	Red **(A)**	—	—	Avenging Daughters	Gray, *FaF* No. 9 (1954)	Olrik I: No. 34		Interp	
194	D183	Herr Ebbes døttre	**Ca**, red	—	—	Sir Ebba	Herbert, *Translations* 22-33 (1804) = *Poems* I,1:22-33 (1804) = *Works* I: 157-62 (1842) =Scott, "Herbert's P." 211-23 (1806) =Scott, *Misc Prose W.* 110-13 (1843)	?		Interp	Omits ref.; Entries simplify Herbert bibliography
194	D183	Herr Ebbes døtre	**Ca**, red	—	—	Sir Ebbe's Daughters	Prior, *ADB* No. 67 (1860)	ANR No. 99		Interp	Omits ref.
194	D183	Herr Ebbes døttre	**B**	Arist	17	Herr Ebbes døttre	G. Jensen, in Præstgaard Anderson 29-30 (1981)	*DgF*	L	Literal	4 st. + prose summ. Omits ref.
194	D183	Herr Ebbes døtre	**B**	Arist	17	Sir Ebbe's Daughters	Syndergaard, Dupl. (1988)	*DgF*		Close	
198	D177	Verkel Vejemandsøn	sole	Arist	16	Verkel Vejemandsøn	Child, *ESPB* 2:281 (1886)	*DgF*		N.A.	Prose
199	D173	Den afhugne haand	sole	Arist	16	Den afhugne Haand	Child, *ESPB* 2:373 (1886)	*DgF*		N.A.	Prose summ

183	D411	Kvindemorderen	—	Comm	?20	Untitled	Kemppinen 51 (1954)	Thyregod No. 81		N.A.	Singing game; Prose summ
183	D411	Kvindemorderen	Red	—	—	Ulver and Vænili	Gray, *Faf* No. 11 (1954)	Olrik 2: No. 3	L	Interp	Omits ref.
183	D411	Kvindemorderen	E	Brds	18	Untitled	Gardner-Medwin, "Paradise" 312 (1963)	*DgF*		Close	2 st. of 57; omits ref.
183	D411	Kvindemorderen	A	Arist	16	Woman-Murderer	Meyer, in Dal, *DBFS* No. 29 (1967)	*DgF*		Close	
183	D411	Kvindemorderen	?Red	—	—	Kvindemorderen	Jacobsen 87 (1988)	?Olrik 2: No. 3		N.A.	Prose summ
184	E64	Den farlige jomfru	F, red	—	—	John Rand's Courtship	Prior, *ADB* No. 96 (1860)	Grimm No. 12		N.A.	From German tr.; omits ref.
185	D308	Stolt Signild	Aa	Arist	16	Fair Signild and the brother whom she rescued	Prior, *ADB* No. 145 (1860)	ANR No. 170		Interp	
185	D308	Stolt Signild	Ab	Comm	19	Proud Snigelse	Syndergaard, "Realiz." 96 (1988)	*DgF*		Close	
188	E31	Den fangne fæstemand	sole	Arist	17	Little Christel and Her Captive Bridegroom	Prior, *ADB* No. 97 (1860)	ANR No. 185		Interp	Omits ref.
189	D168	Mø værger æren	A	Ar/Com	17	Maiden's Defense of Honor	Cox, in Steenstrup, *MPB* 13-14 (1914)	*DgF*		Interp	4 st. of 53; omits ref.
189	D168	Mø værger æren	C	Comm	19	Maiden Defends Honor	Syndergaard, "Realiz." 97-98 (1988)	*DgF*		Close	
193	D354	Døttre hævne fader	B, red	—	—	Two Sisters	Stokes, "Sec. Batch" 89-90 (1855)	ANR No. 171		Interp	Omits ref.
193	D354	Døttre hævne fader	B, red	—	—	Two Sisters Who Avenged their Father	Prior, *ADB* No. 142 (1860)	ANR No. 171		Interp	

231	D97	Den dyre kaabe	A	Arist	16	The Dear Robe	Meyer, in Dal, *DBFS* No. 34 (1967)	*DgF*	Interp	
233	D152	Ellen Ovesdatter	Bb, red	—	—	Miss Ellen	Amateur [Prior], *ODB* No. 29 (1856)	Grimm No. 28	N.A.	From German tr.; omits ref.
233	D152	Ellen Ovesdatter	Bb, red	—	—	Ellen Ove's Daughter	Prior, *ADB* No. 68 (1860)	ANR No. 101	Interp	Omits ref.
233	D152	Ellen Ovesdatter	Red	—	—	Ellen, Daughter of Ove	Gray, *FaF* No. 36 (1954)	Recke No. 132	Interp	
234	D153	Herr Palles bryllup	Red (F)	—	—	Gundelille and Sir Pallé	Prior, *ADB* No. 147 (1860)	ANR No. 198	Interp	
234	D153	Herr Palles bryllup	Red (A)	—	—	Sir Palle's Bridal	Smith-Dampier, *BDB* 2: No. 28 (1939)	Olrik 2: No. 29	Interp	
236	D406	Fru Gundelils Harpeslæt	Red (sole)	—	—	Dame Gundelil's Harping	Smith-Dampier, *BDB* 2: No. 25 (1939)	Olrik 2: No. 26	Close	
238	D399	Tærningspillet	Aa	Comm	17	All's Well that Ends Well	Amateur [Prior], *ODB* No. 10 (1856)	Grimm No. 91	N.A.	From German tr.; omits ref.
238	D399	Tærningspillet	Aa	Comm	17	Little Horseboy	Prior, *ADB* No. 121 (1860)	ANR No. 186	Interp	Omits ref.
238	D399	Tærningspillet	Aa	Comm	17	Bonnie Groom	Buchanan, *BSA* 63-67 (1866)	ANR No. 186	Adapt	
238	D399	Tærningspillet	Compos	—	—	Tærningspillet	Child, *ESPB* 2:458-59 (1886)	*DgF*	N.A.	Prose summ
238	D399	Tærningspillet	Aa	Comm	17	Game of Dice	Smith-Dampier, *DB* No. 23 (1920) ≅ *BDB* 1: No. 39 (1939)	Olrik 1: No. 39	Close Interp	
238	D399	Tærningspillet	Red	—	—	Princess and the Vagabond / Untitled	Rodholm, *Harvest* 152-54 (1953) = Balslev-Clausen No. 70 (1988)	?F. Grundtvig No. 497 from N. Grundtvig 1847	Adapt	11 st. of 22

National Type No.	TSB No.	Title	Version	Tradition	Century	Title of Translation	Translator, Venue, Date	Translator's Source	Lang./Music	Trans. Strategy	Notes
238	D399	Tærningspillet	**Aa**	Comm	17	Game of Dice	Gray, *FæF* No. 43 (1954)	Olrik I: No. 39		Interp	
238	D399	Tærningspillet	U	Comm	18	Dice Game	Meyer, in Dal, *DBFS* No. 33 (1967)	*DgF*		Interp	
239	D397	Møens morgendrømme	Red	—	—	Maiden's Morning Dream	Smith-Dampier, *DB* No. 25 (1920) ≅ *BDB* 1: No. 38 (1939)	Olrik I: No. 38		Close	
239	D397	Møens morgendrømme	Compos	—	—	Morning Dreams of the Maiden	Bredsdorff 14 (1949)	?*DgF*		N.A.	Prose summ
239	D397	Møens morgendrømme	?S	Comm	20	Proud Vesselill	Grainger, *Two Danish F.* (1951)	Own recording		N.I.	2 st. of 25 + prose summ
239	D397	Møens morgendrømme	Red	—	—	Morning Dreams	Gray, *FæF* No. 38 (1954)	Olrik I: No. 38		Interp	
239	D397	Møens morgendrømme	V	Comm	19	Maiden's Morning Dream	Meyer, in Dal, *DBFS* No. 32 (1967) =Rossel, *Scand. Ball.* No. 19 (1982)	*DgF*		Close	
240	D428	Venderkongens jomfrurov	Red (A)	—	—	Stolen Bride	Smith-Dampier, *BDB* 2: No. 15 (1939)	Olrik 2: No. 16		Interp	
240	D428	Venderkongens jomfrurov	Red (A)	—	—	Raid of the King of Norway	Gray, *FæF* No. 44 (1954)	Olrik 2: No. 16		Interp	
244	D14	Den saarede jomfru	Red (sole)	—	—	Wounded Maiden	Smith-Dampier, *BDB* 1: No. 42 (1982)	Olrik I: No. 42		Close	
244	D14	Den saarede jomfru	Red (sole)	—	—	Wounded Maiden	Gray, *FæF* No. 39 (1954)	Olrik I: No. 42		Interp	
250	D195	Esbern og Sidsel	Red (N)	—	—	Esbern and Sidselille	Prior, *ADB* No. 165 (1860)	ANR No. 191		Interp	Omits ref.

252	D198	Troskabsprøven	Ab, red	—	—	Sir Norman and Christine	Prior, *ADB* No. 146 (1860)	ANR No. 206		Close	Omits ref.
254	D200	Tro som guld	A	Arist	17	True as Gold	Cox, in Steenstrup 53, 117 (1914)	*DgF*		Interp	3 st. of II
256	D113	Troskabseden	Red (sole)	—	—	Sir Peter's Harp	Smith-Dampier, *BDB* 1: No. 43 (1939)	Olrik 1: No. 43		Interp	
258	—	Skjøn Anna	Fc	Brds	17	Fair Annie	Jamieson, *PBS* 2:99-116 (1806) =Child, *ESB* 1857-59 3:383-89 =Child, *ESB* 1860 3:383-89	Syv No. 17	L	Adapt	
258	—	Skjøn Anna	Fc	Brds	17	Fair Anna	Prior, *ADB* No. 148 (1860)	ANR No. 177		Interp	
258	—	Skjøn Anna	Compos	—	—	Skjön Anna	Child, *ESPB* 2:65-66 (1885)	*DgF*		N.A.	Prose
258	—	Skjøn Anna	A	Arist	16	Fair Annie	Cox, in Steenstrup, *MPB* 113-14 (1914)	*DgF*		Interp	2 st. of 39
258	—	Skjøn Anna	B	Ar/Com	16	Fair Anna	Cox, in Steenstrup, *MPB* 115 (1914)	*DgF*		Interp	5 st. of 34
259	D229	Lave Stisøn og Fru Eline	Red (H)	—	—	Victory of Patience	Prior, *ADB* No. 42 (1860)	ANR No. 214		Interp	Omits ref.
259	D229	Lave Stisøn og Fru Eline	A	Comm	17	Lave Stisøn and Lady Eline	Meyer, in Dal, *DBFS* No. 27 (1967)	*DgF*		Close	
259	D229	Lave Stisøn og Fru Eline	H	Arist	17	Lave Stisøn and Lady Eline	Meyer, in Dal, *DBFS* No. 75 (1967)	*DgF*		Close	
259	D229	Lave Stisøn og Fru Eline	A	?Comm	17	Lave Stisøn og Fru Eline	G. Jensen, in Præstgaard Anderson 28-29 (1981)	*DgF*	L	Literal	2 st. + prose summ.; omits ref.
263	D416	Liden Kirstins dans	Red (A)	—	—	Little Kirstin's Dance	Prior, *ADB* No. 112 (1860)	ANR No. 219		Interp	Omits ref.
263	D416	Liden Kirstins dans	Red (A)	—	—	Little Christina's Dance	Buchanan, *BSA* 160-65 (1866)	ANR No. 219		Adapt	

National Type No.	TSB No.	Title	Version	Tradition	Century	Title of Translation	Translator, Venue, Date	Translator's Source	Lang./Music	Trans. Strategy	Notes
265	D115	Jomfruens harpeslæt	A, red	—	—	Untitled	Jamieson, *INA* 382-83 (1814)	Syv No. 28		Close	Omits ref.
265	D115	Jomfruens harpeslæt	Ba	Comm	19	Signelil	Prior, *ADB* No. 123 (1860)	ANR No. 182		Interp	
265	D115	Jomfruens harpeslæt	Ba	Comm	19	Signelil the Serving-Maiden	Buchanan, *BSA* 6-11 (1866)	ANR No. 182		Adapt	
265	D115	Jomfruens harpeslæt	Ba	Comm	19	Signelil	Borrow, *Works* 8:73-74 (1923) = *Ball. All Nations* 115-16 (1927)	ANR No. 182		Interp	
267	D396	Jomfru og stalddreng	Gc, red	—	—	Fair Ingeborg's Disguise	Prior, *ADB* No. 103 (1860)	ANR No. 184		Interp	
267	D396	Jomfru og stalddreng	Compos	—	—	Jomfru og Stalddreng	Child, *ESPB* 2:85 (1885)	*DgF*		N.A.	Prose summ
267	D396	Jomfru og stalddreng	Gc, red	—	—	Ingeborg's Disguise	Borrow, *Works* 8:75-76 (1923) = *Ball. All Nations* 117-18 (1927)	ANR No. 184		Interp	Omits ref.
267	D396	Jomfru og stalddreng	Ma	Comm	19	Lord Peter's Stable-Boy	Grainger, *DGMS: Power L* (1950) = T. Lewis, *Source G* 249 (1991)	Kristensen, *JFT* No. 42	M	Interp	4 st. of 26 + prose summ; omits ref.
267	D396	Jomfru og stalddreng	Ma	Comm	19	Lord Peter's Stable-Boy	Grainger, *LPS*, n.d.	Kristensen, *JFT* No. 42		Interp	20 st. of 26; omits ref.
270	D287	Bolde Hr. Nilaus' løn	sole	Arist	17	Bolde Hr. Nilaus' løn	Child, *ESPB* 1:180-81 (1882)	*DgF*		N.A.	Prose summ
271	D288	Redselille og Medelvold	Y	Comm	18	Fair Midel and Kirsten Lyle	Jamieson, *INA* 370, 377-80 (1814)	*Bragur* 3:242	M	Close	
271	D288	Redselille og Medelvold	Z	Comm	18	Fair Midel and Kirsten Lyle	Jamieson, *INA* 368-69 (1814)	*Danske T.*, No. 99-100, 1793		Close	8 st. of 16; omits ref. From Faroes

Page	Code	Title	Y	Comm	No.	Variant Title	Reference	Source	Rel.	Notes
271	D288	Redselille og Medelvold	Red	—	18	Little Christina's Death	Robinson, "Popular" 286-87 (1836)	*Bragur* 3:292	Close	
271	D288	Redselille og Medelvold	Red	—	—	Skion Middel / Sir Middel	Borrow, "Danish P." 306-09 (1823) = *Works* 16:507-09 (1924) ≈ *Rom. Ball.* 28-31 (1826) = *Works* 9:290-92 (1923) = *Ball. All Nations* 139-41 (1927) ≈ *Works* 8:53-56 (1923)	ANR No. 156	Adapt	
						Child Maidelvold			Interp	Uses some *Rom. Ball.*
271	D288	Redselille og Medelvold	Red	—	—	Medelwold and Sidselill	Amateur[Prior], *ODB* No. 35 (1856) = Rev. *ODB* 251 (1856)	Grimm No. 7	N.A.	From German tr.; omits ref.
271	D288	Redselille og Medelvold	Red	—	—	Medelwold and Sidselille	Prior, *ADB* No. 101 (1860) = M. Leach, *Ball. Bk.* 94-96 (1955)	ANR No. 156	Adapt	
271	D288	Redselille og Medelvold	Combos	—	—	Redselille og Medelvold	Child, *ESPB* 1:179-80 (1882)	*DgF*	N.A.	Prose
271	D288	Redselille og Medelvold	Q	Comm	19	Birth in the Grove	Meyer, in Dal, *DBFS* No. 30 (1967)	*DgF*	Close	
274	D421	Brud ikke mø	Ba, red	—	—	Ingfred and Gudrune	Jamieson, *IMA* 340-43 (1814)	Syv No. 62	Close	
274	D421	Brud ikke mø	Ba, red	—	—	Gossiping Nightingales	Amateur[Prior], *ODB* No. 24 (1856)	Grimm No. 47	N.A.	From German tr.; omits ref.
274	D421	Brud ikke mø	Red (Ba)	—	—	Ingfred and Gudrune	Prior, *ADB* No. 157 (1860)	ANR No. 194	Interp	
274	D421	Brud ikke mø	A	Arist	16	Brud ikke Mø	Child, *ESPB* 1:64-65 (1882)	*DgF*	N.A.	
274	D421	Brud ikke mø	Red (Ba)	—	—	Ingfred and Gudrune	Borrow, *Works* 8:77-79 (1923)	ANR No. 194	Interp	

National Type No.	TSB No.	Title	Version	Tradition	Century	Title of Translation	Translator, Venue, Date	Translator's Source	Lang. Music	Trans. Strategy	Notes
275	D420	Hr. Find og Vendelrod	sole	Arist	17	Hr. Find og Vendelrod	Child, *ESPB* I:65 (1882)	*DgF*		N.A.	Prose summ
276	D417	Ingelilles bryllup	Compos	—	—	Ingelilles Bryllup	Child, *ESPB* I:65 (1882)	*DgF*		N.A.	Prose summ
277	D182	Brud i vaande	K	Arist	17	Brud i vaande	Colbert, "Danish" 8 (1978)	*DgF*		Close	4 st. of 61; omits ref.
278	D418	Peder og Malfred	Compos	—	—	Peder og Malfred	Child, *ESPB* I:65 (1882)	*DgF*		N.A.	Prose summ
279	D419	Oluf og Ellinsborg	Compos	—	—	Oluf og Ellinsborg	Child, *ESPB* I:65 (1882)	*DgF*		N.A.	Prose summ
280	D422	Iver Hr. Jonsøn	Compos	—	—	Iver Hr. Jonsøn	Child, *ESPB* I:66 (1882)	*DgF*		N.A.	Prose summ
285	D374	Grevens Datter af Vendel	D, red	—	—	Count of Vendel's Daughter	Prior, *ADB* No. 161 (1860)	ANR No. 138		Interp	
285	D374	Grevens Datter af Vendel	D, red	—	—	Count of Vendel's Daughter	Borrow, "Count" 35-36 (1863) = *Works* 7:399-403 (1923) = *Ball. All Nations* 100-03 (1927)	ANR No. 138		Adapt	Omits ref.
288	D332	Torbens Datter og hendes Faderbane	sole	Arist	17	Torben's Daughter	Smith-Dampier, *DB* No. 21 (1920) ≅ *BDB* I: No. 35 (1939) = Bredsdorff 14 (1949) = Bredsdorff, Mortensen & Popperwell 25-26 (1951)	Olrik I: No. 35	L	Interp Close	3 st. + prose summ 7 st. + prose summ
288	D332	Torbens Datter og hendes Faderbane	sole	Arist	17	Sir Walter's Daughter	Gray, *FæF* No. 10 (1954)	Olrik I: No. 35		Interp	

288	D332	Torbens Datter og hendes Faderbane	sole	Arist	17	Torben's Daughter and His Slayer	Meyer, in Billeskov Jansen & Mitchell 1:11, 13 (1972)	*DgF*		Close	
288	D332	Torbens Datter og hendes Faderbane	sole	Arist	17	Torben's Daughter and His Slayer	Meyer, in Abrahamsen & Dal 16-17 (1965) ≅ Dal, *DBFS* No. 26 (1967)	*DgF*		Close	
293	D123	Ung Axelvold	D, red	—	—	Child Axelvold	Jamieson, *INA* 361-65 (1814) =Longfellow, *PPE* 74-75 (1847)	Syv (Vedel 2: No. 12)		Close	
293	D123	Ung Axelvold	D, red	—	—	Axelwold	Amateur [Prior], *ODB* No. 30 (1856)	Grimm No. 32		N.A.	From German tr.; omits ref.
293	D123	Ung Axelvold	D, red	—	—	Axelwold	Prior, *ADB* No. 152 (1860)	*ANR* No. 166		Interp	Omits ref.
293	D123	Ung Axelvold	D, red	—	—	Young Axelwold	Buchanan, *BSA* 103-11 (1866)	*ANR* No. 166		Adapt	
294	D434	Karl Hittebarn	C, rec	—	—	King's Daugher of Engelland	Jamieson, *INA* 384-88 (1814)	Syv No. 16		Close	
294	D434	Karl Hittebarn	Red (C)	—	—	The Foundling	Prior, *ADB* No. 127 (1860)	*ANR* No. 176		Interp	
297	D352	Liden Engel	Red (E)	—	—	Little Engel	Stokes, "Dan. Ball.," Rev. 214 (1858)	*ANR* No. 127		Close	Omits ref.
297	D352	Liden Engel	Red (E₁)	—	—	Childe Engel	Prior, *ADB* No. 164 (1860)	*ANR* No. 127		Interp	Omits ref.
297	D352	Liden Engel	Red (E₂)	—	—	Liden Engel	Child, *ESPB* 2:298 (1886)	*ANR* No. 127		N.A.	Prose. Called **A**
297	D352	Liden Engel	Red (E₃)	—	—	Little Engel	Borrow, *Works* 7:376-86 (1923)	*ANR* No. 127		Interp	Omits ref.
297	D352	Liden Engel	Red	—	—	Liden Engel	Ker, "On Dan. B." 5:399-400 (1908) =*Coll. Ess.* 2:112-13 (1925)	Olrik I: No. 33		N.A.	Prose summ

National Type No.	TSB No.	Title	Version	Tradition	Century	Title of Translation	Translator, Venue, Date	Translator's Source	Lang./Music	Trans. Strategy	Notes
297	D352	Liden Engel	Red	—	—	Young Engel	Smith-Dampier, *BDB* 1: No. 33 (1939) = Warnock & Anderson 518-20 (1959)	Olrik 1: No. 33		Interp	
298	E96	Svend af Vollersløv	Red (Q)	—	—	Young William	Prior, *ADB* No. 170 (1860)	ANR No. 126		Interp	Omits ref.
298	E96	Svend af Vollersløv	Red (Q)	—	—	Young William	Child, *ESPB* 2:297 (1886)	ANR No. 126		N.A.	Prose
298	E96	Svend af Vollersløv	Red	—	—	Svend of Vollerslov	Smith-Dampier, *BDB* 2: No. 22(1939)	Olrik 2: No. 23		Interp	
303	D333	Elsker dræbt af broder	Red (Dh)	—	—	Fair Ellensborg and Sir Olave	Prior, *ADB* No. 169 (1860)	ANR No. 146		Interp	Omits ref.
303	D333	Elsker dræbt af broder	A	Arist	17	Elsker dræbt af Broder	Colbert, "Danish" 9 (1978)	*DgF*		Literal	1 st. Omits ref.
304	D324	De hurtige svar	Aa	?Arist	17	Wit at Need	Jamieson, *INA* 424-26 (1814) = Longfellow, *PPE* 78-79 (1847)	Syv No. 73		Interp	
304	D324	De hurtige svar	Aa	?Arist	17	Stolen Nuptials	Amateur [Prior], *ODB* No. 3 (1856)	Grimm No. 19		N.A.	From German tr.; omits ref.
304	D324	De hurtige svar	Aa	?Arist	17	Ready Reply	Prior, *ADB* No. 91 (1860) = Drummond-Davies 5-6 (1861)	ANR No. 204		Interp	Omits ref.
304	D324	De hurtige svar	Aa	?Arist	17	Det hurtige Svar	Child, *ESPB* 2:158 (1885)	ANR No. 204		Close	2 st. of 16
304	D324	De hurtige svar	Aa	?Arist	17	Ready Answer	Borrow, *Works* 8:80-81 (1923) = *Ball. All Nations* 119-20 (1927)	ANR No. 204		Interp	Omits ref.
305	D390	Hertug Frydenborg	Compos	—	—	Hertug Frydenborg	Child, *ESPB* 5:31 (1894)	*DgF*		N.A.	Prose summ

311	D255	Adelbrand	Ab, red	—	—	Bridal Robe	Amateur[Prior], *ODB* No. 28 (1856)	Grimm No. 6	N.A.	From German tr.; omits ref.
312	D185	Gade og Hillelille	Bc, red	—	—	Fair Hillelille and Sir Judah	Prior, *ADB* No. 132 (1860)	ANR No. 130	Interp	Omits ref.
314	D178	Ebbe Galt	Rec	—	—	Ebbé Galt	Prior, *ADB* No. 55 (1860)	ANR No. 63	Interp	Omits ref.
314	D178	Ebbe Galt	Red	—	—	Ebbe Galt	Child, *ESPB* 2:458 (1886)	ANR No. 63	N.A.	Prose
315	D175	Oluf Pant	b, red	—	—	Oluf Pant	Jamieson, *IMA* 393-96 (1814) =Longfellow, *PPE* 16-77 (1847)	Syv No. 86	Close	
318	D339	Bueskytte som blodhævner	Ad, red	—	—	Brother Avenged	Borrow, in Borrow-Bowring 61-62 (1830)	ANR No. 173	Adapt	With ref.
							= *Wright* 143-44 (1921) ≈ *Works* 8:68-70 (1923)			Omits ref.
318	D339	Bueskytte som blodhævner	Ad, red	—	—	Archer's Revenge	Prior, *ADB* No. 109 (1860)	ANR No. 173	Interp	Omits ref.
319	D340	Age fælder Tord Iversøn	Red	—	—	Slaying of Thord Iverson	Smith Dampier, *BDB* 2: No. 23 (1939)	Olrik 2: No. 24	Close	
319	D340	Age fælder Tord Iversøn	Red	—	—	Murder of Tord Iverson	Gray, *FaF* No. 7 (1954)	Olrik 2: No. 24	Interp	Omits ref.
325	D342	Nilus og Hillelil	A	Ar/Com	16	Nilus og Hillelil	Ker, "On Dan. B." 5:399 (1908) = *Coll. Ess.* 2:111-12 (1925)	Olrik I: No. 32	N.A.	Prose summ
325	D342	Nilus og Hillelil	A	Ar/Com	16	Nilus og Hillelil	Smith Dampier, *BDB* 1: No. 32 (1939)	Olrik I: No. 32	Interp	
325	D342	Nilus og Hillelil	A	Ar/Com	16	Nilus and Little Hilde	Entwistle, *Eur. Ball.* 225 (1939)	Olrik I: No. 32	Close	5 st. of 31
325	D342	Nilus og Hillelil	A	Ar/Com	16	Nilus og Hillelille	Gray, *FaF* No. 6 (1954)	Olrik I: No. 32	Interp	

National Type No.	TSB No.	Title	Version	Tradition	Century	Title of Translation	Translator, Venue, Date	Translator's Source	Lang. / Music	Trans. Strategy	Notes
325	D342	Nilus og Hillelil	**Ab**	Ar/Com	16	Nilus og Hillelil	Meyer, in Dal, *DBFS* No. 24 (1967) =Rossel, *Scand. Ball.* No. 20 (1982)	*DgF*		Close	
330	D306	Palle, Baard og Liden	Red (**b**)	—	—	Sir Pall, Sir Bear, and Sir Liden	Borrow, *Works* 8:1-2 (1923)	ANR No. 139		Interp	Omits ref.
337	B18	Hr. David og hans stesønner	Red	—	—	Sir David and His Stepsons	Smith-Dampier, *BDB* 2: No. 30(1939)	Olrik 2: No. 31		Adapt	
338	B21	Hr. Truelses døtre	Red (**F**)	—	—	Three Robbers and Their Three Sisters	Prior, *ADB* No. 137 (1860)	ANR No. 164		Interp	
338	B21	Hr. Truelses døtre	Red (**F**)	—	—	Hr. Truels's Døtre	Child, *ESPB* 1:171 (1882)	ANR No. 164		N.A.	Prose. Called **A**
338	B21	Hr. Truelses døtre	**H**	Comm	19	Hr. Truels's Døtre	Child, *ESPB* 1:171 (1882)	Berggreen *FSM* 1869 I: No. 42		N.A.	Prose summ. Called **B**
338	B21	Hr. Truelses døtre	Red (**F**)	—	—	Sir Truels's Daughters	Borrow, *Works* 8:60-63 (1923)	ANR No. 164		Interp	
340	D320	Svend i rosensgaard	**A**	Comm	19	Son, Come tell to me	Karpeles, *FS Eur* No. 2 (1956)	Berggreen *FSM* 1869 I: No. 45; *DgF*	L M	Close	
340	D320	Svend i rosensgaard	**A**	Comm	19	Murdered Brother	Stracke, in Luboff & Stracke 204-05 (1965)	Karpeles, *FS Eur* No. 2	L M	Adapt	

			A	Comm				DgF	Interp	1846 A version
340	D320	Svend i rosensgaard	A	Comm	19	Svend among Rosebuds so Near / Svend in the Rose Garden	Meyer, in Abrahamsen Dal 18-19 (1965) ≅ Dal, DBES No. 31 (1967) = Rossel, Scand. Ball. No. 21 (1982)	Sv. Grundtvig letter	N.A.	Prose summ
341	D321	Den forgivne datter	Ba	Comm	19	Untitled	Child, ESPB 1:154 (1882)		Interp	Omits ref.
342	D271	Volmers hustru levende begravet	Ag, red	—	—	Lyborg and her Mother-in-Law	Prior, ADB No. 171 (1860)	ANR No. 134	Interp	Prose summ
342	D271	Volmers hustru levende begravet	Ag, red	—	—	Cruel Mother-in-Law	Borrow, Works 7:394-98 (1923)	ANR No. 134	Interp	3 st. of 20; omits ref.
343	D272	Fæstemøen levende begravet	sole	Arist	17	Untitled	Cox, in Steenstrup, MPB 184 (1914)	N.I.	Interp	
353	D106	Jon rømmer af land	Rec	—	—	Sir John the Outlaw	Smith-Dampier, BDB 1: No. 36 (1939)	Olrik 1: No. 36	Close	
353	D106	Jon rømmer af land	Red	—	—	The Outlaw	Gray, FaF No. 16 (1954)	Olrik 1: No. 36	Interp	
354	D251	Ebbe Skammelsøn	Red(Ha)	—	—	Ebbé Skammelson	Prior, ADB No. 92 (1860) = M. Leach, Ball. Bk. 217-22 (1955)	ANR No. 120	Adapt	Omits ref.
354	D251	Ebbe Skammelsøn	Red(Ha)	—	—	Ebbe Skammelson	Buchanan, BSA 32-44 (1866)	ANR No. 120	Interp	
354	D251	Ebbe Skammelsøn	Red(Ha)	—	—	Ebbe Skammelsøn	Child, ESPB 2:i28 (1885)	ANR No. 120	N.A.	Prose summ
354	D251	Ebbe Skammelsøn	Red	—	—	Ebbe Skammelsøn	Ker, "On Dan. B." 5:400 (1908) = Coll. Ess. 2:113 (1925)	Olrik 1: No. 44	N.A.	Prose summ

National Type No.	TSB No.	Title	Version	Tradition	Century	Title of Translation	Translator, Venue, Date	Translator's Source	Lang/ Music	Trans. Strategy	Notes
354	D251	Ebbe Skammelsøn	Red	—	—	Ebbe Skammelsøn	Smith-Dampier, *DB* No. 11 (1920) ≅ *BDB* 1: No. 44 (1939)	Olrik I: No. 44		Close	
354	D251	Ebbe Skammelsøn	Compos	—	—	Ebbe Skammelsøn	Brodeur 179-81 (1923)	? *DgF*		N.A.	Prose
354	D251	Ebbe Skammelsøn	Red	—	—	Ebbe Skammelsøn	Gray, *FaF* No. 14 (1954)	Olrik I: No. 44		Interp	
354	D251	Ebbe Skammelsøn	**Ca**	Arist	17	Ebbe Skammelsen	Meyer, in Dal, *DBFS* No. 25 (1967) = Rossel, *Scand. Ball.* No. 23 (1982) = Piø, "Ebbe Sk." 18-23 (1985) = Balslev-Clausen No. 69 (1988)	*DgF*		Close	
354	D251	Ebbe Skammelsøn	Red	—	—	Ebbè Skammelsen	H. Meyer, in Billeskov Jansen & Mitchell I:21-29 (1972)	Olrik I: No. 44	L	Close	
354	D251	Ebbe Skammelsøn	Compos	—	—	Untitled	Jette Andersen & Carol Edwards, in Piø, "Ebbe Sk." 27-51 (1985)	*DgF*	L	Close	
355	D252	Utro fæstemø	**A**	Arist	17	Utro Fæstemø	Brodeur 183-84 (1923)	*DgF*		Close	3 st. + prose summ; omits ref.
360	D220	Fru Mettelils utroskab	Red (**C**)	—	—	Sir Peter and Dame Margaret	Prior, *ADB* No. 95 (1860)	ANR No. 125		Interp	Omits ref.
366	D190	Nidvisen	Red	—	—	Untitled	Cox, in Steenstrup, *MPB* 22-24 (1914)	*DgF*		Close	
369	F26	Rakkerens brud	Red	—	—	Gypsy's Bride	Smith-Dampier, *NKB* 23-26 (1912)	? *DgF*		Interp	

No.	D	Danish title				English title	Source	Reference	L	Type	Notes
372	DI56	Kong Erik og den spotske jomfru	Red	—	—	King Erik and the Scornful Maid	Smith-Dampier, *DB* No. 24 (1920) ≅ *BDB* 1: No. 48 (1939)	Olrik 1: No. 48		Close	
372	DI56	Kong Erik og den spotske jomfru	Red	—	—	Prideful' Lass	Gray, *FaF* No. 31 (1954)	Olrik 1: No. 48		Interp	
375	D360	Jon Remorsøns død paa havet	**Fa, red**	—	—	Sir John Rimord's Son's Shrift	Prior, *ADB* No. 77 (1860) = Drummond-Davies 30-31 (1861)	ANR No. 92		Interp	Omits ref.; 19 st. + prose summ
375	D360	Jon Remorsøns død paa havet	**Fa, red**	—	—	Drowning of John Remorsson	Smith-Dampier, *NKB* 34-38 (1912)	*DgF*		Adapt	
375	D360	Jon Remorsøns død paa havet	**Fa, red**	—	—	John Rimaardson's Confession	Borrow, *Works* 7:334-39 (1923)	ANR No. 92		Interp	
376	D361	Hr. Peders skriftemaal paa havet	**A**	Arist	16	Danish A	Child, *ESPB* 2:13-14 (1885)	Sv. Grundtvig	L	Interp	1 st. + prose summ
376	D361	Hr. Peders skriftemaal paa havet	**C**	Comm	19	Danish C, D	Child, *ESPB* 2:13-14 (1885)	Sv. Grundtvig		Close	2 st. + prose summ
377	D307	Danneved og Svend Trøst	Red **(Be)**	—	—	Childe Danneved and Swain Trusty	Prior, *ADB* No. 172 (1860)	ANR No. 169		Interp	
377	D307	Danneved og Svend Trøst	Red	—	—	Young Danneved and Boy Trust / Young Danneved and Swain Trust	Smith-Dampier, *BfD* 17-20 (1910) ≅ *BDB* 2: No. 20 (1939)	Olrik 2: No. 21		Adapt / Close	Heavily revised
377	D307	Danneved og Svend Trøst	Red **(Be)**	—	—	Little Danneved and Swayne Trost	Borrow, *Works* 8:64-67 (1923)	ANR No. 169		Interp	Omits ref.

National Type No.	TSB No.	Title	Version	Tradition	Cen-tury	Title of Translation	Translator, Venue, Date	Translator's Source	Lang. Music	Trans. Strategy	Notes
381	D90	Svend og hans søster	**Ba**	?Arist	17	Gentle Orphan	Amateur[Prior], *ODB* No. 8 (1856)	Grimm No. 15		N.A.	From German tr.; omits ref.
381	D90	Svend og hans søster	**Ba**	?Arist	17	Orphan Sister	Prior, *ADB* No. 110 (1860)	ANR No. 202		Interp	
383	D407	Verner kommer af fangetaarn	**Ab**, red	—	—	Sir Verner's Escape	Prior, *ADB* No. 158 (1860)	ANR No. 174		Interp	Omits ref.
383	D407	Verner kommer af fangetaarn	**Ab**, red	—	—	Sir Verner and Dame Ingeborg	Borrow, *Works* 8:71-72 (1923)	ANR No. 174		Interp	
383	D407	Verner kommer af fangetaarn	Red	—	—	Sir Verner's Escape	Smith-Dampier, *BDB* I: No. 47 (1939)	Olrik I: No. 47		Interp	
383	D407	Verner kommer af fangetaarn	Red	—	—	Sir Malcolm in Prison	Gray, *FaF* No. 33 (1954)	Olrik I: No. 47		Interp	
387	D45	Lovmand og Tord	**Ea**, red	—	—	Der Rechter Zeit	Anster 615-17 (1842)	Grimm No. 54		N.A.	From German tr.
387	D45	Lovmand og Tord	**D**	Brds	17	Sir Lowman and Sir Thor	Prior, *ADB* No. 99 (1860)	ANR No. 199		Interp	
390	F11	Lave og Jon	**Da**	?Comm	17	Sir Lava and Sir John	Jamieson, *INA* 420-23 (1814)	Syv No. 64		Close	
390	F11	Lave og Jon	**Da**	?Comm	17	Sir Lavé and Sir John	Howitt, *LRNE* 301-03 (1852)	ANR No. 196		Interp	Parital ref.
390	F11	Lave og Jon	**Da**	?Comm	17	Sir John	Borrow, *Rom. Ball.* 40-43 (1826) = *Works* 9:299-300 (1923) = *Ball. All Nations* 144-45 (1927)	ANR No. 196		Adapt	
390	F11	Lave og Jon	**Da**	?Comm	17	Sir John	Amateur[Prior], *ODB* No. 19 (1856)	Grimm No. 22		N.A.	From German tr.; omits ref.

			Da	?Comm	17	Sir John	Prior, ADB No. 143:277-79 (1860)	ANR No. 196		Interp	
390	FII	Lave og Jon	C	Brds	18	Sir John	Prior, ADB No. 143:276 (1860)	ANR 4:356		Interp	6 st. of 24
390	FII	Lave og Jon	Red	—	—	Lovel and John	Smith-Dampier, BfD 34-37 (1910)	Olrik 1: No. 37		Adapt	
390	FII	Lave og Jon	Red	—	—	Lovel and John	Smith-Dampier, DB No. 28 (1920) ≅ Smith-Dampier et al 764-68 (1924) ≅ BDB I: No. 37 (1939) =Hallmundsson, Anth. 18-20 (1965)	Olrik 1: No. 37		Close	Uses some BfD
390	FII	Lave og Jon	Red	—	—	Lovel and John	Gray, FaF No. 41 (1954)	Olrik 1: No. 37		Interp	
390	FII	Lave og Jon	Red	—	—	Laurence and John	Meyer, in Billeskov Jansen & Mitchell 1:31-35 (1972)	Olrik 1: No. 37	L	Close	
391	D213	Tyge Hermandsøn	**Ae** red	—	—	Coward Bridegroom	Prior, ADB No. 90 (1860)	ANR No. 210		Interp	Omits ref.
391	D213	Tyge Hermandsøn	**Ae**, red	—	—	Tygge Hermandsen	Borrow, Works 8:82-85 (1923)	ANR No. 210		Interp	Omits ref.
391	D213	Tyge Hermandsøn	**A**	Arist	17	Tyge Hermandsson	Smith-Dampier, DB No. 29 (1920)	DgF		Interp	
394	D51	Svend Dyrings bruderov	**Ac**, red	—	—	Young Child Dyring	Jamieson, IM 335-39 (1814) =Longfellow, PPE 73-74 (1847) =Child, ESB 1857-59 4:265-69 =Child, ESB 1860 4:265-69	Syv No. 77		Interp	
394	D51	Svend Dyrings bruderov	Red	—	—	Young Svend Dyre	Smith-Dampier, BDB 2: No. 27 (1939)	Olrik 2: No. 28		Interp	
394	D51	Svend Dyrings bruderov	Red	—	—	Young Squire Dyre	Gray, FaF No. 42 (1954)	Olrik 2: No. 28		Interp	

National Type No.	TSB No.	Title	Version	Tradition	Century	Title of Translation	Translator, Venue, Date	Translator's Source	Lang; Music	Trans. Strategy	Notes
408	D36	Hr. Mortens klosterrov	Red (Ba)	—	—	Robbing of the Nunnery	Johnstone (1786)	Sandvig, *Levn* I: No. 4	L	Interp	Omits ref.
408	D36	Hr. Mortens klosterrov	Red (Ba)	—	—	Cloister-Robbing	Prior, *ADB* No. 166 (1860)	ANR No. 212		Interp	
408	D36	Hr. Mortens klosterrov	Red (Ba)	—	—	Cloister Robbing	Buchanan, *BSA* 68-75 (1866) =Rev. *BSA* 1434-35 (1866) =B., W., "Scand. Ball." 293 (1867)	ANR No. 212		Adapt	5 st. of 38; 24 st. + prose summ
408	D36	Hr. Mortens klosterrov	Red (Ba)	—	—	Klosterranet	Child, *ESPB* 1:249 (1882)	ANR No. 212		N.A.	Prose
409	D37	Hr. Karl paa ligbaare	A	Arist	16	Untitled	Child, *ESPB* 1:247 (1884)	Sv. Grundtvig		N.A.	Prose
409	D37	Hr. Karl paa ligbaare	B	Ar/Com	16	Untitled	Child, *ESPB* 1:248 (1884)	Sv. Grundtvig		N.A.	Prose. Called **C**
409	D37	Hr. Karl paa ligbaare	D	Arist	17	Untitled	Child, *ESPB* 1:247-48 (1884)	Sv. Grundtvig		N.A.	Prose. Called **Ba**
409	D37	Hr. Karl paa ligbaare	G	Comm	19	Untitled	Child, *ESPB* 1:248-499 (1884)	Sv. Grundtvig		Close	3 st. + prose summ. Called **E**
409	D37	Hr. Karl paa ligbaare	I	Comm	19	Untitled	Child, *ESPB* 1:248 (1884)	Sv. Grundtvig		N.A.	Prose. Called **D**
409	D37	Hr. Karl paa ligbaare	K	Comm	19	Untitled	Child, *ESPB* 1:249 (1884)	Sv. Grundtvig		N.A.	Prose summ. Called **F**

409	D37	Hr. Karl paa ligbaare	Fed	—	—	Sir Karl's Lykewake Sir Karel's Lyke-Wake	Smith-Dampier, *BfD* 7-9 (1910) ≈ *DB* No. 26 (1920) ≈ *BDB* 2: No. 31 (1939)	Olrik 2: No. 32		Interp Close Interp	
409	D37	Hr. Karl paa ligbaare	Rød	—	—	Sir Karl on His Bier	Gray, *FaF* No. 40 (1954)	Olrik 2: No. 32		Interp	
415	D78	Hr. Hjælmer	**Af**, red	—	—	Sir Helmer Blaa and his Bride's Brothers	Prior, *ADB* No. 162 (1860) = M. Leach, *Ball. Bk.* 570-71 (1955)	ANR No. 209		Interp	
415	D78	Hr. Hjælmer	Red	—	—	Sir Hjelm	Smith-Dampier, *BDB* 2: No. 21 (1939)	Olrik 2: No. 22		Close	
415	D78	Hr. Hjælmer	Red	—	—	Sir Helmer	Gray, *FaF* No. 8 (1954)	Recke No. 3		Interp	
416	D69	Ridder fælder jomfruens syv brødre	Red (**A**)	—	—	Maid in the Wood	Prior, *ADB* No. 134 (1860)	ANR No. 123		Interp	
416	D69	Ridder fælder jomfruens syv brødre	Compos	—	—	Jomfruen i Skoven	Child, *ESPB* 2:170 (1885)	ANR No. 123		N.A.	Prose summ
416	D69	Ridder fælder jomfruens syv brødre	Red (**A**)	—	—	Jomfruen i Skoven	Child, *ESPB* 4:164 (1890)	ANR No. 123		N.A.	Prose summ
416	D69	Ridder fælder jomfruens syv brødre	Red (**A**)	—	—	Damsel of the Wood	Borrow, *Works* 7:372-75 (1923)	ANR No. 123		Interp	
416	D69	Ridder fælder jomfruens syv brødre	**A**, red	—	—	Maiden in the Woods	Cox, in Steenstrup 175-76 (1914)	*DgF*		Close	4 st. of 27
416	D69	Ridder fælder jomfruens syv brødre	Red	—	—	Power of Love	Grainger, *DFMS: Power* L1 (?1950) = *Thirteen* F. 56-61, 67-68 (1981) = T. Lewis, *Source* G. 248 (1991)	Own record. & *DgF*	M	Interp	2 st + prose summ

National Type No.	TSB No.	Title	Version	Tradition	Century	Title of Translation	Translator, Venue, Date	Translator's Source	Lang; Music L M	Trans. Strategy	Notes
416	D69	Ridder fælder jomfruens syv brødre	C	Comm	20	Power of Love	Grainger, *Power* (1991)	Own record.		N.A.	1 st.
421	D304	Daniel Bosøn	Red (H)	—	—	Sir Dalebo's Vengeance	Smith-Dampier, *MKB* 39-44 (1912)	? *DgF*		Interp	
424	D369	Nilus Strangesøns Stenstue	a	Comm	19	Niels Strangeson's Stone Tower	Smith-Dampier, *BDB* 2: No. 19 (1939)	Olrik 2: No. 20		Interp	Omits ref.
424	D369	Nilus Strangesøns Stenstue	a	Comm	19	Nilus Strangeson's Stone-House	Gray, *HBD* No. 16 (1958)	Olrik 2: No. 20		Interp	Omits ref.
425	D9	I grevens tjæneste	Red	—	—	Lowly Squire	Smith-Dampier, *MKB* 31-33 (1912)	? *DgF*		Interp	
429	D101	Bjørn og den norske kongebrud	Red	—	—	Norse King's Bridal	Smith-Dampier, *MKB* 19-22 (1912)	? *DgF*		Interp	
431	D29	Karl og Rigmor	Red (Ac)	—	—	Lover's Strategem	Buchanan, *BSA* 56-62 (1866)	ANR No. 190		Adapt	
435	D92	Hr. Peder og hans søster	sole	Comm	19	Herr Peder og hans søster	Child, *ESPB* 1:447-48 (1884)	Grundtvig		N.A.	Prose summ
436	D88	Sverkel og hans søster	A	Arist	17	Sir Swerkel	Prior, *ADB* No. 135 (1860)	ANR No. 155		Interp	
436	D88	Sverkel og hans søster	A	Arist	17	Sir Swerkel	Borrow, *Works* 8:50-52 (1923) = *Ball. All Nations* 113-14 (1927)	ANR No. 155		Interp	Omits ref.
437	D91	Søster beder broder	A	Arist	17	Brother and Sister	Prior, *ADB* No. 113 (1860)	ANR No. 151		Interp	Omits ref.
437	D91	Søster beder broder	B	Arist	17	Sister Woos Brother	Meyer, in Dal, *DBFS* No. 35 (1967)	*DgF*		Close	

438	D95	Broder myrder søster			18	Liden Ellen og hendes Broder	Child, *ESPB* 1:447 (1884)	Sv. Grundtvig, *ESF* No. 50	N.A.	Prose summ
442	D133	Fortvivelsen	A	Arist	17	The Despair	Stokes, "Sec. Batch" 90 (1855)	ANR No. 159	Interp	
443	D297	Lindens varsel	Red	—	—	Luck of the Linden-Tree	Smith-Dampier, *NKB* 45-47 (1912)	*DgF*	Interp	
460	D284	Fæstemanden dør	C	?Arist	17	Sir Olave and Fair Metté	Prior, *ADB* No. 98 (1860)	ANR No. 193	Interp	Omits ref.
460	D284	Fæstemanden dør	Red	—	—	Lover's Death	Smith-Dampier, *BDB* 2: No. 24 (1939)	Olrik 2: No. 25	Interp	
460	D284	Fæstemanden dør	Fed	—	—	Dying Lover	Gray, *FaF* No. 18 (1954)	Olrik 2: No. 25	Interp	
464	D71	Jomfruens straf	Compos	—	—	Maiden's Punishment	Cox, in Steenstrup, *MPB* 63n (1914)	*DgF*	N.A.	Prose summ
465	D227	Haagens dans	**b**, red	—	—	Hero Hogen and the Queen of Denmark	Jamieson, *IMA* 306-09 (1914) =Longfellow, *PPE* 69-70 (1847)	Syv No. 25	Close	
465	D227	Haagens dans	**b**, red	—	—	Hogen's Dance and Song	Prior, *ADB* No. 163 (1860)	ANR No. 181	Interp	
465	D227	Haagens dans	a	Arist	16	Hagen at the Dance	Smith-Dampier, *NKB* 27-30 (1912)	*DgF*	Interp	
465	D227	Haagens dans	a	Arist	16	Hagen's Dance	Cox, in Steenstrup, *MPB* 12, 26 (1914)	*DgF*	Close	5 st. of 20
469	D387	Allegast	Red (**A**)	—	—	Allegast	Borrow, *Works* 8:86-89 (1923)	ANR No. 221	Interp	
470	D384	Tistram og Isold	sole	Arist	16	Untitled	Schach, "Tristan" 287-88 (1964)	*DgF*	N.A.	Prose summ
470	D384	Tistram og Isold	sole	Arist	16	Thisterom and Isall	S.A.J. Bradley, in Hill 146-48 (1977)	*DgF*	Literal	Stanzaic prose
471	D385	Tistram og Jomfru Isolt	Compos	—	—	Untitled	Schach, "Tristan" 289 (1964)	*DgF*	N.A.	**D. E.** Prose summ
471	D385	Tistram og Jomfru Isolt	**A**	Ar/Com	16	Sir Tistrum and Maid Isallt	S.A.J. Bradley, in Hill 148-49 (1977)	*DgF*	Literal	Stanzaic prose

National Type No.	TSB No.	Title	Version	Tradition	Century	Title of Translation	Translator, Venue, Date	Translator's Source	Lang; Music	Trans. Strategy	Notes
471	D385	Tistram og Jomfru Isolt	**B**	Arist	16	Sir Tistrum and Maid Isallt	S.A.J. Bradley, in Hill 149-50 (1977)	*DgF*		Literal	Stanzaic prose
471	D385	Tistram og Jomfru Isolt	**C**	Arist	17	Sir Tistrum and Maid Isallt	S.A.J. Bradley, in Hill 150-51 (1977)	*DgF*		Literal	Stanzaic prose
471	D385	Tistram og Jomfru Isolt	**D**	Arist	16	Sir Tistrum and Maid Isallt	S.A.J. Bradley, in Hill 152-53 (1977)	*DgF*		Literal	Stanzaic prose
471	D385	Tistram og Jomfru Isolt	**E**	Arist	17	Sir Tistrum and Maid Isallt	S.A.J. Bradley, in Hill 153-55 (1977)	*DgF*		Literal	Stanzaic prose
475	D87	Aslag Tordsøn og skøn Valborg	**Ca**	Brds	17	Axel Thordsen and Fair Valborg	Thorpe 43-46 (1851)	ANR No. 143		N.A.	Prose summ
475	D87	Aslag Tordsøn og skøn Valborg	**Ca**	Brds	17	Axel and Walborg	Prior, *ADB* No. 78 (1860)	ANR No. 143		Interp	Omits ref.
475	D87	Aslag Tordsøn og skøn Valborg	**Ca**	Brds	17	Axel and Walborg	Buchanan, *BSA* 117-58 (1866)	ANR No. 143		Interp	
475	D87	Aslag Tordsøn og skøn Valborg	**Ca**	Brds	17	Axel Thordson and Fair Valborg	Borrow, *Works* 8:3-31 (1923)	ANR No. 143		Interp	Omits ref.
475	D87	Aslag Tordsøn og skøn Valborg	N.I.			Axel Thordson and Fair Walborg	Morris, "Axel Thordson," n.d.	N.I.			Unpublished
476	D327	Hertugen af Skare	**b**	Arist	17	Duke's Daughter of Skage	Borrow, *Works* 7:321-27 (1923) = *Ball. All Nations* 87-93 (1927)	ANR No. 88		Close	42 of 98 st.; omits ref.
477	D74	Giselmaar	**Bb**, red	—	—	Maiden Gisselmore	Prior, *ADB* No. 168 (1860)	ANR No. 218		Close	
480	D201	Terkel Trundesøn	**Ce**	Brds	17	Torkild Trundeson	Prior, *ADB* No. 100 (1860)	ANR No. 200		Adapt	Omits ref.

No.	D	Danish title	Red (D)			English title			Interp	
482	D86	Sallemand dør af elskov	Red (D)	—	—	Sir Sallemand	Prior, *ADB* No. 106 (1860)	ANR No. 153	Interp	Omits ref.
486	D391	Fæstemand løskøber fæstemø	D	Comm	19	Untitled	Melby 102-03 (1914)	Thuren	Literal	3 st. of 20; prose
487	—	Den udkaarne ridder	Red	—	—	Elected Knight	Longfellow, *Ballads* 53-56 (1842) = *PPE* 82 (1847) = *Poetical Works* 90-92 n.d. = *Complete P. Works* 608 (1893) = Van Doren, *Anthol.* 976-78 (1928) = Van Doren & Lapolla, *World's* 403-05 (1928) = Van Doren & Lapolla, *Anthol. High Sch. ed.* 403-05 (1929) = Creekmore, *Lyrics* 224-25 (1959) = Longfellow, *Works* 6:256-58 (1966)	ANR No. 152	Close	Many similar eds. Multiple later eds.
487	—	Den udkaarne ridder	Rel	—	—	Chosen Knight	Borrow, *Works* 8:48-49 (1923)	ANR No. 152	Interp	
494	D24	Hr. Magnus faar sin elskede	A	Arist	16	Hr. Magnus faar sin elskede	Colbert, "Danish" 12-13 (1978)	*DgF*	Literal	
507	—	Falken og duen	Red	—	—	Song of the Falcon	Smith-Dampier, *BDB* 1: No. 49 (1939) = Hallmundsson, *Anth.* 17-18 (1965)	Olrik I: No. 49	Interp	
509	—	Ungersvends drøm	A	Arist	16	Young Man's Dream	Meyer, in Dal, *DBFS* No. 36 (1967)	*DgF*	Close	
513	D376	Nonnens klage	Red	—	—	Cloister-Maiden	Cox, in Steenstrup, *MPB* 63-64, 223 (1914)	Sv. Grundtvig 1867 146-48	Close	8 st. of 14; omits ref.
513	D376	Nonnens klage	G, red	—	—	Maiden's Complaint	Meyer, in Dal, *DBFS* No. 37 (1967)	*DgF*	Close	Also "Pigens klage"

National Type No.	TSB No.	Title	Version	Tradition	Century	Title of Translation	Translator, Venue, Date	Translator's Source	Lang/Music	Trans. Strategy	Notes
516	—	Jeg ved saa dejlig en urtegaard	sole	Comm	19	I Know Where so Lovely a Garden Grows	D. Colbert, in Rossel, *Scand. Ball.* No. 32 (1982)	*DgF*		Close	
518	F61	Limgris	sole	Arist	16	Limgrises Vise	Child, *ESPB* 1:210 (1882)	*DgF*		N.A.	Prose summ
528	B35	Fru Ingelil og hendes døtre	Red (**A**)	—	—	Fru Ingelil's Daughters	"Fru Ingelisl's D." (1924)	Sv. Grundtvig 1882:374		Literal	Adds ref.
529	B36	Barnemordersken	**Aa**	Comm	19	Untitled	Child, *ESPB* 1:219 (1884)	Kristensen, *JFT* 1: No. 121A		Close	Omits ref.
537	B26	De søfarne mænd	**A**	Brds	18	An Old Danish Ballad	Sv. Grundtvig, *Acta C.* 95-98 (1880) =Kolozsvar (1880) =*Folk-lore Record* 255-57 (1881)	Own Ms	L	Close	
GrN 1	—	Visesangeren		Arist	16	Song Carrier	D. Colbert, in Rossel, *Scand. Ball.* No. 30 (1982)	GrN *DSk* No. 1		Close	
10	F58	Den store krage		Brds	17	The Corbie	Gray, *FaF* No. 32 (1954)	Erk & Böhme 55		N.A.	From German tr.
14	F67	Fluens bryllup	A	?Comm	17	Wedding of the Fly	Meyer, in Dal, *DBFS* No. 77 (1967)	Ravn 115		Interp	1 st.
14	F67	Fluens bryllup	B	?Comm	17	Wedding of the Fly	Meyer, in Dal, *DBFS* No. 77 (1967)	Ravn 115		Close	1 st.
14	F67	Fluens bryllup	C	Brds	18	Wedding of the Fly	Meyer, in Dal, *DBFS* No. 38 (1967)	GrN, *DSk* No.14		Close	

24	—	sole	Arist	17	Mesterens råd	Master's Counsel	Meyer, in Dal, *DBFS* No. 40 (1967)	GrN, *DSk* No.24		Close	
26	F7	Red	—	—	Hvormed vil du føde mig	Last Resort	Smith-Dampier, *BDB* I: No. 50 (1939) =Abrahamsen & Dal 241-43 (1965)	Olrik I: No. 50		Interp	
27	F13	sole	Arist	17	Her bliver vel bedre køb	Better Bargain	Meyer, in Dal, *DBFS* No. 41 (1967)	GrN, *DSk* No.27		Close	
31	F17	?	—	—	Møllerdatteren	Three Rascals	William Wright in Botsford, *FSMP* 2:188-90 (1922) = *Botsford CFS* 2:56-59 (1931)	Cf. Berggreen, *FSM* (1860) I: No. 151a	L M	Interp	9 st.
31	F17	?	—	—	Møllerdatteren	Three Rascals	Ostlund & Krone, in Krone & Ostlund, *SWD* 36-38 (1941)	Unidentified	M	Adapt	4 st.
31	F17	?	—	—	Møllerdatteren	Cat in the Sack	Anon., in Read 19-20 (1965)	Cf. Berggreen, *FSM* (1860) I: No. 151a	L M	N.A.	
56	F42	C	Arist	17	Bondens kone besøger hovmand	Peasant's Wife Visits Courtier	Meyer, in Dal, *DBFS* No. 43 (1967)	GrN, *DSk* No. 27		Close	
58	F41	sole	Arist	16	Munken i vaande	Munken i Vaande	Child, *ESPB* 5:101 (1894)	Sv. Grundtvig 1867 No. 24		N.A.	Prose summ
69	F45	?	—	—	Nis Bossens fedel	The Fiddler	G. & M. Bidstrup, in Campbell 17 (1932) =Campbell 21 (1941) =Coop. R.S., *Handy FSB* 105 (195-)	?	M	N.A.	Singing game. 2 st.
91	—	—	Arist	16	Bagvendt vise	Upside Down Ditty	Meyer, in Dal, *DBFS* No. 45 (1967)	GrN, *DSk* No.91		Close	

National Type No.	TSB No.	Title	Version	Tradition	Century	Title of Translation	Translator, Venue, Date	Translator's Source	Lang/Music	Trans. Strategy	Notes
ETK 2	F56	Den store brud	Red	—	—	Bride of Ribe	Smith-Dampier, *BDB* 1: No. 51 (1939) = Warnock & Anderson 243-44 (1959)	Olrik I: No. 51		Interp	
3	—	Kællingen til barsel	cf. **C**	Comm	20	Old Woman at the Christening	Grainger, *Old W.* (1994)	Own record.	L M	Interp	Dialect
9	F58	Den store krage	—	Comm	20	The Big Crow	Meyer, in Dal, *DBFS* No. 44 (1967)	Frydendahl 30		Close	
13	—	Fuglegildet	—	?	—	I skoven skulde være gilde	Unknown, in Haugaard 1:5 (1957)	≅ Berggreen, *FSM*1860 I: NO. 110	L	Literal	Sound recording
13	—	Fuglegildet	**A**	Comm	19	Banquet of the Birds	Meyer, in Dal, *DBFS* No. 39 (1967)	ETK 13		Interp	
25	—	Mand leger med kone	—	Comm	20	Hubby & Wifey	Grainger, *Hubby*, n.d.	Own record.	M	?Interp	3 st; Cf. *ETK*25
52	F12	Den narrede ungersvend	**B**	Comm	19	Lad Who Was Fooled	Meyer, in Dal, *DBFS* No. 42 (1967) = Rossel, *Scand. Ball.* No. 31 (1982)	ETK 52 B		Interp	
—	—	Rejsen efter hø	—	?Comm	N.I.	A Farmer Lived on a Danish Farm	Allwood, *Scand S. Ball.* 9-10 (1957)	N.I.		N.A.	cf. GrN, *DSk*60, *ETK*60
—	—	De to kongebørn	—	Comm	19	Two Royal Children	Meyer, in Dal, *DBFS* No. 53 (1967) = Rossel, *Scand. Ball.* No. 33 (1982)	Thuborg 254-56		Close	
—	—	Det var en Lørdag aften	—	Red	—	On Saturday, T'wards Evening	Heepe, in Haraldsted 31 (1939)	Boisen, *NG Viser*		Close	Sv. Grundtvig adapt. 1849

—	—	Det var en Lørdag aften	—	Red	—	Unhappy Love	Rodholm, in *World of Song* Pt. 4:32-33 (1941) = *World of Song* 275 (1958) = *Harvest* 155-56 (1953) = Balslev-Clausen No. 71 (1988)	Boisen, *NG Viser* or FL Grundtvig, *Sangbog*	M	Interp	*Sv.* Grundtvig adapt. 1849
—	—	Det var en Lørdag aften	—	Comm	19	'Twas on a Saturday Evening	Meyer, in Dal, *DBFS* No. 71 (1967)	Sneedorff-Birch No. 2		Interp	Traditional
—	—	Det var en Lørdag aften	—	Red	—	On Saturday I Waited	Allwood, *Scand. S. Ball.* 35-36 (1957)	Boisen, *NG Viser*	L M	Interp	*Sv.* Grundtvig adapt. 1849
—	—	Det var en Lørdag aften	—	Red	—	Det var en Lørdag aften	Unknown, in Haugaard 1:4 (1957)	=Boisen, *NG Viser*	L	Close	*Sv.* Grundtvig adapt. 1849. Sound recording
—	—	Det var en Lørdag aften	—	Comm	19	I Waited up All Evening	D. Colbert in Rossel, *Scand. Ball.* No. 34, P. 60 (1982)	Sneedorff-Birch No. 2		Interp	Traditional
—	—	Det var en Lørdag aften	—	Red	—	I Waited up All Evening	D. Colbert in Rossel, *Scand. Ball.* No. 34, P. 61 (1982)	Boisen, *NG Viser*		Interp	*Sv.* Grundtvig adapt. 1849

TABLE 2. TRANSLATIONS FROM THE FAROESE AND THE SHETLAND NORN

The comprehensive scholarly national edition is Sv. Grundtvig and J. Bloch, *Føroya Kvæði: Corpus Carminum Færoensium*, ed. N. Djurhuus and Chr. Matras. *CCF* is the abbreviation used here; readers should be aware that *FKv* is sometimes used elsewhere. An important earlier edition, V. U. Hammershaimb's *Færöiske Kvæder*, is also sometimes abbreviated *FKv* or *Fkv* in the literature, but here designated *FKvr*.

The organization of *CCF* is such that one "version" (**A**, **B**, etc.) of what the editors have designated as one ballad type may comprise multiple narratives, each with its own classification in *The Types of the Scandinavian Medieval Ballad*. Thus CCF 1 "Sjúrðar kvæði" version **H** is the source for translations of both "Regin Smiður," TSB E51, and "Høgna táttur," TSB E55.

Establishing the genuineness of the source version for earlier translations of the Faroese ballads is often difficult or impossible. The editors of two of the collections most often used by translators—Hammershaimb, in *Færöiske Kvæder* and Lyngbye, in *Færøiske Qvæder*—often offer redacted texts. (Hammershaimb's texts are printed in reduced type in *CCF*.) *CCF* lacks the thorough comparative discussions of variants and earlier editing and printing history that Svend Grundtvig provides in *DgF*. Thus the frequency of question marks in the "Version" column here.

A more recent source for some translations, Jóannes Patursson, *Kvæð(a)bók* 1–2, does not seem to be available in North America and has not been seen. For some translations from Patursson the table provides cross-references to *FKvr*, whose versions Patursson sometimes follows (Erik Dal. "Tyske, franske og engelske oversættelser af færøkvæder." *Fróðskaparrit* 18 [1970]: 91).

National Type No.	TSB No.	Title	Version	Tradition	Century	Title of Translation	Translator, Venue, Date	Translator's Source	Lang; Music	Trans. Strategy	Notes
CCF 1	E51	Sjúrðar kvæði. Regin smiður	**Ab,** ?red	—	—	Regin the Smith	Cox, in Steenstrup *MPB* 75 (1914)	Lyngbye, *FQ* No. 1		Interp	2 st. of 132; omits refr.
—	E51	Sjúrðar kvæði. Regin smiður	Red **(H)**	—	—	Ballad of Regin	Smith-Dampier, *SD-S* 33-52 (1934)	Patursson, from *FKvr* I: No. 1		N.I.	
—	E51	Sjúrðar kvæði. Regin smiður	Red	—	—	Sigurd and the Dragon	Karpeles, *FSEur* 8-9 (1956) = Masters, *Waldorf* 36-37 (1987)	*CCF*; Thuren, *Folkes.*	L M	Interp	5 st. of 123
—	E51	Sjúrðar kvæði. Regin smiður	**H,** ?red	—	—	Regan smiður	Hughes 37-45 (1978)	*FKvr* I: No. 1	L	Literal	5 st. of 131; prose
—	E51	Sjúrðar kvæði. Regin smiður	**H,** ?red	—	—	Sigurd the Dragon Slayer	Margolin, in Wylie & Margolin 85 (1981)	*FKvr* I: No. 1	L	Literal	3 st. of 131; prose
—	E51	Sjúrðar kvæði. Regin smiður	**Aa**	Comm	19	Sigurd the Dragon Slayer	Margolin, in Wylie & Margolin 85 (1981)	Schrøter I (1951-53)	L	N.I.	
—	E100	Sjúrðar kvæði. Brynhildar táttur	Red	—	—	Ballad of Brynhild	Smith-Dampier, *SD-S* 53-85 (1934) = H. Leach, *Pageant* 110-12 (1946)	Patursson		N.I.	
—	E55	Sjúrðar kvæði. Høgna táttur	Red **(H)**	—	—	Ballad of Høgni	Smith-Dampier, *SD-S* 87-122 (1934)	Patursson, from *FKvr* I: No. 3		N.I.	
2	D401	Ragnars kvæði	Red **(G)**	—	—	Ballad of Ragnar	Smith-Dampier *SD-S* 135-52 (1934)	Patursson, from *FKvr* I: No. 4		N.I.	

			Da	Comm			CCF		
2	E156	Ragnars kvæði. Ragnars táttur		19	Ragnars táttur	Conroy, "Oral" 45 (1980)		Literal	3 st. of 56
3	D402	Gests ríma ella Áslu ríma	C, ?red	—	Rime of Ásla	Smith-Dampier, SD-S161-66 (1934)	Patursson, from *FKvr* I: No. 5	N.I.	
4	E2	Nornagests ríma	D, red	—	Faroese Ballad of Nornagest	Kershaw, *St. & Ball.* 176-81 (1921)	*FKvr* I:72-73	Interp (L M)	
4	E2	Nornagests ríma	D, red	—	Rime of Nornagest	Smith-Dampier, SD-S153-59 (1934)	Patursson, from *FKvr* I: No. 6	Interp	
5	E74	Ísmal fræga kempa	C, red	—	Ballad of Ísmal	Smith-Dampier, SD-S123-33 (1934)	Patursson, from *FKvr* I: No. 7	N.I.	
6	E153	Sjúrður og dvørgamoy, ella Dvørgamoy I	C, ?red	—	Sigurd's Song	Crawford 18 (1909)	Garborg, *SW* 25-35	N.A. (L M)	From Norwegian tr.; 1 st. of 59
6	E153	Sjúrður og dvørgamoy, ella Dvørgamoy I	C, ?red	—	Song of Sigurd	Smith-Dampier, *MBfD* 3-7 (1914)	Garborg, *SW* 25-35	Adapt	From Norwegian tr.; 25 st. of 59
6	E153	Sjúrður og dvørgamoy, ella Dvørgamoy I	C, ?red	—	Dwarfie-Maiden, I	Smith-Dampier, SD-S167-73 (1934)	Patursson from *FKvr* I: No. 8	Adapt	27 st. of 60: Adapts *MBfD* lines
13	E114	Lokka táttur	D, ?red	—	Loki's Song	Carpenter 410-13 (1882)	*FKvr* I:140-45	Close	
13	E114	Lokka táttur	D, ?red	—	Lay of Skrymner (2)	Borrow, *Works* 8:211-19 (1923)	?Lyngbye, *FQ* 500-19	Interp	Danish tr. in source
15	E89	Hjálmar og Angantýr	C, ?red	—	Ballad of Hjalmar and Angantyr	Kershaw 182-85 (1921)	*FKvr* 2:12-13	Interp (L M)	

National Type No.	TSB No.	Title	Version	Tradition	Century	Title of Translation	Translator, Venue, Date	Translator's Source	Lang. Music	Trans. Strategy	Notes
15	E89	Hjálmar og Angantýr	Red(**C**) **C**, ?red	—	—	Rival Brothers	Grainger, *Sketches*, n. d. ≈ *Rival Br.* (1943) = *Rival Br.* (1905), n. d.	*FKvr* 2:12-13	L L M M	Interp	9 st. of 21 2 st. of 21
16	ES3, E90	Arngríms synir	**D**, red	—	—	Ballad of Arngrim's Sons	Kershaw 193-211 (1921)	*FKvr* 2: No. 3	L M	Interp	
17	E34	Gátu ríma	a, ?red	Comm	19	Riddle Rimes	Prior, *ADB* 1:334-42 (1860)	*FKvr* 2: No. 4		Interp	6 conjectural st.
17	E34	Gátu ríma	a, ?red	Comm	19	Faroese Riddle Ballad	Kershaw 212-16 (1921)	*FKvr* 2: No. 4		Close	
22	E30	Sigmundar kvæði	Red	—	—	Ballad of Sigmund	Powell, *Tale* xix-xxvi (1896) = Annandale 63 (1905)	*FKvr* 2: No. 9 & other texts		Close	
26	E83	Finnur hin fríði	**Ac**	Comm	19	Finn the Fair	Kingsley, *Lectures* 70 (1875) = *Hist. Lectures* 241-42 (1880)	Rafn, *Ant. Am.* 319-35		Adapt	2 st. of 97
29	E148	Gongurólvs kvæði	**G**, ?red	—	—	Gongu-Rólvs kvæði	Grøndahl, in Liestøl 44 (1946)	*FKvr* 2:131-43	L	Literal	2 st. of 131
30	E3	Geyti Áslaksson, l. Geyta táttur	**E**, ?red	—	—	Geyti Aslaksson	Metcalfe 14-16 (1861)	*FKvr* 2: No. 17	L	Close	3 st. + prose summ
31	D94	Magnus Kongr í Noregi ella Margretu kvæði	**Ab**, ?red	Comm	19	Margretu kvæði	Child, *ESPB* 1: 444-45 (1884)	*FKvr* 2: No. 18		Close	1 st. + prose summ; omits refr.
36	E86	Ásmundur Aðalsson	**A**	Comm	18	Ásumundur Aðalsson	Grøndahl, in Liestøl 45 (1946)	*CCF*	L	Literal	1 st. of 101; omits refr.
45	D368	Ellindur bóndi á Jaðri	Compos	—	—	Ellindur Bóndi á Jaðri	Flom 167 (1945)	*CCF* in Ms.	L	N.A.	Prose summ

No.	Code	Title		Comm	Cent.	Title	Reference	Source		Transl.	Notes
52	E125	Gríms ríma	Aa	Comm	19	Grims Ríma	Conroy, "Faroese Ball." 183-90 (1974)	CCF	L	Literal	
53	E106	Grímur á Bretlandi	Ba	Comm	19	Grímur á Bretlandi	Conroy, "Faroese Ball." 119-59 (1974) ="Oral" 41 (1980)	CCF	L	Literal	Omits refr. 17 st. of 220
53	E106	Grímur á Bretlandi	A	Comm	18	Grímur á Bretlandi	Conroy, "Oral" 44 (1980)	CCF	L	Literal	10 st. of 65
66	E85	Hermundur illi	A	Comm	18	Hermund the Evil	Grainger, Two MR No. 1 (1924)	Thuren "Tanz" 255 (1902)	L M	N.A.	1 st. of 124
66	E85	Hermundur illi	D	Comm	19	Hermundur illi	Conroy, "Ball. Comp." 80-81, 98-100 (1979)	CCF	L	Literal	18 st. of 113; literal and prose
66	E85	Hermundur illi	E	Comm	19	Hermundur illi	Conroy, "Ball. Comp." 90-91,99 (1979)	CCF	L	Literal	4 st. of 154
67	E33	Hernilds kvæði	Sole	Comm	19	Hernilds kvæði	Conroy, "Ball. Comp." 99-100 (1979)	CCF	L	Literal	8 st. of 76; omits refr.
77	C22	Margretu kvæði. 2. Frúgvin Margreta	C	Comm	19	Frúgvin Margreta	Grøndahl, in Liestøl 42-43 (1946)	F Anth I: No. 17	L	Literal	1 st. of 172; omits refr.
90	E113	Skrímslið	C, red	—	—	Lay of Skrymnir. I.	Borrow, Works 8:205-II (1923)	Lyngbye 480-99		Interp	Omits refr.; Danish tr. in source
91	—	Sniolvs kvæði. Hildardalsstríð	Ca	Comm	19	Stríðið í Hildardal	Conroy, "Creativity" 32, 36-42 (1979)	CCF	L	Literal	3 st. + prose summ
91	—	Sniolvs kvæði. Stríðið í Hildardal	G	Comm	19	Stríðið í Hildardal	Conroy, "Creativity" 32, 35-47 (1979)	CCF	L	Literal	18 st. + prose summ
91	E18	Sniolvs kvæði. Risin á Blálandi	Ca	Comm	19	Risin á Blálandi	Conroy, "Creativity" 32, 34 (1979)	CCF	L	Literal	2 st. + prose summ

National Type No.	TSB No.	Title	Version	Tradition	Century	Title of Translation	Translator, Venue, Date	Translator's Source	Lang; Music	Trans. Strategy	Notes
106	E28	Karlamagnusar kvæði. Runsivals stríð	near **D**	Comm	20	Untitled	Smith-Dampier, "Faroese" 89 (1932)	Own recording		N.I.	2 st.
106	E28	Karlamagnusar kvæði. Runsivals stríð	Red	—	—	Song of Roland	Smith-Dampier, "Song" 244-46 (1936) = "Song," *A-SR* 39-43 (1952)	Unidentified		N.I.	26 st. 21 st.
106	E28	Karlamagnusar kvæði. Runsivals stríð	Compos	—	—	Runsivals Stríð	Ólason, "Literary B." 123-24 (1991)	*CCF*		N.A.	Prose
106	E28	Karlamagnusar kvæði. Runsivals stríð	**B**	Comm	19	Runsivals Stríð	Conroy, "Faroese Ball." 195-215 (1974)	*CCF*	L	Literal	
106	—	Karlamagnusar kvæði. Viljorm Kornus	Red	—	—	Ballad of William Curt-Nose	Smith-Dampier, "Ballad" 247-49 (1936)	? Patursson		N.I.	16 st.; omits refr.
110	D386	Tístrams táttur	sole	Comm	19	Tístrams táttur	Schach, "Tristan" 286-87 (1964)	*F Anth* 1: No. 26		N.A.	Prose
110	D386	Tístrams táttur	sole	Comm	19	Faroese Ballad of Tristan	W.B. Lockwood, in Hill 156-58 (1977)	*CCF*		Literal	Stanzaic Prose
117	E37	Blikimans kvæði	**B**	Comm	19	Iron-Wolf	Cox, in Steenstrup, 162-63 (1914)	*DgF* 4:693-98	L	Close	Refrain only
124	D324	Faðir og dóttir	**A**	Comm	19	Faðir og dóttir	Child, *ESPB* 2: 157 (1885)	Hammershaimb "Faðir" 88		N.A.	Prose
124	D324	Faðir og dóttir	**D**	Comm	19	Father and Daughter	Grainger, *Faðir* [5], n.d.	*CCF* Ms. or *F Anth* I: No. 31	L M	Adapt	24 st. of 42
124	D324	Faðir og dóttir	**D**	Comm	19	Father and Daughter	A. Strettell in Grainger, *Faðir* [6], n.d.	*CCF* Ms. or *F Anth* I: No. 31	L M	Interp	Full. Also German tr.
129	D391	Frísa vísa	a	Comm	19	Frísa Vísa	Child, *ESPB* 2:347 (1886)	Hammershaimb, "Frísa"		N.A.	Prose

			a	Comm	19				L M		
129	D39I	Frísa vísa	a	Comm	19	Frísa Ballad	Melby 100-02 (1908)	F Anth 1: No. 34	L	Literal	"Dance game." 2 st + prose summ.
140	B7	Sankta Jákup	A, ?red	—	—	Saint Jacob	Borrow, Works 9:200-03 (1923) = Ball. All Nations 320-22 (1927)	Lyngbye 520-29		Adapt	Omits refr.; Danish version in source
154	A63	Ólavur Riddararós og álvamoy	Compos	—	—	Untitled	Child, ESPB 1:374-75 (1884)	DgF 4: 849-52		N.A.	Prose
163	D148	Riddarin hjá jomfrúbúðini	sole	Comm	19	Riddarin hjá jomfru budini	Gardner-Medwin, "Paradise" 315 (1963)	CCF	L	Literal	3 st. of 22
166	D231	Roysningur	A	Comm	19	Untitled	Christophersen 222-27 (1952)	DgF 1:209-10; 10:4	L	Close	Called D
166	D231	Roysningur	B	Comm	19	Untitled	Christophersen 227-30 (1952)	DgF 1:210-11; 10:4	L	Close	Called E
167	B8	Rudisar vísa	A	Comm	19	Rudisar vísa	Child, ESPB 1:234 (1884)	Hammershaimb, "Rudisar"		Close	3 st. + prose summ.
167	B8	Rudisar vísa	A	Comm	19	Stephen He Looked Out	J.A. Arengo Jones in Seeman, et al 186-91 (1967)	F Anth 1: No. 11	L M	Interp	
176	B21	Torkils døtur	A, ?red	—	—	Torkilds Riim	Child, ESPB 1:172-73 (1882)	Lyngbye 534-44 (1822)		Close	2 st. + prose summ.
215	—	Ólavur Trygvason	Red	—	—	Ormen Lange	Kastman & Köhler 86-88 (1913)	Hellgren, No. 97	M	N.A.	From Swedish tr. of Norwegian tr; song-game; 10 st. of 84
215	—	Ólavur Trygvason	Red	—	—	Viking Ship	Van Cleve 178-79 (1916)	Hellgren No. 97	M	N.A.	From Swedish tr. of Norwegian tr; song-game; 7 of 84

National Type No.	TSB No.	Title	Version	Tradition	Century	Title of Translation	Translator, Venue, Date	Translator's Source	Lang; Music	Trans. Strategy	Notes
215	—	Ólavur Trygvason	Red (sole)	—	—	Great Serpent	West 19-21 (1983-84)	F Anth I: No. 35		Adapt	36 st. of 85
DgF 109	B20	Møen paa Baalet	C	Comm	19	Maid on the Pyre	Prior, ADB No. 51 (1860)	DgF 109C		Interp	Faroese/Danish
—	—	Brúnsveins vísa	Pastiche	—	—	Merry Wedding	P. Grainger and R. Grainger in Grainger, "Merry W." iv-vii [1916]	F Anth Nos. 3, 13, 28, 30, 31, 33	L M	Close	Grainger pastiche, "bridal dance"
—	—	[Multiple]	—	Comm	19	[sailing theme]	Conroy, "Oral" 41 (1980)	CCF (2D, 14B, 53B, 99C)	L	Literal	Theme in 8 ball. by 1 singer
Shet-land	E97	Hildina	sole	Comm	18	Earl of Orkney and King of Norway's Daughter	Low 113 (1879) =Hægstad 31-32 (1900)	Own recording	L	N.A.	Prose summ.
	E97	Hildina	Red	—	—	Hildina	Kershaw 217-19 (1921) =H. Leach, Pageant 275-76 (1946)	Hægstad 14-20	L	?Close	12 st. of 35; Reconstr. orig.

Table 3. Translations from the Icelandic

In order to link the translations of Icelandic ballads with their national type (ÍF) numbers and their context one needs to consider two scholarly national editions and one comprehensive commentary.

Grundtvig and Sigurðsson, *Íslenzk fornkvæði* (1854–55) establishes sixty-six national types and prints a limited number of versions, **A**, **B**, etc., or a composite, for each. The general model is *Danmarks gamle Folkeviser*, though this Icelandic edition is certainly less thorough.

The comprehensive national edition is Jón Helgason, *Íslenzk fornkvæði. Islandske folkeviser*, which expands the canon to 110 types. This is the only national edition organized chronologically by *ballad manuscript*, not ballad type. Thus one could find versions of a given ballad type in several different volumes. Volume 8 provides an index to the national type numbers and earlier printing history, including the Grundtvig and Sigurðsson version designations (**A**, **B**, etc.), but no additional versions are so designated.

Here the abbreviation ÍF is used for ballad type numbers, *ÍF* for Helgason, and *Ífkv* for Grundtvig and Sigurðsson. Under "Version" the *Ífkv* designation is given where available, otherwise *ÍF* volume and pages.

For comparative or contextual discussion organized by ballad type one turns to Vésteinn Ólason's indispensable *The Traditional Ballads of Iceland: Historical Studies* (Reykjavík: Stofnun Árna Magnússonar, 1982). Besides type-by-type discussions of internal and international relationships Vésteinn provides a generic or composite English summary by Sverrir Hólmarsson for the collective versions of each type except fragments and non-traditional ballads. *Because this nearly full translation coverage can be cited in the single present reference, separate entries are not made in the table.*

Judging the genuineness of translators' source texts is often straightforward. Earlier translators tend to use the responsibly edited *Ífkv*, in which composite versions are identified. Later translators may use Briem's popular and sometimes redacted *Fornir Dansar*, against which one can compare the scholarly editions.

National Type No.	TSB No.	Title	Version	Tradition	Century	Title of Translation	Translator, Venue, Date	Translator's Source	Lang; Music	Trans. Strategy	Notes
ÍF 1	A63	Kvæði af Ólafi liljurós	Aa	Comm	17	Kvæði af Ólafi Liljurós	Child, ESPB 1:375 (1884)	Íłkv No. 1		N.A.	Prose
	A63	Kvæði af Ólafi Liljurós	M	Comm	19	Olaf and the Fairy	Anon., in Sveinbjörnsson 6-9, n.d.	Magnusson & Þorð. 200-06	L M	Close	3 st. of 25
	A63	Kvæði af Ólafi Liljurós	Ib	Comm	19	Olaf and the Fairy-Maiden	Smith-Dampier, MBID 17-19 (1914)	Berggreen FSM 1869 I: No. 20e		Interp	Danish tr. in source
	A63	Kvæði af Ólafi Liljurós	Ib	Comm	19	Oliver and the Fairy Maid	Karpeles, FSE No. 6 (1956)	Berggreen FSM 1869 I: No. 20e	L M	Adapt	11 st. of 20 Danish tr. in source
	A63	Kvæði af Ólafi Liljurós	Red	—	—	An old ballad	Johnson, NL 73-75 (1959)	Unidentified		N.A.	
	A63	Kvæði af Ólafi Liljurós	Red	—	—	Olaf and the Elf-Maid	Simpson, NT 261-62 (1965)	Briem 1-4		Close	
	A63	Kvæði af Ólafi Liljurós	Ib	Comm	19	Olaf Along the Mountains Rode	Halkett, in Seemann, et al 14-19, 230 (1967)	Berggreen FSM 1845 No. 8	L M	Close	
3	A50	Gauta kvæði	Red	—	—	Ballad of Gauti	Hallmundsson, "A Northern Orpheus" 267-71 (1962)	Briem 8-11		Interp	
7	A26	Hildibrands kvæði	Red	—	—	Hildibrand	Simpson, NT 253-56 (1965)	Briem 21-25		Close	
9	A66	Stafrós kvæði	Red	—	—	The She-Troll	Simpson, NT 284-87 (1967)	Briem 34-39		Close	
12	D231	Kvæði af Rögnvaldi og Gunnhildi	Sole	Comm	17	Ravengaard og Memering	Child, ESPB 2:36 (1885)	Íłkv No. 12		N.A.	Prose summ.

No.	Code	Title				Title (trans.)	Reference	ÍFkv	L		Notes
12	D231	Kvæði af Rögnvaldi og Gunnhildi	Sole	Corrm	17	Gunnhildar kvæði	Batho, "Icel. B." 168 (1928-29)	ÍFkv No. 12		Close	2 st. of 28
12	D231	Kvæði af Rögnvaldi og Gunnhildi	Sole	Corrm	17	Untitled	Christophersen 230-35 (1952)	ÍFkv No. 12	L	Close	
13	A38	Hörpu kvæði	A	Corrm	17	Untitled	Child, ESPB 1:122 (1882) =H. Leach, Angevin Br. 367 (1921)	ÍFkv No. 13		Interp	6 st. of 24; omits ref.
13	A38	Hörpu kvæði	A	Comm	17	Hörpu kvæði	Batho, "Icel. B." 169-70 (1928-29)	ÍFkv No. 13		Interp	
13	A38	Hörpu kvæði	Red	—	—	The Harp Song	Simpson, NT 272-74 (1965)	Briem 51-59		Close	
14	D94	Margrétar kvæði	—	Comm	17	Margrétar kvæði	Grøndahl, in Liestøl 43 (1946)	ÍF 1:98	L	Literal	1 st. of 42; omits refr.
15	B21	Kvæði af vallara systra-bana	Compos	—	—	Vallara kvæði	Child, ESPB 1:173 (1882)	ÍFkv No. 15		N. A.	Prose
16	A41	Kvæði af Ribbaldi og Gullbrúnu	Red	—	—	Lord Ribbald	Simpson, NT 274-76 (1965)	Briem 74-77		Close	
16	A41	Kvæði af Ribbaldi og Gullbrúnu	Red	—	—	Ribold and Goldborg	Smith-Dampier, BDB 247-49 (1939)				Danish-Icelandic mix. See DgF 82
17	D289	Sonarharmur	Compos	—	—	Sønnens Sorg	Child, ESPB 1:180 (1882)	ÍFkv No. 17		N. A.	Prose summ
17	D289	Sonarharmur	A	Comm	18	Son's Sorrow	Morris, Poems 144-46 (1891) =Poems/Love 166-68 (1896) =Coll. Works 9:206-07 (1911)	ÍFkv No. 17		Interp	

National Type No.	TSB No.	Title	Version	Tradition	Century	Title of Translation	Translator, Venue, Date	Translator's Source	Lang. Music	Trans. Strategy	Notes
18	D374	Kristínar kvæði	Sole	Comm	17	Lay of Christine	Morris, *Poems* 138-40 (1891) =*Poems/Love* 159-61 (1896) =*Coll. Works* 9:201-02 (1911)	*Íslfkv* No. 18		Interp	
21	D335	Bjarnarsona kvæði	A	Comm	17	Bjarnasona Kvæði	Batho, "Icel. B.," 184-86 (1928-29)	*Íslfkv* No. 21		Adapt	19 st. of 25
23	D383	Tristrams kvæði	C	Comm	17	Ballad of Tristram	Ker, "On Dan. Ball." 1:372-73 (1904) =*Collected Essays* 2:84-85 (1925) =Batho, "Icel. B.," 186-87 (1928-9)	*Íslfkv* No. 23	L	Interp	6 st. of 30
23	D383	Tristrams kvæði	A, red	—	—	Icelandic Ballad of Tristram	Schlauch, *Med. Narr.* 169-74 (1928)	Ranke 262-75		Interp	German tr in source
23	D383	Tristrams kvæði	A, red	—	—	Ballad of Tristram	Kirkconnell, 93-98 (1930) =H. Leach, *Pageant* 328-32 (1946) =Rossel, *Scand. B.* 55-56 (1982)	*Íslfkv* No. 23		Interp	
23	D383	Tristrams kvæði	Red	—	—	Tristran	Simpson, *NT* 257-60 (1965)	Briem 101-07		Close	
23	D383	Tristrams kvæði	Red	—	—	Ballad of Tristran	Hallmundsson, *Anthol.* 208-12 (1965)	Briem 101-07		Interp	
23	D383	Tristrams kæði	near A	Comm	18	Icelandic Ballad of Tristran	Hill, *Tristan L.* 34-36 (1977)	*ÍF* 4:221-26		Literal	Stanzaic prose
23	D383	Tristrams kvæði	B	Comm	17	Icelandic Ballad of Tristran	Hill, *Tristan L.* 32-34 (1977)	*ÍF* 3:198-201		Literal	Stanzaic prose
23	D383	Tristrams kvæði	C	Comm	17	Icelandic Ballad of Tristran	Hill, *Tristan L.* 30-32 (1977)	*ÍF* 1:137-43		Literal	Stanzaic prose
23	D383	Tristrams kvæði	D	Comm	18	Icelandic Ballad of Tristran	Hill, *Tristan L.* 36-38 (1977)	*ÍF* 5:22-25		Literal	Stanzaic prose

28	E96	Kvæði af Loga í Vallar-hlíð	A	Comm	18	Logi í Vallarhlíð	Batho, "Icel. B." 171-72 (1928-29)	ÍFkv No. 28		Close	2 st. of 55; omits refr
28	E96	Kvæði af Loga í Vallar-hlíð	Red	—	—	Logi of Vallarahlíd	Simpson, NT 277-84 (1965)	Briem 123-34		Close	Omits refr
30	D183	Ebbadætra kvæði	Red	—	—	Ebbi's Daughters	Simpson, NT 266-71 (1965)	Briem 141-50		Close	
31	D172	Kvæði af Knúti í Borg	Red	—	—	Kvæði af Knúti í Borg	Batho, "Icel. B." 179-83 (1928-29)	ÍFkv No. 31		Close	32 st. + prose summ
31	D172	Kvæði af Knúti í Borg	D	Comm	18	Kvæði af Knúti í Borg	Grøndahl, in Liestøl 43 (1946)	ÍFkv	L	Close	1 st. of 33; omits refr.
33	D350	Magna dans	Sole	Comm	17	Magna Dans	Batho, "Icel. B." 172-73 (1928-29)	ÍFkv No. 33		Interp	2 st. of 57; omits refr
34	D324	Ólöfar kvæði	Compos	—	—	Ólöfar kvæði	Child, ESPB 2:157 (1885)	ÍFkv No. 34		N. A.	Prose summ
38	D399	Taflkvæði	A	Comm	17	Game at Dice	Cox, in Steenstrup, 174, 183 (1914)	ÍFkv No. 38		N. A.	From Danish tr.
49	D355	Kvæði af Gunnari á Hlíðarenda	a	Comm	17	Gunnars kvæði	Batho, "Icel. B." 173-74 (1928-29)	ÍFkv No. 49		Interp	16 st. of 20 + prose summ
50	D206	Ólafs vísur	Sole	Comm	17	Ólafs vísur	Batho, "Icel. B." 176-78 (1928-29)	ÍFkv No. 50		Close	13 st. of 32
50	D206	Ólafs vísur	Sole	Comm	17	Untitled	Ólason, "Saint Olaf" 2-5 (1985)	ÍF 4:11-15	L	N. A.	Prose
51	D207	Karlamagnúsar kvæði	Sole	Comm	17	Karla-Magnusar Vísa	Batho, "Icel. B." 176 (1928-29)	ÍFkv No. 51		Close	2 st. of 22; omits refr
53	D258	Kvæði af Tófu og Suffaralín	Red	—	—	Valdemar and Tove	Smith-Dampier, DB 15-18 (1920) = BDB 133-35 (1939)	Ólrik I: No. 17		N.A.	From Danish tr.

National Type No.	TSB No.	Title	Version	Tradition	Century	Title of Translation	Translator, Venue, Date	Translator's Source	Lang/Music	Trans. Strategy	Notes
53	D258	Kvæði af Töfu og Suffaralín	Red	—	—	Valdemar and Tove, version **A**	Gray, *HBD* No. 2 (1958)	Olrik I: No. 17		N.A.	From Danish tr.
54	D232	Kvæði af frúnni Kristínu	**A**	Comm	17	Kvæði af Kristínu drottningar elju	Grøndahl, in Liestøl 43 (1946)	*Íslkv*	L	Literal	1 st. of 35; omits refr
60	D412	Ásu kvæði	**A**	Comm	17	Untitled	Child, *ESPB* I:28-29 (1882)	*Íslkv* No. 60		Literal	Omits refr
60	D412	Ásu kvæði	**D**, red	—	—	Untitled	Child, *ESPB* I:28-29 (1882)	*Íslkv* No. 60		Literal	4 st. of 12; omits refr
60	D412	Ásu kvæði	Compos	—	—	Ásu kvæði	Nygard, "Icel. Ásu" 43-48 (1955)	*Íslkv* No. 60	L	Literal	Omits refr
84	—	Ísungs kvæði	Sole	Lit.	17	Iceling	Simpson, *NT* 263-66 (1965)	*Briem 358-62*		Close	
86	F33	Konuríki	*ÍF2:* 29-32	Comm	17	The Goodman and the Goodwife	Simpson, *NT* 288-90 (1965)	Briem 354-57		Close	
—	—	Krumma-kvæði	—	—	—	Raven-song	Metcalfe, *Oxonian* 254-55 (1861)	Unidentified		N.A.	Marginal type

TABLE 4. TRANSLATIONS FROM THE NORWEGIAN

Norway has been blessed with many popular and school editions of the ballads and other folksongs, but the national scholarly edition has been often delayed. Such an edition began with Ådel Blom's *Legendeviser* (1982), volume 1 of *Norske Mellomalderballadar*, but the editor's subsequent death has led to a change in plans. The new national edition will be in a CD-ROM format including all texts and melodies, produced at Visearkivet in Oslo. Whereas *Norske Mellomalderballadar* used NMB numbers and "national" titles, the electronic edition will use titles and type designations from *The Types of the Scandinavian Medieval Ballad*.

There are problems in keying translations to two national editions (incomplete and projected, respectively) of differing philosophies. While respecting the rationale of the projected edition, I have still supplied NMB type numbers (from *The Types*) and titles (from *Norske Mellomalderballadar* and from Blom and Bø, *Norske Balladar*, 1973) when possible. When Norwegian titles are not known, TSB titles are supplied in brackets.

Without an edition discussing primary materials and past editing it is often hard to know whether the source text for a translation is genuine. Of two very important sources for translators, Landstad, *Norske Folkeviser* (1853) presents many redacted texts, and Liestøl and Moe, *Norske Folkeviser* (1920–24) presents mainly redacted texts for a general audience.

The classification (indeed perception) of the visionary materials called "Draumkvede" (NMB 54) has long been a vexed question. The tradition is thoroughly discussed in Michael Barnes' *Draumkvæde: An Edition and Study* (Oslo, 1974). The table here provides Blom's *NMB* classifications in the "Version" column and Barnes's classifications under "Notes." Barnes provides a concordance to others' classifications (103–10).

For the abbreviated translations in some songbooks the connection with the ballad as originally recorded often has too many twists and reprintings (e.g., later popular songbooks and earlier anthologies by Lindeman, Bugge, Berggreen, and Berge) to follow at this distance. Thus "Translator's Source" is occasionally blank.

National Type No.	TSB No.	Title	Version	Tradition	Century	Title of Translation	Translator, Venue, Date	Translator's Source	Lang; Music	Trans. Strategy	Notes
NMB 6	A16	Jomfruva Ingebjørg	—	Comm	19	Maiden in the Shape of a Hind and an Eagle	Richmond, "Esse" 320-21 (1990)	Unpublished Ms		N.I.	
18	A38	Dei tvo systar (Horpa)	—	Comm	20	Two Sisters	Grainger, in Olsen, *NFS*, [1946]	Olsen record.	L M	N.A.	1 st.
26	A50	Vilemann og Magnhild	—	?Red		Villeman and Magnhild	Jorgenson, *MB* n.pag. (1950) =Jorgenson, *Trumpet* 193-96 (1954)	Liestøl/Moe No. 9		Interp	
?29	A54	Liti Kjersti	—	N.I.	—	Little Kersti	Anderson, in Forestier/Anderson 52 (1881) = *Warmuth's Coll.* No. 30, n.d.	Landstad No. 42	L M	Interp	2 st. of 24
?30	A54	Liti Kjersti	Red	—	—	Margit Hjukse	Jorgenson, *MB*, n.pag. (1950) =Jorgenson, *Trumpet* 197-200 (1954)	Liestøl & Moe No.53		Interp	
31	A57	Margit og Targjei Risvollo	—	Comm	19	Margit and Targjei Risvollo	Bø, "Margit" 284-91 (1985)	Blom & Bø No. 11 (1973)	L	Close	
36	A63	Olav Liljekrans	—	?	—	Olav Liljekrans	Child, *ESPB* 1:377 (1884)	Landstad No. 40		Close	2 st. of 39
36	A63	Olav Liljekrans	—	?	—	Olav Liljekrans	Child, *ESPB* 1:377 (1884)	Landstad 843-44		Close	2 st. of 15
36	A63	Olav Liljekrans	—	Comm	19	Olav Liljekrans	Child, *ESPB* 1:377 (1884)	Bugge Ms. via Sv. Grundtvig		N.I.	2 st.
39	A69	[Hedebys gjenganger]	—	Comm	19	Untitled	Cox, in Steenstrup, *MPB* 59 (1914)	Bugge, *GW* No. 15		Close	4 st. of 13; omits refr.

									L M		
46	B16	Maria	I	Comm	19	Maria	Child, *ESPB* 1:229 (1882)	*DgF* 3:891		Interp	3 st. + prose summ; omits refr.
47	D367	Olav og Kari	Red	—	—	Olav and Kari	Jørgenson, *NB* n.pag. (1950) =Jørgenson, *Trumpet* 188-92 (1954)	Liestøl/Moe No. 32		Interp	
47	D367	Olav og Kari	Red	—	—	Olav and Kari	Haugen, in Beyer 69-71 (1956)	Liestøl/Moe No. 32		N.A.	Prose
50	B22	Tora liti	?Red	—	—	Little Torø	Peed 129 (1989)	Grieg, *Album* No. 3	L M	Literal	3 st. of 14
50	B22	Tora liti	?Red	—	—	Little Torø	Peed 129 (1989)	Grieg, *Album* No. 3	L M	Close	3 st. of 14
50	B22	Tora liti	?Red	—	—	Little Torø	Peed 176-79 (1989)	Grieg, *Album* No. 3	L M	Interp	3 st. of 14
54	B31	Draumkvedet	Red	—	—	Draumkvæde	Ruud 52-57 (1922)	Lammers, *NF* 1:9-15		Interp	
54	B31	Draumkvedet	Red	—	—	Draumkvæde	Unknown, in Moe, *SS* 387-400 (1927)	?Moe, *SS* 199-209	L	Close	Stanzaic prose
54	B31	Draumkvedet	Red	—	—	Draumkvæde	Unknown, in Moe, *SS* 385 (1927)	?Moe, *SS* 199-209	L	N.A.	Prose
54	B31	Draumkvedet	Red	—	—	Draumkvæde	Grøndahl, in Liestøl 7-16 (1946) =Hallmundsson, *Anth.* 103-08 (1965) ==Olsen, *Draumk.* 3-39 (1952) =Beyer 65-66 (1956)	Liestøl/Moe No. 1	L M	Close / Interp / Close	20 st. of 52 / 3 st. of 52
54	B31	Draumkvedet	XIII	Comm	19	Draumkvæde	Grøndahl, in Liestøl 33 (1946)	Ms.	L	Close	=Barnes L6; 1 st. of 14
54	B31	Draumkvedet	XV	Comm		Draumkvæde	Grøndahl, in Liestøl 34 (1946)	Ms.	L	Close	=Barnes K5; 11 st. of 21
54	B31	Draumkvedet	—	Comm	19	Draumkvæde	Grøndahl, in Liestøl 34 (1946)	Ms.	L	Close	=Barnes M14; 1 st.

National Type No.	TSB No.	Title	Version	Tradition	Century	Title of Translation	Translator, Venue, Date	Translator's Source	Lang. Music	Trans. Strategy	Notes
54	B31	Draumkvedet	—	Comm	19	Draumkvæde	Grøndahl, in Liestøl 34 (1946)	Ms.	L	Interp	1 st.
54	B31	Draumkvedet	—	Comm	19	Two Old stev	Grøndahl, in Liestøl 66-67 (1946)	Landstad 410	L	Literal	2, free-floating st.
54	B31	Draumkvedet	Red	—	—	Dream Vision of Olav Åsteson	Jorgenson, *NB*, n.pag. (1950) =Jorgenson, *Trumpet* 139-49 (1954)	Liestøl/Moe No. 1	L	Interp	
54	B31	Draumkvedet	Red	—	—	Dream Vision of Olaf Aasteson	Jorgenson, *NB* n.pag. (1950) =Jorgenson, *Trumpet* 150-76 (1954)	Mortensson-Egnund 151-77	L	Interp	
54	B31	Draumkvedet	Red	—	—	Dream Song	Norman, in *Norway S.* 25 (1950)	Liestøl/Moe No. 1 & Landstad 7A	L M		5 st. of 52
54	B31	Draumkvedet	Red	—	—	Dream-Lay	?Grøndahl, in Olsen, *Draumk* 2 (1952)	Liestøl/Moe No. 1	M	N.A.	Prose summ
54	B31	Draumkvedet	Red	—	—	Dream Song of Olaf Åsteson	Merry 15-41 (1961) =Steiner, *Festivals* 53 (1955-57)	Trummler	L M	N.A.	From German tr.; Illus. by trans.
54	B31	Draumkvedet	Red	—	—	Untitled	B. Wood, in Merry 44-47 (1961)	Trummler	M	N.A.	From German tr.; 4 st. of 39
54	B31	Draumkvedet	II	Comm	19	Dream Journey	Halkett, in Seeman, et al 198-209, 243 (1967) =Rossel, *Scand. Ball.* No. 11 (1982)	Landstad No. 7B	L M	Close	=Barnes K1
54	B31	Draumkvedet	XIV	Comm	19	Untitled	Barnes, "Draumkvæde" 104 (1972)	Ms.	L	Literal	=Barnes R2a. Stanzaic prose

54	B31	Draumkvedet	—	Comm	19	Untitled	Folkvor Lommansson	Barnes, "Draumkvæde" 104 (1972)	Ms.	L	Literal	=Barnes M14; 1 st. Stanzaic prose
54	B31	Draumkvedet	➤	Comm	19	Untitled	Folkvor Lommansson	Barnes, "Draumkvæde" 104-05 (1972)	Ms.	L	Literal	=Barnes L4; stanzaic prose
54	B31	Draumkvedet	—	Comm	19	Untitled	Folkvor Lommansson	Barnes, "Draumkvæde" 105 (1972)	Ms.	L	Literal	=Barnes T3; stanzaic prose
61	C15	Falkvor Lommansson	?Red	—	—	Folkvor Lommansson		Smith-Dampier, *MBfD* 12-16 (1914)	Landstad No. 29		Interp	
76	D61	[Samson]	?Red	—	—	Dalebu Jonson		Anderson, in Forestier/Anderson 59 (1881) = *Warmuth's Coll.* No. 34 n.d. = *Hals Album* No. 26 [c. 1890] = *Norsk Nat.* 30, n.d. = *Norw. Nat. M.* 30, n.d.	≅ Landstad No. 24	L M	Interp	1 st. of 16
76	D61	[Samson]	?Red	—	—	Dalebu Jonson		Hansen, in Hansen & Wick 144 (1948)	Woll, Sønner	L M	Close	1 st. of 19
76	D61	[Samson]	Red	—	—	Dalebu Jonson		Unknown, in *Folk-SOL* 70, n.d.	Unidentified	M	N.I.	1 st. Pseudo-trans.
96	D153	[Herr Palles Bryllup]	—	Comm	19	Ballad of the Wedding of Sir Palle		Grøndahl, in Liestøl 46 (1946)	*DgF* 4:393	L	Literal	2 st. of 23; omits refr.
99	D169	Herreper og Gjøali	Compos	—	—	Herre Per og Gjøalin		Richmond, "D. Utrue" 72 (1963)	Landstad No. 68, other vars		N.A.	Prose summ
103	D205	Den utrue egtemann	—	Comm	19	Den utrue egtemann		Richmond, "D. Utrue" 63-64 (1963)	Ms.	L	N.A.	Prose summ. First pub. of orig.

National Type No.	TSB No.	Title	Version	Tradition	Century	Title of Translation	Translator, Venue, Date	Translator's Source	Lang; Music	Trans. Strategy	Notes
103	D205	Den utrue egtemann	—	Comm	19/20	Den utrue egtemann	Richmond, "D. Utrue" 64 (1963)	Ms.	L	N.A.	Prose summ. First pub. of orig.
108	D245	[Herr Peders slegfred]	?Red	—	—	Liti Kerstis hevn	Child, *ESPB* 2:181 (1885)	Landstad No. 67	L	Interp	4 st. + prose summ; omits refr.
117	D279	[Herr Magnus og hans møy]	Compos	—	—	Maarstig aa hass möy	Child *ESPB* 2:205 (1885)	Bugge, *GNF* No. 26		N.A.	Prose summ
118	D280	[Kærestens død]	N.I.	—	—	I Laid Me Down to Rest	Forestier, in Forestier & Anderson 34 (1881) = *Warmuth's Coll.* No. 16, n.d. = *Hals Album* No. 23 [c. 1890] = *Norsk Nat.* 28, n.d. =Bantock 106-07 (1911) = *Norw. Nat. M.* 28, n.d. = *Norway S.* 53 (1950) Vanberg 136-37 (1970)	Lindeman, *ÆWNF* No. 300	L M	Interp	3 st.
118	D280	[Kærestens død]	—	—	—	I Laid Me Down to Slumber	Grainger, in Grieg, *Excerpts* 3-4 (1925)	Grieg, *Album* No. 1	M	N.A.	1 st.
118	D280	[Kærestens død]	—	—	—	I Came Home Late One Evening	Karpeles, *FS Eur* No. 7 (1956)	Lindeman, *ÆnnF* No. 300	L M	Interp	6 st.
118	D280	[Kærestens død]	—	—	—	Folksong from Valdres	Unknown, *Den Norske Stud.* 1939 23-24	≃Lindeman, *HNF* No. 29	L	Close	2 st.
118	D280	[Kærestens død]	—	—	—	I Lay Me so Late	Peed 127 (1989)	Grieg, *Album* No. 1	L M	Interp	1 st.

									L	M		
118	D280	[Kærestens død]	—	—	—	I Lay Me so Late	Peed 127 (1989)	Grieg, *Album* No. 1	L	M	Close	1 st.
118	D280	[Kærestens død]	—	—	—	Untitled	Peed 166-68 (1989)	Grieg, *Album* No. 1	L	M	Interp	1 st.
118	D280	[Kærestens død]	—	—	—	He Ole	Peed 131 (1989)	Grieg, *Album* No. 7	L	M	Literal	2 st.
118	D280	[Kærestens død]	—	—	—	He Ole	Peed 131 (1989)	Grieg, *Album* No. 7	L	M	Interp	2 st.
118	D280	[Kærestens død]	—	—	—	Han Ole	Peed 194-97 (1989)	Grieg, *Album* No. 7	L	M	Interp	2 st.
122	D289	[Sønnens sorg]	Compos	—	—	Sønnens Sorg	Child, *ESPB* 1:180 (1882)	*DgF5*, 1:297-301			N.A.	Prose summ
122	D289	[Sønnens sorg]	—	Comm	19	Son's Sorrow	Cox, in Steenstrup, *MPB* 51 (1914)	*DgF5*, 1:298			Close	4 st. of 14
123	D291	[Esben og Malfred]	Compos	—	—	Maalfri	Child, *ESPB* 2:310 (1886)	Bugge, *GNF* No. 25			N.A.	Prose summ
137	D354	[Døttre hævne fader]	?Red	—	—	Sigrid and Astrid	Grøndahl, in Liestøl 45-46 (1946)	Liestøl & Moe No. 66	L		Literal	2 st. of 31; omits refr.
144	D381	[Paris og Dronning Ellen]	—	Comm	19	Paris og Helen i Trejeborg	Richmond, "Paris" 231-36 (1970)	Ms.	L		N.A.	Prose summ
146	D392	[Kong David og Solfager]	?Red	—	—	Solfager and the King of Worms	Forestier, in Forestier & Anderson 47 (1881)	≅ Landstad No. 56	L	M	Adapt	1 st. of 21
146	D392	[Kong David og Solfager]	?Red	—	—	Solfager og Ormekongin	Child, *ESPB* 5:7 (1894)	Landsted No. 56	L		N.A.	Prose
146	D392	[Kong David og Solfager]	?Red	—	—	Solfager and the King of Serpents	Unknown, *Den Norske Stud.* 1939 23-24	≅ Landstad No. 56	L		Close	3 st. of 21

National Type No.	TSB No.	Title	Version	Tradition	Century	Title of Translation	Translator, Venue, Date	Translator's Source	Lang./Music	Trans. Strategy	Notes
146	D392	[Kong David og Solfager]	?Red	—	—	Sunfair and the Dragon King	Norman, in *Norway* S. 23 (1950)	≅ Landstad No. 56	L M	Adapt	5 st. of 21
151	D399	[Tærningspillet]	—	—	—	Guldterning	C. Kappey in Kappey 126 [c. 1905]	Unidentified	M	Adapt	3 st.
151	D399	[Tærningspillet]	Red	—	—	The Dice Game	Beal, *Dances* 182-84 (1989)	Liestøl & Semb 44-45	L M	Close	Song-dance
154	D405	[Den fortryllande sang]	—	—	—	Inga Litamor	Peed, 134 (1989)	Grieg, *Saml. V.* 17:54	L M	Literal	1 st.
154	D405	[Den fortryllande sang]	—	—	—	Inga Litamor	Peed, 134 (1989)	Grieg, *Saml. V.* 17:54	L M	Close	1 st.
154	D405	[Den fortryllande sang]	—	—	—	Inga Litamor	Peed, 217-19 (1989)	Grieg, *Saml. V.* 17:54	L M	Interp	1 st.
158	D411	Kvinnemordaren (Svein nordmann)	?Red	—	—	Svein Norðmann	Gardner-Medwin, "Paradise" 313 (1963)	Landstad No. 69	L	Interp	2 st. of 20
158	D411	Kvinnemordaren (Svein nordmann)	?Red	—	—	Svein Norðmann	Arengo Jones, in Seeman, et al 52-57, 233 (1967)	Landstad No. 69	L M	Interp	
164	D432	Bendik og Årolilja	Red	—	—	Bendix and Olrun, the Lily Fair	Jorgenson, *NB,* n.pag. (1950) ≅ Jorgenson, *Trumpet* 177-87 (1954)	Liestøl & Moe No. 19		Interp	
164	D432	Bendik og Årolilja	Red	—	—	Bendik and Aarolilja	Unknown, in Semb, *Dances* 28-30 (1951)	Liestøl & Semb No. 19	M	Adapt	Song-dance

164	D432	Bendik og Árolilja	Red	—	—	Untitled	Haugen, in Beyer 70 (1956)	Liestøl & Moe No. 19		Close	1 st. of 58; omits refr.
164	D432	Bendik og Árolilja	Red	—	—	Bendik and Aarolilja	M. Shirley in Krogsæter 46-48 (1968)	?Liestøl & Semb No. 19	M	Interp	Echoes Semb, *Dances*
171	E29	Roland og Magnus Kongjen	Compos	—	—	Roland og Magnus Kongjen	Ólason, "Literary B." 125-26 (1991)	Blom & Bø No. 36		N.A.	Prose
171	E29	Roland og Magnus Kongjen	—	Comm	19	Roland og Magnus Kongjen	Ólason, "Literary B." 127 (1991)	Blom & Bø 218-19	L	Literal	3 st. of 26
184	E85	[Hermundur illi]	?Red	—	—	Hermoð Ille	Conroy, "Ballad Comp." 86-88, 98-99 (1979)	Landstad No. 17B	L	N.A.	12 st. of 90 Stanzaic prose
188	E126	Torekall	—	Comm	18	Thorekarl of Asgarth	D. Colbert, in Rossel, *Scand. Ball.* (1982)	Blom & Bø 262-64		Close	
191	E140	Kappen Illugjen	—	Comm	19	Untitled	Richmond, "From Edda" 307, 309-10 (1980)	Ms.	L	Close	3st. + prose summ
192	E143	[Sigurd og trollbruri]	?Red	—	—	Sigurd and the Troll-Bride	Anderson, in Forestier & Anderson 50 (1881) = *Warmuth's Coll.* No. 28, n.d.	=Landstad No. 50	L M	Interp	1 st. of 10
192	E143	[Sigurd og trollbruri]	?Red	—	—	Sjugar and the Troll	Norman, in *Norway S.* 47 (1950)	=Landstad No. 50	L M	Interp	3 st. of 10
196	E147	Steinfinn Fefinnsson	?Red	—	—	Steinfinn Fefinnsson	Jorgenson, *MB,* n.pag. (1950) =Jorgenson, *Trumpet* 201-08 (1954)	Liestøl & Moe No. 10		Interp	
204	FI	Gjenta som ville gifte seg	—	Comm	19	Girl Who Wanted to Get Married	Solberg, "Jocular" 21 (1992)	Ms.		N.I.	1 st. + prose summ

National Type No.	TSB No.	Title	Version	Tradition	Cen-tury	Title of Translation	Translator, Venue, Date	Translator's Source	Lang; Music	Trans. Strategy	Notes
208	F9	[Kælling og hovmand]	—	Comm	19	Old Woman and the Nobleman	Solberg, "Jocular" 22 (1992)	Ms.		N.I.	1 st. + prose summ
213	F17	Myllardottera	—	—	—	Miller's Daughter	Anderson, in Forestier/Anderson 53 (1881) = *Warmuth's Coll.* No. 31, n.d. = *Hals Album* 26 [c. 1890] = *Norsk Nat.* 26, n.d. = *Norw. Nat. M.* 26, n.d.	= Lindeman, *ÆNNF* No. 116	L M	Adapt	1st.
213	F17	Myllardottera	Red	—	—	Miller's Daughter	M.L. Baum, in Gilbert 78 (1910)	Unidentified	M	N.I.	4 st.
213	F17	Myllardottera	—	Comm	20	Miller's Daughter	Solberg, "Norwegian" 39-40 (1990)	Berge, *NV* No. 36.1		Interp	
215	F23	[Sorte Iver]	—	Comm	19	Black Iver and Lucy	Solberg, "Jocular" 19 (1992)	Ms.		N.I	1 st. + prose summ
216	F26	Fanteguten	—	?Comm	N.I.	Beggar Boy	Unknown, *Den Norske Stud. 1939* 27	≅ Landstad No. 91	L	Close	5 st. of 26
216	F26	Fanteguten	?Red	—	—	Raggedy Boy	Haugen, in Beyer 72 (1956)	Liestøl/Moe No. 92		Close	3 st. of 30; omits refr.
216	F26	Fanteguten	N.I.	—	—	Fante Boy	Peed 133 (1989)	Grieg, *Album* No. 11	L M	Interp	3 st.
216	F26	Fanteguten	N.I.	—	—	Fante Boy	Peed 133 (1989)	Grieg, *Album* No. 11	L M	Close	3 st.
216	F26	Fanteguten	N.I.	—	—	Untitled	Peed 209-12 (1989)	Grieg, *Album* No. 11	L M	Adapt	3 st.
220	F40	[Hovmand og præstens hustru]	—	Comm	20	Nobleman, the Vicar, and the Vicar's Wife	Solberg, "Jocular" 19 (1992)	Ms.		N.I.	1 st. + prose summ

221	F45	[Nis Bossens fedel]	Red	—	The Fiddler	Kastman & Köhler No. 48 (1913)	Hellgren No. 98, from Garborg?	Adapt			3 st. Song-dance
221	F45	[Nis Bossens fedel]	Red	—	Peter the Fiddler	Van Cleve 180-81 (1916)	Hellgren No. 98, from Garborg?	Adapt		M	3 st. Song-dance
221	F45	[Nis Bossens fedel]		—	Norwegian [sic] Folk Song	Knudsen 31, n.d.	Unidentified	N.I.			3 st.
221	F45	[Nis Bossens fedel]		—	Peter, the Player	B. Krone in Krone & Ostlund, *SSF*9-10 (1942)	Hellgren No. 98, from Garborg?	Adapt		M	From Swedish tr.? 3 st.
221	F45	[Nis Bossens fedel]		—	Per Spelmann	E. Haugen in Vornholt 24 (1943)	Unidentified	N.I.		M	4 st.
221	F45	[Nis Bossens fedel]		—	Tom Fiddler	Norman, in *Norway S.* 49 (1950)	Unidentified	N.I.	L	M	3 st.
221	F45	[Nis Bossens fedel]		—	Per the Fiddler	M. Bryne in *UNEF*31 (1958)	Unidentified	N.I.	L	M	3 st.
221	F45	[Nis Bossens fedel]		—	Per the Fiddler	Hansen, in Hansen & Wick 142 (1967)	Woll, *Sønner*	Close	L	M	3 st.
221	F45	[Nis Bossens fedel]		—	Per, the Fiddler	Sevig & Gundersen, in Sevig 79(1985)	Unidentified	N.I.	L	M	5 st.
224	F54	[Bjørneskindet]		—	Mass and Lass	Anderson, in Forestier & Anderson 45 (1881)	≅ Lindeman, *ÆNNF* No. 221	Adapt	L	M	1 st.
224	F54	[Bjørneskindet]		—	Mass and Lasse	Anderson, in Forestier & Anderson 73 (1881) =Forestier & Anderson 46 (1881) =*Warmuth's Coll.* No. 26, n.d.	≅ Lindeman, *ÆNNF* No. 168	Interp	L	M	1 st. of ?10 — Different tune
224	F54	[Bjørneskindet]		—	Han Mass og Han Lasse	Hansen, in Hansen & Wick 142 (1967)	Woll, *Sønner*	Interp	L	M	1 st. of ?10
225	F54	[Bjørneskindet]	Compos	—	Mats and Lars	Solberg, "Jocular" 18-19 (1992)	Unidentified	N.A.			Prose summ

National Type No.	TSB No.	Title	Version	Tradition	Cen-tury	Title of Translation	Translator, Venue, Date	Translator's Source	Lang. Music	Trans. Strategy	Notes
—	D231	Ravengård og Memering	—	—	—	Runda Ballad	Christophersen 235-36 (1952)	*DgF* 2:644-45		N.A.	Summ of lost ball.
[Grn 91]	—	Den bakvende visa	—	—	—	Awkward Ballad	Anderson, in Forestier & Anderson 36 (1881) = *Warmuth's Coll.* No. 21, n.d.	≅ Lindeman, *ÆNWF* No. 587	L M	Adapt	1 st.
[Grn 91]	—	Den bakvende visa	—	—	—	Backwards Song	Beal, *Dances* 181-82 (1989)	≅ Lindeman, *ÆNWF* No. 587	L M	Close	4 st. Song-dance
—	—	Kjærringa med staven	—	—	—	Here Comes on Crutches Sally	Anderson, in Forestier/Anderson 25 (1881) = *Warmuth's Coll.* No. 12, n.d.	Unidentified	L M	Interp	1 st.
—	—	Kjærringa med staven	—	—	—	Old Crone with a Staff	Unknown, *Den Norske Stud. 1939* 32	Unidentified	L	Close	1 st.
—	—	Kjærringa med staven	—	—	—	Old Woman with a Cane	B. Krone, in Krone/Ostlund, *SND* 21-23 (1941)	Unidentified	M	N.I.	With dance music
—	—	Kjærringa med staven	—	—	—	Old Woman with the Cane	Sevig & Gundersen, in Sevig 53 (1985)	Unidentified	L M	Close	4 st.
—	—	Der stander et slot i Oesterrige	—	—	—	There Stands in Austria a Castle	Forestier, in Forestier & Anderson 13 (1881)	= Lindeman, *ÆNWF* No. 10	L M	Close	1 st. of 25; cf. DgF 57
—	—	Paa Vossevangen	—	—	—	Sweet Home	Van Cleve 86-88 (1916)	Hellgren No. 50	M	Adapt	Song-dance; cf. Swed. "Till Øster-land"

Den bergtekne	—	Comm	19	Mountain Thrall	Ellingboe 88 (1988)	Grieg, *Bergentr.* =Landstad 394f.	L	M	Literal	6 st. of 12. *Stev*
Den bergtekne	—	Comm	19	Mountain Thrall	Ellingboe 33-35 (1988)	Grieg, *Bergentr.* =Landstad 394f.	L	M	Adapt	6 st. of 12. *Stev*
Den bergtekne	—	Comm	19	Mountain Thrall (Alone)	W.H. Halverson, in Grieg, *Saml. V.* 14:147-55 (1990)	Grieg, *Bergentr.* =Landstad 394f.	L	M	Adapt	6 st. of 12. *Stev*

TABLE 5. TRANSLATIONS FROM THE SWEDISH

Ballads from the Swedish are indexed when possible to the SMB numbers in *Sveriges Medeltida Ballader*, the comprehensive scholarly edition for Sweden and Swedish-speaking Finland. Andersson, *Finlands Svenska Folkdigtning*. 5. *Folkvisor*. I. *Den Äldre Folkvisan* (1934) has its own validity as an edition of the Swedo-Finnish ballads, however. Numbers and titles for ballads forthcoming in *SMB* have been established and are used here. *SMB* is a model of scholarly care, and—unique among the comprehensive editions—it presents texts and melodies together. Also unlike the other editions, *SMB* prints no more than 25 versions for any one ballad type (the earliest, and a selection of later ones); all other known records are listed only. Although this departs from Svend Grundtvig's fundamental "All that there is, all as it is" principle of ballad editing, it is a practical necessity where widespread collecting has recorded hundreds of texts for some SMB types. Volume 1 has a brief, useful commentary in English.

Commentary on the texts and melodies is segregated into yet unpublished volumes of *SMB*. For the present work this lack to some extent has been made up with the help of Bengt Jonssons's encyclopedic *Svensk balladtradition*. 1. *Balladkällor och balladtyper* (Stockhom, 1967).

The most common sources for translators are editions which, following the tendency of their time, often redacted or combined their sources. Geijer and Afzelius, *Svenska Folk-visor från Forntiden* (GA) and Arwidsson, *Svenska Fornsånger (SF)* both exhibit this freedom, especially GA (Jonsson 817-30, 846-54). Especially for SMB numbers 132 ff., not yet published, the judgments in the "Version" and "Tradition" columns are often tentative.

The revised and reorganized edition of Geijer and Afzelius, *Svenska Folk-visor från Forntiden* by Bergström and Höijer, is more widely available than the original, so references to the revision (GAB) are given along with those to the original (GA). The several = and ≅ signs under "Translator's Source" mark cases in which the translator possibly or probably worked from an unidentified intermediate source, itself sometimes redacted, but obviously close to the standard edition indicated.

National Type No.	TSB No.	Title	Version	Tradition	Century	Title of Translation	Translator, Venue, Date	Translator's Source	Lang; Music	Trans. Strategy	Notes
2	A11	Sömnrunorna	A		17	Sömn-runorna	Child, *ESPB* I:391 (1884)	*SF* 133		N.A.	Prose
3	A12	Kung Erik och spåkvinnan	D	Comm	19	King Eric and the Wise Woman	Howitt, *LRME* I:274-75 (1852)	GA 63=GAB 94		Interp	
9	A26	Ravnen Rune	Ad, red	—	—	Runè, the Raven	Kenealy, *Poems* 386-89 (1864) =*Poetical W.* 3:310-13 (1879)	GA 59=GAB 52		Adapt	Omits refr.
10	A27	Jungfrun i hindhamn	A	Arist	16	Enchanted Maiden Slain in Form of a Hind	G. Stephens, Rev. 25:40 (1840)	*SF* 136		Interp	2 st. of 13
10	A27	Jungfrun i hindhamn	Red	—	—	Untitled	Ker, "On Dan. B." 1:368 (1904) =*Coll. Ess.* 2:78 (1925)	Olrik I: No. 12		N.A.	From Danish tr.; 10 st. of 12; prose
10	A27	Jungfrun i hindhamn	Red	—	—	Maiden Hind	Smith-Dampier, *BDB* I: No. 12 (1939) =Creekmore, *Little Tr.* 506-07 (1952) =Creekmore, *Lyrics* 227-28 (1959) =Abrahamsen/Dal 12-13 (1965)	Olrik I: No. 12			From Danish tr.
10	A27	Jungfrun i hindhamn	Red	—	—	Girl in Hind's Skin	Gray, *FaF* No. 24 (1954)	Olrik I: No. 12		N.A.	From Danish tr.
11	A29	Lindormen	Red	—	—	Lindworm	Kenealy, *Poems* 374-75 (1864) =*Poetical W.* 3:298-99 (1879)	GA 88[:] =GAB 72:1		Adapt	Omits refr.
12	A30	Jungfrun förvandlad till lind	B	?Comm	19	King Magnus	Kenealy, *Poems* 384-86 (1864) =*Poetical W.* 3:308-10 (1879)	GA 87[:] =GAB 71:1		Interp	

13	A38	De två systrarna	AA, red	—	—	Two Sisters	Kenealy, "Sw. Anth." 115-17 (1846) =Poems 366-69 (1864) =Poetical W. 3:290-93 (1879)	GA 69=GAB 16:2	Interp	
13	A38	De två systrarna	Ab	Comm	19	Wonderful Harp	Peterson 109-15 (1883)	GA 17=GAB16:1	Interp	
14	A40	Den förtrollade barnaföderskan	A	?Comm	17	Liten Kerstins Förtrollning	Child, ESPB 1:84 (1882)	Sv. Formm. T. 2:72f.	N.A.	Prose summ
14	A40	Den förtrollade barnaföderskan	Compos	—	—	Liten Kerstins Förtrollning	Child, ESPB 1:83-84 (1882)	SF 134 A, B	N.A.	Prose summ
15	A41	Redebold och Gullborg	I	Comm	19	Hillebrand	Stephens, Rev. 25:41-43 (1840) =Longfellow, PPE 133-34 (1847)	GA 2=GAB 2:1	Interp	
16	A42	Hilla lilla	E, red	—	—	Proud Hilla Lilla	Kenealy, Poems 371-74 (1864) =Poetical W. 3:295-98 (1879)	GA 32=GAB 26	Interp	
16	A42	Hilla lilla	Compos	—	—	Hildebrand and Hilde	Child, ESPB 1:92 (1882)	SF 107 & GA 32=GAB26	N.A.	Prose summ.
20	A48	Näcken bortför jungfrun	G	Comm	19	Necken, the Water-King	Stephens, Rev. 25:33 (1840)	GA89[:1]=GAB73:1	Interp	4 st. of 23
20	A48	Näcken bortför jungfrun	Ha	Comm	19	Necken Chooses Him a Bride	Stephens, Rev. 25:33 (1840)	GA11=GAB74	Interp	4 st. of 19
20	A48	Näcken bortför jungfrun	G	Comm	19	Necken	Kenealy, Poems 378-80 (1864) =Poetical W. 3:302-04 (1879)	GA89[:1]=GAB73:1	Adapt	Omits refr.
21	A49	Ungersven och havsfrun	B	Comm	19	Untitle	Lloyd 193-94 (1870)	GA21=GAB78	Adapt	9 st. + prose summ

National Type No.	TSB No.	Title	Version	Tradition	Century	Title of Translation	Translator, Venue, Date	Translator's Source	Lang; Music	Trans. Strategy	Notes
22	A50	Harpans kraft	Ja, ?red	—	—	Power of the Harp	Keightley, *FM*1:237-40 (1828) = *FM*150-52 (1850) = *World G.*150-52 (1978)	GA91[:III] = GAB75:3		Close	
22	A50	Harpans kraft	Ja, ?red	—	—	Power of the Harp	Robinson, "Popular" 295-97 (1836) =Longfellow, *PPE*139 (1847)	GA91[:III] = GAB75:3		Close	
22	A50	Harpans kraft	Ha, red	—	—	Power of the Harp	Stephens, Rev. 25:34-35 (1840) ≃ [Bushby], "Ballads" 130:489-90 (1864)	GA91[:I]=GAB75:I		Interp	
22	A50	Harpans kraft	Ha, red	—	—	Power of the Harp	Kenealy, "Sw. Anth." 118-19 (1846) = *Poems* 376-78 (1864) = *Poetical W.* 3:300-02 (1879)	GA91[:I]=GAB75:I		Interp	
22	A50	Harpans kraft	Red (D)	—	—	Might of the Harp	Halkett, in Seeman 26-31, 231 (1967)	*SF*149B	L M	Interp	
23	A51	Havsfruns tärna	C	Comm	19	Mer-lady	Prior, *ADB*3:468-71 (1860) = Rev. *ADB*344 (1860)	*SF*150A		Interp	
24	A54	Den bergtagna	I, red	—	—	Proud Margaret	Keightley, *FM*1:172-80 (1828) = *FM*103-08 (1850) = *World G.*103-08 (1978)	GA35=GAB29		Close	
24	A54	Den bergtagna	Red (Ba)	—	—	Mountain-Taken Maid / Maid Carried Off to the Mountains	Stephens, Rev. 25:35-36 (1840) =Longfellow, *PPE*132 (1847) ≃ [Bushby], "Ballads" 130:492-93 (1864)	GAI[:I]=GABI:I		Interp	

									L	M		
24	A54	Den bergtagna	I, red	—	—	Mountain King and His Bride Maid Carried Off to the Mountains	Stephens, Rev. 25:37 (1840) ≃ [Bushby], "Ballads" 130:493 (1864)	GA35=GAB29			Interp	5 st. of 41; omits refr.
24	A54	Den bergtagna	Red (Ba)	—	—	Mountain-King	K. Gercke, in Berens 14, n.d.	GAI[:l]=GAB I:l	L	M	Close	1 st. of 21
24	A54	Den bergtagna	Red (Ba)	—	—	Mountain-King	Chapman, in Hägg 22-24 (1909)	GAI[:l]=GAB I:l	L	M	Interp	
24	A54	Den bergtagna	Red (Ba)	—	—	Taken by Fairies	Adams-Ray, in Stockholms St. 22-23 (1925)	GAI[:l]=GAB I:l	L		Interp	3 st. of 21
24	A54	Den bergtagna	Red (Ba)	—	—	Mountain King	Unidentified, Coll. Sw. NM17 [c. 1925]	GAI[:l]=GAB I:l	L	M	Interp	1 st. of 21
24	A54	Den bergtagna	Red (Ba)	—	—	Mountain Captive	C. Stork, in Botsford, FSMP2:216-17 (1922) = Botsford CFS2:69-71 (1931)	GAI[:l]=GAB I:l	L	M	Interp	14 st. of 21
24	A54	Den bergtagna	Red (Ba)	—	—	Captive Mountain Maid	Krone, in Krone & Ostlund, SSF4-5 (1942)	GAI[:l]=GAB I:l		M	Adapt	5 st. of 21
26	A59	Herr Magnus och havsfrun	Red (C)	—	—	Duke Magnus and the Mermaid	Keightley, FM1:242-44 (1828) =FM154-55 (1850) =World G. 154-55 (1978)	GA96=GAB83:2			Close	
26	A59	Herr Magnus och havsfrun	Red (C)	Comm	19	Duke Magnus	Robinson, "Popular" 294-95 (1836) =Longfellow, PPF138-39 (1847)	GA96=GAB83:2		M	Adapt	

National Type No.	TSB No.	Title	Version	Tradition	Century	Title of Translation	Translator, Venue, Date	Translator's Source	Lang; Music	Trans. Strategy	Notes
26	A59	Herr Magnus och havsfrun	**F**	Comm	19	Sir Magnus and the Sea-Witch	Kenealy, *Poems* 380-81 (1864) = *Poetical W.* 3:304-05 (1879)	GA95[:I]=GAB83:I		Interp	
28	A62	Riddar Tynne	**D**, ?red	—	—	Sir Thynne	Keightley, *FM* I:163-72 (1828) = *FM* 97-103 (1850) = *World G.* 97-103 (1978)	GA7[:I]=GAB7:I		Close	Omits refr.
28	A62	Riddar Tynne	**D**, ?red	—	—	Ridder Tynne	Howitt, *LRNE* I:72-73 (1852)	GA7[:I]=GAB7:I		Interp	5 st. of 49
28	A62	Riddar Tynne	**D**, ?red	—	—	Sir Tynnè	Kenealy, *Poems* 341-49 (1864) = *Poetical W.* 3:265-73 (1879)	GA7[:I]=GAB7:I		Interp	Omits refr.
29	A63	Herr Olof och älvorna	**A**	Comm	17	Elf-Woman and Sir Olof	Keightley, *FM* I:144-47 (1828) = *FM* 84-86 (1850) = *World G.* 84-86 (1978)	GA94[:II] = GAB80:2		Close	
29	A63	Herr Olof och älvorna	**Dc**, red	—	—	Sir Olof in the Elve-Dance	Keightley, *FM* I:141-43 (1828) = *FM* 82-83 (1850) = *World G.* 82-83 (1978)	GA93=GAB79		Close	
29	A63	Herr Olof och älvorna	**Dc**, red	—	—	Sir Olof's Bridal	Robinson, "Popular" 292-93 (1836) = Longfellow, *PPE* 138 (1847)	GA93=GAB79		Close	
29	A63	Herr Olof och älvorna	**Dc**, red	—	—	Master Olof at the Elfin Dance	Howitt, *LRNE* I:269-70 (1852)	GA93=GAB79		Interp	
29	A63	Herr Olof och älvorna	N.I.	—	—	Sir Olaf and the Fairy Dance	Dixon (1868)	Unknown		N.I.	

29	A63	Herr Olof och älvorna	A	Comm	17	Sir Olaf and the Fairies	Halkett, in Seeman, et al 12-15 (1967) = Rossel, *Scand. Ball.* No. 3 (1982)	Jonsson 1966 No. 2	L	Close	
31	A65	Älvefärd	A	Comm	17	Young Swain and the Elves	Keightley, *FM* 1:147-49 (1828) = *FM* 86-87 (1850) = *World G.* 86-87 (1978)	GA3:170-71 = GAB81		Close	
31	A65	Älvefärd	A	Comm	17	Rosegrove-Side	Robinson, "Popular" 291-92 (1836) = Longfellow, *PPE* 137 (1847)	GA95[:II]=GAB81		Interp	Echoes Keightley
32	A67	Sorgens makt	A, red	—	—	Sorrow's Might	C. Kappey, in Kappey 112-15 [c. 1905]	GA6[:I]=GAB6:I	M	Adapt	
33	A68	Styvmodern	B	Comm	19	Step-mother Rebuked	Stephens, Rev. 25:45 (1840)	SF90A		Interp	2 st. of 28; omits ref.
33	A68	Styvmodern	Da	Comm	19	Step-mother Rebuked	Stephens, Rev. 25:45 (1840)	GA72[:I]=GAB58:I		Close	2 st. of 20; omits ref.
33	A68	Styvmodern	Da	Comm	19	Sir Ulf and Lady Sölfverlind	Howitt, *LRNE* 1:277-74 (1852)	GA72[:I]=GAB58:I		Close	
33	A68	Styvmodern	Da	Comm	19	Sir Ulfver and His Wife Silverlind	Kenealy, *Poems* 351-53 (1864) = *Poetical W.* 3:275-77 (1879)	GA72[:I] = GAB58:I		Interp	
33	A68	Styvmodern	B	Comm	19	Untitled	B. Jonsson, "Oral" 143 (1991)	SF90A	L	Literal	6 st. of 29
33	A68	Styvmodern	Ia	Comm	19	Untitled	B. Jonsson, "Oral" 143 (1991)	SF90B	L	Close	6 st. of 31
39	B8	Sankte Staffan	Be	B'rds	19	Staffan's Visa	Lloyd 207 (1870)	GA99[:II] = GAB91:2		Close	1 st. of 30
39	B8	Sankte Staffan	—	B'rds	19	Untitled	Child, *ESPB* 1:235 (1882)	GAB2:360-61		Close	1 st. + prose summ

National Type No.	TSB No.	Title	Version	Tradition	Century	Title of Translation	Translator, Venue, Date	Translator's Source	Lang. Music	Trans. Strategy	Notes
39	B8	Sankte Staffan	**Be**	Brds	19	Staffans Visa	Child, *ESPB*1:234-35 (1882)	GA99[:II] = GAB91:2		Close	1 st. of 30
39	B8	Sankte Staffan	**D**	Comm	19	Staffans Visa	Child, *ESPB*1:234-35 (1882)	GA99[:I] = GAB91:1		Close	1 st. of 7
39	B8	Sankte Staffan	**Be**	Brds	19	Carol of Saint Staffan	Mrs. J.H. Monrad, Anna Monrad, & Reed, in Reed 17-19 (1934)	GA99[:II] = GAB91:2	M	Interp	10 st. of 30
39	B8	Sankte Staffan	**C**	Comm	19	Staffan Var en Stalledräng	Underwood, in Cagner 90 (1955)	Unidentified	M	Interp	1 st. of 7
39	B8	Sankte Staffan	**?D**	?Comm	19	Staffan Var en Stalledräng	Underwood, in Cagner 88-89 (1955)	?GA99[:I]=GAB 91:1	M	Interp	2 st. of 7
39	B8	Sankte Staffan	**Nb**	Comm	20	Sankt Staffan Han Rider Sina Hästar till Vanns	Underwood, in Cagner 89 (1955)	=*Folkminnen* 1916: 15-16	M	Close	1 st. of 20
39	B8	Sankte Staffan	**?Red**	—	—	Stefan Was a Stable Boy	de Cormier & Löfgren, in Shekerjian 116-17 (1963)	Unidentified	M	N.A.	7 st.
39	B8	Sankte Staffan	**X**	Comm	20	Stephen and Herod	Arengo Jones, in Seeman, et al 183-87, 242 (1967) =Strömbäck 140 (1968) =Rossel, *Scand. Ball.* No. 8 (1982)	Andersson No. 23	L M	Interp	Swedish Finland
39	B8	Sankte Staffan	**D**	Comm	19	Stephen Stableboy	D. Colbert, in Rossel, *Scand. Ball.* No. 9 (1982)	GA99[:I] = GAB91:1		Adapt	

42	B14	Liten Karin	**Da**	Comm	19	Little Karin's Death	Robinson, "Popular" 297-98 (1836) =Longfellow, *PPE* 139-40 (1847)	GA3[:I]=GAB3:I		Close	13-st. version
42	B14	Liten Karin	**Da**	Comm	19	Little Karin	Stephens, Rev. 26:44-45 (1840)	GA3[:I]=GAB3:I		Interp	13-st. version
42	B14	Liten Karin	—	—	—	Little Katie	E.N-n, in *Swed. Nat. S.* 10 (1877)	Unidentified		N.I.	Not seen
42	B14	Liten Karin	**Da**	Comm	19	Little Karin	Peterson 55-58 (1883)	GA3[:I]=GAB3:I		Close	13st. version
42	B14	Liten Karin	**Da**	Comm	19	Little Karin	K. Gercke, in Berens 13, n.d.	=GA3[:I]=GAB3:I	L M	Interp	1 st. of 13
42	B14	Liten Karin	**Da**	Comm	19	Little Karin	Chapman, in Hägg 109-11 (1909)	=GAB3[:I]=GAB3:I	L M	Interp	13-st. version
42	B14	Liten Karin	**Da**	Comm	19	Little Katie	C. Kappey, in Kappey 116-17 [c. 1905] =Bantock 114-15 (1911)	=GA3[:I]=GAB3:I	M / L M	Interp	
42	B14	Liten Karin	**Da**	Comm	19	Little Carin	Unidentified, in *Coll. Sw NM7* [c. 1925]	=GA3[:I]=GAB3:I	L M	Interp	1 st. of 12
43	B16	Maria Magdalena	**C**	Comm	19	Magdalena	Howitt, *LRMET*:282-84 (1852)	GA2:229-33 = GAB85		Adapt	
43	B16	Maria Magdalena	**F**	Comm	19	Untitled	Child, *ESPB*1:229 (1882)	*DgF* 2:533-36		Close	3 st. + prose summ; omits refr.
43	B16	Maria Magdalena	**I**	Comm	19	Mary Magadalen	D. Colbert, in Rossel, *Scand. Ball.* No. 10 (1982)	Säve No. 28		Close	
46	B20	Herr Peder och hans syster	Red (**D**)	—	—	Brother's Revenge	Stephens, Rev. 26:46 (1840)	*SF* 47A		Close	2 st. of 24; omits refr.
47	B21	Herr Töres' döttrar	**D**	Comm	17	Pehr Tyrson's Döttrar i Wänge	Child, *ESPB*1:172 (1882)	*SF* 166		N.A.	Prose summ

National Type No.	TSB No.	Title	Version	Tradition	Century	Title of Translation	Translator, Venue, Date	Translator's Source	Lang. Music	Trans. Strategy	Notes
47	B21	Herr Töres' döttrar	Compos	—	—	Pehr Tyrson's Döttrar i Wänge	Child, *ESPB* 1:172 (1882)	GA98[:I-III]= GAB84:1-3		N.A.	Prose summ
47	B21	Herr Töres' döttrar	Red	—	—	Untitled	Malmström & Kushner, in Isaksson ix-xiii (1960) =Hallmundsson, *Anth.* 275-77 (1965)	Unidentified		N.I.	Bergman film
48	B22	Duvans sång	Red	—	—	Dove's Song	Unidentified, in Brown & Moffat 173 (1901)	Unidentified	M	N.I.	Lyric of loss
48	B22	Duvans sång	Red (BPa)	—	—	Song of the Dove	Gilchrist 47-48 (1940)	Andersson No. 19B, A	M	Interp	Swedish Finland
54	B32	Den rike mannens själ	A	Brds	18	Rich Man's Soul. A	Prior, *ADB* No. 47A (1860)	*DgF* 2:572		Interp	
54	B32	Den rike mannens själ	C	Comm	19	Rich Man's Soul. C	Prior, *ADB* No. 47C (1860)	*DgF* 2:572-73		Adapt	2 st. of 6
59	C8	Vreta klosterrov	B	?Comm	17	Abduction from Vreta Abbey	D. Colbert, in Rossel *Scand. Ball.* No. 18 (1982)	Jonsson 1962 No. 27		Close	
60	C15	Folke Algotssons brudrov	A	Arist	16	Swain Carrieth off His Mistress	Stephens, Rev. 26:33 (1840)	*SF* 22		Interp	2 st. of 14
66	D7	Dansen i rosende lund	A	Cleric	16	Dance in the Grove of Roses	Stephens, Rev. 26:30 (1840) =Longfellow, *PPE* 134 (1847) ≅Stephens, *Revenge* 48-49 (1857)	*SF* 127		Interp / Adapt	
70	D37	Herr Karl och klosterjungfrun	J, red	—	—	Sir Carl, or The Cloister Robbed	Stephens, Rev. 26:49-51 (1840) =Longfellow, *PPE* 136-37 (1847)	GA26-GAB24		Interp	

		Swedish title				English title	Reference	GA		Notes
70	D37	Herr Karl och klosterjungfrun	J, red	—	—	Sir Carl; or The Cloister Robbing	Kenealy, "Sw. Anth." 121-22 (1846) = Poems 338-40 (1864) = Poetical W. 3:262-64 (1879)	GA26=GAB24	Adapt	
70	D37	Herr Karl och klosterjungfrun	J, red	—	—	Master Carl, or the Nunnery-Raid	Howitt, LRNE 1:292-94 (1852)	GA26=GAB24	Close	
70	D37	Herr Karl och klosterjungfrun	BCa	Comm	19	Herr Carl, eller Klosterrofvet	Child ESPB 1:249 (1882)	Rancken No. 4 ≅ Andersson No. 55D	Interp	2 st. of 12; omits refr.; Swedish Finland
80	D69	Ung Hillerström	Ba	?Comm	19	Ung Hillerström	Kenealy, "Sw. Anth." 119 (1846) = Poems 389-90 (1864) = Poetical W. 3:313-14 (1879)	GA55=GAB48	Interp	
85	D87	Axel och Valborg	Ad	Brds	18	Axel Thordson and Fair Valborg	Stephens, Rev. 25: 46 (1840)	GA25=GAB23	Interp	3 st. of 200
86	D90	Broder prövar syster	?Red	—	—	The Proof	Kenealy, Poems 354-57 (1864) = Poetical W. 3:278-81 (1879)	GA8[:1]=GAB8:1	Interp	
88	D96	Herr Axel och hans syster	A	Comm	17	Herr Axel	Child, ESPB 1:447 (1884)	SF 46	N.A.	Prose summ
93	D118	Den falska tärnan	Red (E)	—	—	...A False Maid	Stephens, Rev. 26:34 (1840)	GA 12=GAB 11	Interp	2 st. of 28; omits refr.
93	D118	Den falska tärnan	Red (E)	—	—	Sir Holkin and Little Kerstin	Kenealy, Poems 382-84 (1864) = Poetical W. 3:306-08 (1879)	GA 12=GAB 11	Interp	
97	D139	Riddar Stigs bröllop	Aa	:Comm	19	Untitled	Entwistle, Eur. Ball. 214 (1939)	GA 53=GAB 46	Interp	6 st. of 9

National Type No.	TSB No.	Title	Version	Tradition	Century	Title of Translation	Translator, Venue, Date	Translator's Source	Lang/ Music	Trans. Strategy	Notes
111	D214	Ungersvens klagan	A	Cleric	16	Too Late	Stephens, Rev. 26:43 (1840)	SF 125		Close	2 st. of 11; omits refr.
122	D245	Herr Peder och liten Kerstin	Red	—	—	Sir Peter and Little Kerstin	Howitt, LRNE 1:258-61 (1852) = Kaines, Love P. 294-98 (1870)	GA 9=GAB 9		Interp	
129	D258	Kung Valdemar och Tova	Red (D)	—	—	Little Tofva	Kenealy, "Sw. Anth." 119-21 (1846) = Poems 334-38 (1864) = Poetical W. 3:258-62 (1879)	GA49[:]=GAB43 :]		Interp	
132	D279	Dödsbudet	—	?Comm	19	Dream Fulfilled	Stephens, Rev. 25:44 (1840)	SF 72		Interp	2 st. of 24
132	D279	Dödsbudet	—	?Comm	19	Sir Malmsten's Dream	Kenealy, Poems 370-71 (1864) = Poetical W. 3:294-95 (1879)	GA85=GAB69		Adapt	
132	D279	Dödsbudet	—	?Comm	19	Ballad	Wm. Morris, in M. Morris 1:517-18 (1936)	GA85=GAB69		Interp	Omits refr.
135	D283	Hustrun dör	—	Cleric	16	Dying Bride	Stephens, Rev. 26:48 (1840)	SF 131		Close	4 st. of 9
138	D288	Lisa och Nedervall	—	Brds	18	Sir Wal and Lisa Lyle	Jamieson, IMA 373-76 (1814)	=DgF 5.1:281	L	Literal	
138	D288	Lisa och Nedervall	—	?Comm	19	Sir Redevall	Kenealy, Poems 349-51 (1864) = Poetical W. 3:273-75 (1879)	GA58=GAB51		Interp	
139	D289	Sonens sorg	—	?Arist	17	First Love in the Deep	Stephens, Rev. 26:39 (1840)	SF 70		Interp	2 st. of 20
151	D311	Ribbolt och Göta lilla	—	?Comm	17	Ribbolt	Child, ESPB 1:92 (1882)	SF 78		N.A.	Prose summ

153	D320	Sven i rosengård	—	Comm	19	Youth of Rosengord	Howitt, *LRNE* 1:263-65 (1852) =Child, *ESB* 1857-59 2:347-49 =Child, *ESB* 1860 2:347-49	GA67[:ll]= GAB54:2		Interp	
153	D320	Sven i rosengård	Red	—	—	Thou Swain in the Rosy Bower	M. Walker, in Marzo 78-79 (1928)	Unidentified	M	Adapt	2 st.; omits refr.
153	D320	Sven i rosengård	—	—	—	Sven i rosengården	Unknown, in Taube (1954)	Unidentified	L	N.I.	Sound recording. Not seen
154	D321	Den lillas testamente	?Red	—	—	Child's Last Wishes	Halliwell-Phillips 262 (1849)	GA68=GAB55	L	Close	1 st. of 9
154	D321	Den lillas testamente	—	Comm	19	Child's Last Wishes	Halliwell-Phillips 262 (1849)	=*SF* 88	L	Close	1 st. of 10
154	D321	Den lillas testamente	?Red	—	—	Child's Last Will	Howitt, *LRNE* 1:265-66 (1852) =Child, *ESB* 1857-59 2:366-67 =Child *ESB* 1860 2:366-67	GA68=GAB55		Close	
154	D321	Den lillas testamente	?Red	—	—	Den lillas Testamente	Child *ESPB* 1:154 (1882)	GA68=GAB55		N.A.	Prose summ
154	D321	Den lillas testamente	—	Comm	19	Den lillas Testamente	Child *ESPB* 1:154 (1882)	*SF* 88		N.A.	Prose summ
154	D321	Den lillas testamente	—	Comm	19	Ballad	Wm. Morris, in M. Morris 1:517 (1936)	=*SF* 88		Interp	
154	D321	Den lillas testamente	Red	—	—	Child's Testament	Haywood 169-70 (1966)	≅ *SF* 88	L M	Close	
156	D324	Tore och hans syster	—	?Comm	19	Cruel Brother	Howitt, *LRNE* 1:261-63 (1852)	GA86=GAB70		Interp	
163	D359	Riddar Malkom fängslas för hasttöld	?Red	—	—	Knight Malkom	Howitt, *LRNE* 1:288-89 (1852)	GA84=GAB68		Close	
164	D361	Herr Peders sjöresa	Red	—	—	Sir Peter's Voyage	Howitt, *LRNE* 1:276-78 (1852)	GA36[:l]=GAB30: l		Close	

National Type No.	TSB No.	Title	Version	Tradition	Century	Title of Translation	Translator, Venue, Date	Translator's Source	Lang. Music	Trans. Strategy	Notes
164	D361	Herr Peders sjöresa	—	Comm	19	Untitled. "Swedish E"	Child, *ESPB* 2: 14n (1885)	Fagerlund 194 No. 4		Interp	2 st. + prose summ Swedish Finland
164	D361	Herr Peders sjöresa	—	?Comm	?19	Sir Peder	Widén 29-31 (1947)	Personal commun.	L	N.I.	Immigrant memory
166	D367	Herren Båld	—	?Comm	19	Untitled	Stephens, Rev. 26:42 (1840)	GAI6=GABI5		Interp	3 st. of 28
166	D367	Herren Båld	—	?Comm	19	Herr Båld	Kenealy, *Poems* 363-65 (1864) = *Poetical W.* 3:287-89 (1879)	GAI6=GABI5		Interp	
172	D390	Hertig Fröjdenborg och fröken Adelin	?Red	—	—	Love Faithful in Death	Stephens, Rev. 26:40 (1840)	GAI9=GABI8		Interp	3 st. of 47
172	D390	Hertig Fröjdenborg och fröken Adelin	Compos	—	—	Hertig Fröjdenborg och Fröken Adelin	Child, *ESPB* 5:30-31 (1894)	Various		N.A.	Prose
173	D391	Den bortsålda	?Red	—	—	Maiden that Was Sold Sweet Rescue	Stephens, Rev. 26:31-32 (1840) =Longfellow, *PPE* 134-35 (1847) =Stephens, *Revenge* 29-33 (1857)	GAI5[:I]=GABI4: I		Interp	
173	D391	Den bortsålda	Compos	—	—	Den Bortsålda	Child, *ESPB* 2:348 (1886)	Various		N.A.	Prose
174	D392	David och Solfager	—	?Comm	17	Jungfru Solfager	Child, *ESPB* 5:7 (1894)	*SF* 25A		N.A.	Prose
174	D392	David och Solfager	—	?Comm	19	Jungfru Solfager	Child, *ESPB* 5:7 (1894)	*SF* 25 B		N.A.	Prose
175	D393	Hertig Henrik	—	?Comm	18	Hertig Henrik	Child, *ESPB* 1:194 (1882)	*SF* 168		N.A.	Prose

177	D395	Per svinaherde	—	?Comm	19	Love's Disguise	Stephens, Rev. 26:34 (1840)	SF 104A		Interp	2 st. of 46
177	D395	Per svinaherde	—	?Comm	19	Peter Swineherd	Unknown, in Coll. Sw. MM23, n.d.	=SF 104B	L M	Interp	1 st. of 7
177	D395	Per svinaherde	—	?Comm	19	Peter, the Swineherd	K. Gercke, in Berens 27, n.d.	=SF 104B	L M	Interp	1 st. of 7
177	D395	Per svinaherde	Rec	—	—	Peer Swineherd	Chapman, in Hägg 30-31 (1909) =People's Inst. 7 (1919)	=SF 104B	L M / L	Interp	6 st. of 7
177	D395	Per svinaherde	Red	—	—	Peter the Swineherd	Adams-Ray, in Sångsällsk. 40-41 (1927)	≅SF 104B	L	Interp	4 st. of 7
177	D395	Per svinaherde	—	?Comm	19	Peter, the Swineherd	Paul, in Ganschow 15-16 (1937)	≅SF 104B	L M	Interp	
181	D399	Liten båtsman	?Red	—	—	Little Seaman	Stephens, Rev. 26:35-37 (1840) =Longfellow, PPE 135-36 (1847)	GA37[:I]=GAB31:I		Interp	
181	D399	Liten båtsman	?Red	—	—	Little Boatman	Howitt, LRNE 1:279-81 (1852)	GA37[:I]=GAB31:I		Interp	
182	D405	Liten vallpiga	?Red	—	—	Power of Music	Stephens, Rev. 26:47 (1840)	GA74[:I]=GAB60:I		Interp	2 st. of 24
182	D405	Liten vallpiga	Red	—	—	Herdsmaid	Karpeles, FS Eur. 32-33 (1956)	Hollmérus/Andersson=Andersson No. 48C	L M	Interp	Swedish Finland
189	D421	Riddar Olle	—	?Comm	19	Riddar Olle	Child, ESPB 1:63-64 (1882)	GA39[:IV]=GAB 33:3		Close	2 st. + prose summ
195	D435	De borttstulna konungadöttrarna	Red	—	—	King's Two Daughters	Howitt, LRNE 1:270-71 (1852)	GA73=GAB59		Close	
205	E52	Sven Svanevit	—	?Comm	19	Untitled	Stephens, Rev. 26:51-52 (1840)	GA45=GAB38		Interp	6 st. of 11

National Type No.	TSB No.	Title	Version	Tradition	Century	Title of Translation	Translator, Venue, Date	Translator's Source	Lang. Music	Trans. Strategy	Notes
205	E52	Sven Svanevit	—	?Comm	19	Sven Svanehvit	Kenealy, "Sw. Anth." 117 (1846) =Poems 332-34 (1864) =Poetical W. 3:256-58 (1879)	GA45=GAB38		Interp	
212	E126	Tors hammarhämtning	—	N.I.		Untitled	Keightley, "Scand. M." 119-20 (1829)			Close	6 st. of 16
212	E126	Tors hammarhämtning	—	Comm	17	Untitled	B. Jonsson, "Oral" 145 (1991)	Noreen/Lundell 351, 392	L	Literal	2 versions same singer; 1 st.
215	E132	Orm ungersven	—	Arist	17	N.I.	Greenwood (1836)	N.I.		N.I.	Not seen
217	E139	Ramunder	—	?Brds	18	Young Ramunder	Stephens, Revenge 54-56 (1857)	SF 12		Interp	9 st. of 25
218	E144	Hemming och bergtrollet	—	?Comm	17	Knight Rescues His Maiden	Stephens, Rev. 25:37-38 (1840)	SF 13		Interp	3 st. of 24
229	F17	Mjölnarens dotter	—	?Comm	?19	Three Rascals	Widén 31-33 (1947)	Personal commun.	L	N.I.	Immigrant memory
244	F45	Per spelman				Peter, the Player	Krone, in Krone/Ostlund, SSF 9-10 (1942)				See NMB 221
248	F58	Bonden och kråkan	?Red	—	—	Farmer and the Sparrow	Misses Carter, Day, and Whealen, in Bolin No. 13 (1908)	Unidentified	M	N.I.	Song-dance
248	F58	Bonden och kråkan	?Red	—	—	Ye Goode Manne and ye Crowe	Gordon 102-03 (1936)	Unidentified		N.I.	

									M	N.I.	
248	F58	Bonden och kråkan	?Red	—	—	Farmer and the Crow	Per Stensland, in Tobitt 42 (1946)	Unidentified		N.I.	
248	F58	Bonden och kråkan	—	Comm	20	The Crow / Swedish Folk Song / The Crow	Mrs. Magnuson, in Rohrbough 126 (1940) =Zanzig No. 70 (1941) =Vornholt 19 (1943) =Y.W.C.A. 30 (1947)	Learned fr. father	M	N.I.	Song-dance; 5 st.
256	F70	Sven den unge	—	Comm	19	Untitled	Child, ESPB I:21 (1882)	Rancken No. 10		Close	Swedish Finland
260	F75	Tjuvarna	—	Comm	?19	Three Honest Men	Widén 33-34 (1947)	Personal commun.	L	N.I.	Immigrant memory
—		Oväntad bröllopsgäst	Red	—	—	Unexpected Marriage Guest	Stephens, Rev. 26:41 (1840)	GA31[:I]=GAB25:I		Interp	2 st. of 15
—		Oväntad bröllopsgäst	**M**	?Comm	?	Unexpected Wedding Guest	Howitt, LRME I:285-87 (1852)	GA31[:II]=GAB25:2		Interp	"Ballad echo"
—		Svennens svek	—	?Comm	18	Maiden Resolveth to Flee	Stephens, Rev. 26:29-30 (1840)	SF 124A		Interp	"Ballad echo"; cf. DgF306. 5 st. of 11
—		Greven i Rom	—	?Arist	16	Untitled	Stephens, Rev. 26:38 (1840)	GA2;244-51 = GAB53		Interp	2 st. of 31
—		Den förtrollade prinsessan	—	Brds	18	Enchanted Princess	Kenealy, Poems 357-62 (1864) =Poetical W. 3:281-86 (1879)	GA41=GAB35		Adapt	Cf. DgF57
—		Den förtrollade prinsessan	Compos	Brds	18	Den förtrollade Prinsessan	Child, ESPB I:336-37 (1884)	Various		N.A.	Prose summ. Cf. DgF57

National Type No.	TSB No.	Title	Version	Tradition	Century	Title of Translation	Translator, Venue, Date	Translator's Source	Lang: Music	Trans. Strategy	Notes
—	—	Konungabarnen	—	Comm	19	Royal Children	Howitt, *LRNE* 1:290-92 (1852)	GA20[:III]=GAB 19:3		Close	"Ballad echo"
—	—	Underbar syn	—	?Comm	19	Wonderful Vision	Howitt, *LRNE* 1:284-85 (1852)	GA2:233=GAB86		Adapt	
—	—	Resan til Österland	—	?Brds	?	To Easterland I am Going	K. Gercke, in Berens 34 n.d.	=GA2:235-39= GAB87	L M	Interp	Lyric. Cf. *DgF* 517; 1 st. of 28
—	—	Resan til Österland	—	?Brds	?	Far Eastward I'll Hie Me	Chapman, in Hägg 14-15 (1909) =People's Inst. 7 (1919)	=GA2:235-39= GAB 87	L M	Interp	Lyric. Cf. *DgF* 517; 8 st. of 28
—	—	Resan til Österland	—	?Brds	?	To the East	Bratli, No. 7 (1911)	=GA2:235-39= GAB87	L	Interp	Lyric. Cf. *DgF* 517; 1 st. of 28
—	—	Resan til Österland	—	?Brds	?	My Homeland	Unidentified, in McConathy, et al 9 (1936) = *Delaware Tercent.* 19 (1938)	=GA2:235-39= GAB87	L M	Adapt	Lyric. Cf. *DgF* 517; 3 st. of 28
—	—	Resan til Österland	—	?Brds	?	Swedish Folksong	Unidentified, in *Norske Stud.* 37 (1939)	=GA2:235-39= GAB87		Close	Lyric. Cf. *DgF* 517; 1 st. of 28
—	—	Resan til Österland	—	?Brds	?	My Homeland	Unidentified, in E. Thomas 65 (1950)	=GA2:235-39= GAB87	M	Adapt	Lyric. Cf. *DgF* 517; 2 st. of 28
—	—	Resan til Österland	—	?Brds	?	I Would Go to that Eastern Country	Wirén & Eyre, in J. Jonsson 40 (1955)	=GA2:235-39= GAB87	L M	Close	Lyric. Cf. *DgF* 517; 2 st. of 28

				Arist	17			SF3: No. 5	L M	Close	Lyric. Cf. *DgF* 516
—	—	Appelgården	—	Arist	17	I Know Where so Lovely a Garden Grows	D. Colbert, in Rossel, *Scand. Ball.* No. 32 (1982)	*SF*3: No. 5		Close	Lyric. Cf. *DgF* 516
—	—	Två jungfrur	Red	—	—	Two Maidens	Karpeles, *FS Eur.* No. 22 (1956)	Hollmérus/Andersson, =Andersson No. 60	L M	Interp	Swedish Finland Lyric
—	—	Unidentified	—	?Comm	?	Fair Gundela	Halliwell-Phillips 121-23 (1849)	Unidentified		N.I.	Ring-dance
—	—	Harald och unge Thor	Red	—	—	Untitled	Stephens, Rev. 26:33 (1840)	*SF*170		Interp	"Ballad pastiche"; 2 st. of 12

BIBLIOGRAPHY OF WORKS INCLUDING TRANSLATED BALLADS

The bibliography is organized conventionally by author, editor, or title, not by translator. In the tables, the author's or editor's name or the abbreviated title usually follows "in" when the translator is not also the editor or author. In some cases the translator is unidentified.

Included are occasional cross-references to abbreviations used in the tables and to names, pseudonyms, or abbreviations the user may encounter in the scholarly literature even though not used in the present work, e.g., "Talvj" for Therese Albertine Robinson. Works not seen are so indicated in brackets.

Capital letters in bold-face following each entry indicate the *original* languages of the ballads translated in the work. Some works, e.g., M. G. Lewis, *Tales of Wonder*, present translations of intermediate translations (see the "Notes" column in the tables).

Reviews of a work follow its entry, indented and in alphabetical order. Reviews which do not deal directly with the ballad translations in a work may be included if they throw some light on the aims, context, or expectations of that work. Reviews containing translations are also listed as main entries.

Abrahamsen, Povl and Erik Dal. *The Heart Book: The Tradition of the Danish Ballad.* Copenhagen: Royal Danish Ministry of Foreign Affairs, 1965. **DS**

Allwood, Martin S., ed. *Scandinavian Songs and Ballads: Modern Swedish, Danish and Norwegian Songs.* Trans. Martin S. Allwood, et al. 4th ed. Mullsjö, Sweden: Anglo-American Center, 1957. **D**

An Amateur [Richard Chandler Alexander Prior]. *Old Danish Ballads: Translated from Grimm's Collection.* London: Hope, 1856. **D**

   Rev. *Literary Gazette* 38 (1856): 250–51.

Rev. of *Ancient Danish Ballads*, by R. C. Alexander Prior. *Athenæum* [London] No. 1716 (15 Sept. 1860): 343–45. **DS**

Annandale, Nelson. *The Faroes and Iceland: Studies in the Island Life.* Oxford: Clarendon, 1905. **F**

[Anster, John], trans. "Nursery Rhymes." *Dublin University Magazine* 20 (1842): 614–17. D

B., W. "Scandinavian Ballad Poetry." Rev. of *Ballad Stories of the Affections, from the Scandinavian*, by Robert Buchanan. *St. James's Magazine* 18 (1867): 285–94. D

Ball. All Nations   See Borrow, George. *Ballads of All Nations.*

Rev. of *Ballad Stories of the Affections, from the Scandinavian*, by Robert Buchanan. *Spectator* 39 (1866): 1434–35. D

Balslev-Clausen, Peter, ed. *Songs from Denmark: A Collection of Danish Hymns, Songs and Ballads in English Translation.* Copenhagen: Danish Cultural Institute, 1988. D

Bantock, Granville, ed. *One Hundred Folksongs of All Nations.* Boston: O. Ditson, 1911. DNS

Barnes, Michael. "Draumkvæde—How Old Is It?" *Scandinavica* 2 (1972): 85–105. N

Batho, Edith. "Icelandic Ballads." *Saga-Book of the Viking Society* 10 (1928–29): 165–87. I

BDB   See Olrik, Axel. *A Book of Danish Ballads.*

Beal, Daniel. *Dances from Norway.* 2d ed. Minneapolis: [Sons of Norway], 1989. N

Berens, Herman, Jr. *Die Schönsten Volkslieder Schwedens. The Most Beautiful Swedish National Songs. Sveriges Skönaste Folkvisor.* Stockholm: Carl Gehrmans Musikforlag, [18—]. S

Beyer, Harald. *A History of Norwegian Literature.* Trans., ed. Einar Haugen. N.p.: New York UP, for American-Scandinavian Foundation, 1956. N

BfD   See Smith-Dampier, E. M. *Ballads from the Danish.*

Billeskov Jansen, F. J. and P. M. Mitchell, eds. *Anthology of Danish Literature.* Bilingual ed. 2 vols. Carbondale, IL: Southern Illinois UP, 1972. D

Bolin, Jakob, ed. *Swedish Song-Plays Used at the New York Normal School of Physical Education*. New York: Jakob Bolin, 1908. s

Borrow, George, trans. *Ballads of All Nations*. Ed. P. Brimley Johnson. London: Alston Rivers, 1927. DF

> Rev. *Bookman* 74 (1928): 66.

———, trans. "The Count of Vendil's Daughter." *Once a Week* 8 (Jan. 3, 1863): 35–36. D

———. "Danish Poetry and Ballad Writing." *The Monthly Magazine* 56 (1823): 306-09. D

———, trans. "The Deceived Merman." *The Monthly Magazine* 59 (1825): 143–44. D

———. *Romantic Ballads Translated from the Danish, and Miscellaneous Pieces*. Norwich: S. Wilkin and London: John Taylor, 1826. Norwich: Jarrold and New York: G. Putnam's, 1913. D

———, trans. *Targum: Or, Metrical Translations from Thirty Languages and Dialects*. St. Petersburg, Russia: Schulz and Beneze, 1835. D

———. *Works*. Ed. Clement Shorter. 16 vols. London: Constable, and New York: Gabriel Wells, 1923–24. Vols. 7–9 published as *The Songs of Scandinavia and Other Poems and Ballads*. 3 vols. DF

Borrow, George and John Bowring. Rev. of *Dansk-norsk Litteraturlexicon* and *Den Danske Digtekunsts Middelalder fra Arrebo til Tullin*, by K. L. Rahbek and R. Nyerup. *The Foreign Quarterly Review* 6 (June 1830): 48–87. D

Botsford, Florence Hudson, comp. and ed. *Botsford Collection of Folk-Songs: With English Versions by American Poets. Vol. 2. Northern Europe*. New York: G. Schirmer, 1931. DS

———, comp. and ed. *Folk-Songs of Many Peoples: With English Versions by American Poets*. 2 vols. New York: Woman's Press, 1922. DS

Bratli, Charles, trans. *Den Danske Studenter-Sangforenings Amerikafærd: 1911*. Copenhagen: Danish University Students' Choral Union, 1911. DS

Bredsdorff, Elias. "Medieval Danish Ballads." *Denmark* (London) Oct. 1949: 13–15. D

Bredsdorff, Elias, Brita Mortensen, and Ronald Popperwell. *An Introduction to Scandinavian Literature.* Cambridge, England: Cambridge UP, 1951. D

Brix, Hans. "The Spirit of the Ballad." *American-Scandinavian Review* 12 (1924): 761–64. D

Brodeur, Arthur G. "The Ballad of 'Ebbe Skammelson' and the 'Lover's Return.'" *Scandinavian Studies and Notes* 7, No. 7 (1923): 179–200. D

Brown, James Duff, ed. and Alfred W. Moffat. *Characteristic Songs and Dances of All Nations.* London: Bayley and Ferguson, 1901. DS

BSA   See Buchanan, Robert. *Ballad Stories of the Affections.*

Buchanan, Robert, trans. *Ballad Stories of the Affections, from the Scandinavian.* London: George Routledge, 1866. D

> Rev. W. B. "Scandinavian Ballad Poetry." *St. James's Magazine* 18 (1867): 285–94.
> Rev. *Spectator* 39 (1866): 1434–35.

———. *Master-Spirits.* London: Henry S. King, 1874. D

———. "The Old Ballads of Denmark." *The Fortnightly Review* 1 (1865): 685–96. D

[Bushby, Anne S.] "The Ballads and Traditions of Northern Europe." *New Monthly Magazine* 130 (1864): 479–99; 131 (1864): 39–49. DS

Bushby, [Anne S.], trans. "Holger Danske and Stark Diderik. Translated from the Danish." *Bentley's Miscellany* 49 (Jan. 1861): 53–54. D

Bushby, Anne S. *Poems by the Late Anne S. Bushby.* London, 1876. D

Butler, Pierce, trans. *Axel and Valborg: A Tragedy in Five Acts.* By Adam Oehlenschläger. Ed. Professor Palmer. London: Trübner, 1874. D

Bø, Olav. "'Margjit og Targjei Risvollo': The Classic Triangle in a Norwegian Medieval Ballad." *Narrative Folksong: New Directions. Essays in*

Appreciation of W. Edson Richmond. Ed. Carol L. Edwards and Kathleen E. B. Manley. Boulder, CO: Westview, 1985. 284–301.   N

Cagner, Ewert, comp. and ed. *Swedish Christmas Celebration.* Trans. Yvonne Aboav-Elmquist. Songs, poems trans. Byron E. Underwood. Gothenburg: Tre Tryckare, 1963. Reprint of *Swedish Christmas.* 1955.   S

Campbell, Olive D., ed. *Singing Games and Folk Dances.* Trans. Georg Bidstrup and Marguerite Bidstrup. Brasstown, NC: John C. Campbell Folk School, 1941.   D

———, ed. *Singing Games Old and New.* Trans. Georg Bidstrup and Marguerite Bidstrup. Swannanoa, NC: Asheville Farm School, 1932.   D

Carpenter, William H. "Folk-Songs of the Faroe Islands." *New Englander* 41 (1882): 406–13.   F

Carrick, J. and J. Carrick, comps. *The Charms of Melody.* Dublin, 1810 to 1820. [Not seen.]   D

Chadwick, Nora. See Kershaw, Nora.

Child, Francis James, ed. *English and Scottish Ballads.* 8 vols. The British Poets. Boston: Little, Brown, 1857–59.   D

———, ed. *English and Scottish Ballads.* 2nd ed. 8 vols. The British Poets. Boston: Little, Brown, 1860.   D

———, ed. *The English and Scottish Popular Ballads.* 5 vols. Boston: Houghton Mifflin, 1882-98.   DFINS

Christophersen, Paul. *The Ballad of Sir Aldingar: Its Origins and Analogues.* Oxford: Oxford UP, 1952.   DFIN

Colbert, David. "The Danish Bower Ballad: A Seminal Type." *Ballads and Ballad Research. Selected Papers of the International Conference on Nordic and Anglo-American Ballad Research. University of Washington, Seattle, May 2–6, 1977.* Ed. Patricia Conroy. Seattle: U Washington, 1978. 7–16.   D

A Collection of Swedish National Music: Containing the Most Beautiful Folk-Songs and Dances for Piano. Stockholm: A. Lundquist, [c. 1925].   s

Conroy, Patricia. "Ballad Composition in Faroese Heroic Tradition: The Case of Hernilds kvæði." *Fróðskaparrit* 27 (1979): 75–101.   FN

———. "Creativity in Oral Transmission. An Example from Faroese Ballad Tradition." *ARV* 35 (1979): 25–48.   F

———. "Faroese Ballads and Oral-Formulaic Composition." Diss. U California Berkeley, 1974.   F

———. "Oral Composition in Faroese Ballads." *Jahrbuch für Volksliedforschung* 25 (1980): 34–50.   F

Cooperative Recreation Service. *The Handy Folk Dance Book.* Delaware, Ohio: Cooperative Recreation Service, [c. 1955].   D

Coppée, Henry, ed. *The American Library of Art Literature & Song.* 6 vols. Philadelphia: Carson, Stuart, 1886.   D

Crawford, Caroline. *Folk Dances and Games.* New York: A. S. Barnes, 1909.   F

Creekmore, Hubert, ed. *A Little Treasury of World Poetry.* New York: Charles Scribner's Sons, 1952.   DS

———, ed. *Lyrics of the Middle Ages.* New York: Grove, 1959. New York: Greenwood, 1969.   DS

Dal, Erik, ed. *Danish Ballads and Folk Songs.* Trans. Henry Meyer. Copenhagen: Rosenkilde og Bagger; New York: American-Scandinavian Foundation, 1967.   D

   Rev. Jan H. Brunvand. *Journal of American Folklore* 81 (1968): 364–65.
   Rev. David Fowler. *Scandinavian Studies* 40 (1968): 166–69.
   Rev. Alisoun Gardner-Medwin. *Scandinavica* 7 (1968): 77–78.
   Rev. Aage Jørgensen. *Folk-lore* 79 (1968): 77–78.
   Rev. Douglas J. McMillan. *Medium Ævum* 37 (1968): 221–23.
   Rev. Daniel W. Patterson. *Southern Folklore Quarterly* 32 (1968): 70–71.

Rev. Archer Taylor. *American-Scandinavian Review* 56.2 (1968): 196.
Rev. *Times Literary Supplement* 14 Sept. 1967: 821.

DB See Smith-Dampier, E. M. *Danish Ballads*.

DBFS See Dal, Erik. *Danish Ballads and Folk Songs*.

Delaware Tercentenary, 1638–1938. Wilmington, DE: Delaware Tercentenary Commission, 1938. s

Deutsch, Leonhard, comp. and arr. *A Treasury of the World's Finest Folk Song*. Trans. Willard Trask. N.Y.: Howell, Soskin, 1942. d

———, comp. and arr. *A Treasury of the World's Finest Folk Song*. New ed. Trans. Willard Trask. New York: Crown, 1967. d

Dixon, James H. "Contributions from Foreign Ballad Literature: Sir Olaf and the Fairy Dance." *Notes and Queries* 4th ser. 1 (1868): 292. s

[Drummond-Davies, F. M.] "Ancient Danish Ballads." Rev. of *Ancient Danish Ballads*, by R. C. Alexander Prior. *Westminster Review* 75 (1861): 1–33. d

Ellingboe, Bradley, trans. and ed. *Forty Five Songs of Edvard Grieg*. Geneseo, NY: Leyerle, 1988. n

Entwistle, William J. *European Balladry*. London: Oxford UP, 1939. ds

F., J., trans. "Elvershöh." *Blackwood's Edinburgh Magazine* 1 (1817): 624. d

Fausböll, Annie J., see Smith-Dampier, et al.

Flom, George T. "The Faroese Ballad of Ellindur Bóndi á Jadri." *Scandinavian Studies* 18 (1945): 165–82. f

FM See Keightley, Thomas. *The Fairy Mythology*.

Folk-Songs of Other Lands. London: Novello, n.d. n

Forestier, Auber [Anna Aubertine Woodward Moore] and Rasmus B. Anderson, eds. and trans. *The Norway Music Album: A Selection for Home Use*. Boston: Oliver Ditson, 1881. n

Freeland, H. W., trans. *Axel and Valborg: A Tragedy*. By Adam Oehlenschläger. London: n.p., n.d.   D

"Fru Ingelil's Daughters." *American-Scandinavian Review* 12 (1924): 753–60. D

Ganschow, Theodore F., comp. *Memories of Sweden: A Collection of It's [sic] Best-loved Melodies with English and the Original Swedish Text for Voice and Piano or Guitar*. Trans. Olga Paul. New York: Edward B. Marks, 1937. S

Gardner-Medwin, Alisoun. "Miss Reburn's Ballads: A Nineteenth-Century Repertoire from Ireland." *Ballad Studies*. Ed. E[mily] B. Lyle. Cambridge: D. S. Brewer for The Folklore Society, 1976. 93–116.   D

———. "Paradise on Earth? A Study of a Motif in Danish Ballads." *Folklore* (London) 74 (1963): 305–17.   DN

Gilbert, Henry F., ed. *One Hundred Folk-Songs: From Many Countries*. Boston: C. C. Birchard, 1910.   DN

Gilchrist, Anne G. "'Death and the Lady' in English Balladry." *Journal of the English Folk Dance and Song Society* 4 (1940): 37–48.   S

Gordon, Elias, ed. and trans. *Bards of the North: Favorite Verses and Folk Songs from the Russian, Scandinavian and Finnish*. New York: American Cultural Foundation P, 1936.   S

Grainger, Percy. *Danish Folk-Music Suite: The Power of Love*. New York: G. Schirmer, [c. 1950].   D

———, trans. *Hubby & Wifey, for Voices (Woman's & Man's) and Piano*. Danish Folk-Music Settings Nr. 5. Aylesbury, England: Bardic Edition, n.d. D

———, trans. *Lord Peter's Stableboy: Chosen Verses*. Ts. n.d. Grainger Society Archive, Aylesbury, England.   D

———. *The Merry Wedding (Brúnsveins Visa): Bridal Dance*. Trans. Rose Grainger and Percy Grainger. For 9 Solo Voices, Mixed Chorus, and Orchestra. Bryn Mawr, PA: Oliver Ditson, [1916].   F

————. *The Nightingale and the Two Sisters.* New York: G. Schirmer, 1931. **D**

————, trans. *The Old Woman at the Christening: For Voice (Woman's or Man's), Piano and Harmonium.* Danish Folk-Music Settings No. 11. Aylesbury, England: Bardic Edition, 1994. **D**

————, trans. *The Power of Love: for Voice . . . and Piano.* Aylesbury, England: Bardic Edition, 1991. **D**

————, trans. *The Rival Brothers (Hjálmar og Angantýr).* Short version for piano solo. Sketched for solo voices, chorus & chamber-music, 1905, 1931, 1938, 1943. Photocopy of ts. Grainger Society Archive, Aylesbury, England. **F**

————, trans. *The Rival Brothers (1905).* Collated from the set of manuscript parts in the National Library of Scotland. Aylesbury, England: Bardic Edition, n.d. **F**

————, trans. *Sketches for The Rival Brothers (Hjálmar og Angantýr).* Ms. Grainger Society Archive, Aylesbury, England. n.d. **F**

————. *Thirteen Folksongs.* Ed. David Tall. Vol. 1. London: Thames, 1981. **D**

————, trans. *Two Danish Folksongs: Collected in Jutland by Evald Tang Kristensen and Percy Aldridge Grainger.* Ts. 1951. Grainger Society Archive, Aylesbury, England. **D**

————, trans. *Two Musical Relics of My Mother. Nr. 1. "Hermundur Illi" (Hermund the Evil).* New York: G. Schirmer, 1924. **F**

Gray, Alexander, trans. *Arrows: A Book of German Ballads and Folk-Songs Attempted in Scots.* Edinburgh: Grant and Murray, 1932. **D**

————, trans. *Four-and-Forty: A Selection of Danish Ballads Presented in Scots.* Edinburgh: Edinburgh UP, 1954. **D**

Rev. Erik Dal. *Danske Studier* 1955: 129–30.

————, trans. *Historical Ballads of Denmark.* Edinburgh: Edinburgh UP, 1958. **DI**

Rev. D. P. Bliss. *The Twentieth Century* 166 (1959): 122–23.

Rev. Erik Dal. *Scandinavica* 1 (1962): 75.

Rev. Douglas Young. *Scottish Historical Review* 39 (1960): 61.

————, trans. *Songs and Ballads, Chiefly from Heine.* Edinburgh: Grant Richards, 1920. Chicago: Corici-McGee, 1924.   D

Greenwood, Thomas. *The First Book of the History of the Germans.* London, 1836. [Not seen]   S

Grieg, Edvard. *Excerpts from Album for Male Voices Based on Norwegian Folksongs.* Op. 30. Trans. Percy Grainger. Leipzig: C. F. Peters, 1925.   N

————. *Samlede Verker. Gesamtausgabe. Complete Works.* Vol. 14. Ed. Dan Fog and Nils Grinde. Trans. W. H. Halverson. Frankfurt: C. F. Peters, 1990.   N

Grimm, Wilhelm [Carl], ed. *Drei Altschottische Lieder in Original und Uebersetsung aus Zwei Neuen Sammlungen.* Heidelberg: Mohr & Zimmer, 1813.   D

Grundtvig, Svend. "En Märkelig Vise om de Söfarne Mänd. An Old Danish Ballad." *Acta Comparationis Litterarum Vniversarum,* novae seriei 3, no. 7–8 (1880): 95–98.   D

————. *En Märkelig Vise om de Søfarne Mänd: An Old Danish Ballad.* Kolozsvár, 1880.   D

————. "En Märkelig Vise om de Söfarne Mänd. An Old Danish Ballad." *Folklore Record* 3 Pt. 2 (1881): 253–57.   D

Hägg, Gustaf, comp. and ed. *Songs of Sweden: Eighty-Seven Swedish Folk- and Popular Songs.* Trans. Henry Grafton Chapman. New York: G. Schirmer, 1909.   S

Halliwell-Phillips, James Orchard. *Popular Rhymes and Nursery Tales.* London: John Russell Smith, 1849.   S

Hallmundsson, Hallberg, ed. *An Anthology of Scandinavian Literature: From the Viking Period to the Twentieth Century.* New York: Collier; London: Collier-Macmillan, 1965.   DINS

————, trans. "A Northern Orpheus." *American Scandinavian Review* 50 (1962): 267–71. I

The Hals Album: A Collection of Norse National Music, Containing the Most Popular Folk-songs, Dances &c., and also Compositions by Various Norse Composers. Kristiania: Brödrene Hals, [c. 1890]. N

[Hansen, Carl G. O. and Frederick Wick, eds.] *Sons of Norway Songbook: A Collection of Norway's Most Popular Folk Songs, Patriotic Songs, and Ballads.* [Trans. Carl G. O. Hansen.] 1948. Minneapolis: Sons of Norway, 1967. N

Haraldsted, Leif, comp. *Danish National Music: National Songs, Morning and Evening Songs, Folk Songs and the Most Popular Danish Music to Operas and Plays.* Trans. Evelyn Heepe and Charles Bratli. København: W. Hansen, 1939. D

Haugaard, Dan. *Songs of Denmark.* LP. New York: Folkways, 1957. D

Haywood, Charles, ed. *Folk Songs of the World.* New York: John Day, 1966. New York: Bantam, 1968. S

Herbert, William. *Herbert's Poems.* 2 vols. London, 1804–38. D

————. *Translations from the German, Danish, &c. to Which is Added Miscellaneous Poetry.* London, 1804. D

　　Rev. *The Critical Review* 3rd ser. 10 (1807): 37–52.
　　Rev. [John Finlay]. *The Monthly Review* 52 (1807): 355–66.
　　Rev. Walter Scott. "Herbert's Poems." *Edinburgh Review* 9 (1806): 211–23.

————. *Works.* Vol. 1. London: H. G. Bohn, 1842. D

Hill, Joyce, ed. *The Tristan Legend: Texts from Northern and Eastern Europe in Modern English Translation.* Leeds: U of Leeds Graduate Center for Medieval Studies, 1977. DFI

Holst, Olav. "Engelske Oversættelser af danske Folkeviser." *Danske Studier* 36 (1941): 113–20. D

Holzapfel, Otto. "Narrative Technique in the German and Danish Ballads—A Stylistic Sample." *The Ballad as Narrative.* Ed. Flemming G. Andersen, Otto Holzapfel, and Thomas Pettitt. Odense: Odense UP, 1982. 110–52.   D

Howitt, William and Mary Howitt. *The Literature and Romance of Northern Europe.* 2 vols. London: Colburn, 1852.   DS

> Rev. Edward Charlton. *Dublin Review* 33 (1852): 112–39.
> Rev. *Eclectic Review* 95 (1852): 592–605.
> Rev. Hannah Lawrance. *British Quarterly Review* 15 (1852): 425–53.

Hughes, S[ean] F. D. "'Völsunga rímur' and 'Sjúrðar kvæði': Romance and Ballad, Ballad and Dance." *Ballads and Ballad Research: Selected Papers of the International Conference on Nordic and Anglo-American Ballad Research, University of Washington, Seattle, May 2–6, 1977.* Ed. Patricia Conroy. Seattle: U Washington, 1978. 37–45.   F

Hull, Myra E. "The Merman Lover in Ballad and Song." *Studies in English in Honor of Raphael Dorman O'Leary and Selden Lincoln Whitcomb.* University of Kansas Humanistic Studies 6. Lawrence, KS: U of Kansas English Department, 1940.   D

Hægstad, Marius, ed. *Hildinakvadet: med utgreiding um det norske maal paa Shetland i eldre tid.* Videnskabsselskabets skrifter. II. Historisk-filosofiske klasse. 1900. No. 2. Christiania: Jacob Dybwad, 1900.   **Shetl.**

INA   See Weber, Henry.

Isaksson, Ulla. *The Virgin Spring.* Trans. Lars Malmström and David Kushner. New York: Ballantyne, 1960.   S

Jacobsen, Per Schelde and Barbara Fass Leavy. *Ibsen's Forsaken Merman: Folklore in the Late Plays.* New York: New York UP, 1988.   D

Jamieson, Robert. *Illustrations of Northern Antiquities.*   See Weber, Henry, Robert Jamieson, and Walter Scott.

———. *Popular Ballads and Songs.* 2 vols. Edinburgh: Archibald Constable, 1806.   D

Rev. *The Critical Review* 3rd ser. 9 (1806): 303–13.
Rev. [John Finlay.] *Monthly Review; or Literary Journal* 52 (1807): 19–31.
Rev. *Literary Panorama and National Register* 1 (Dec. 1806): col. 472–81.
Rev. [? William Taylor]. *Annual Review and History of Literature* 5 (1806): 534–35.

Johnson, Jakobina, trans. *Northern Lights: Icelandic Poems.* Reykjavík: Bókaútgáfa Menningarsjóðs, 1959. I

Johnstone, James, trans. *The Robbing of the Nunnery; or The Abbess Out-Witted.* [Copenhagen], 1786. D

Jonsson, Bengt. "Oral Literature, Written Literature: The Ballad and Old Norse Genres." *The Ballad and Oral Literature.* Ed. Joseph Harris. Cambridge, MA: Harvard UP, 1991. 139–70. S

Jonsson, Josef. *Sweden Sings: Ballads, Folk-Songs and Dances.* Photogr., text by Karl Werner Gullers. Trans. Noel Wirén and Leonard B. Eyre. Stockholm: Nordiska Musikförlaget, 1955. S

Jorgenson, Theodore, trans. *Norwegian Ballads.* Duplicated ts. Various pagings. St. Olaf College Library. 1950. N

———, ed. and trans. *The Trumpet of Nordland by Petter Dass and Other Masterpieces of Norwegian Poetry from the Period, 1250–1700.* Northfield, MN: St Olaf College P, 1954. N

Rev. R. Dittman. *Scandinavian Studies* 27 (1955): 32–35.
Rev. Erik J. Friis. *American-Scandinavian Review* 43.2 (1955): 206.

Kaines, Joseph, comp. *Love Poems of All Nations.* London: Basil Montagu Pickering, 1870. DS

Kappey, J. A., ed. *Songs of Scandinavia and Northern Europe: A Collection of 83 National and Popular Songs of Russia, Poland, Lithuania, Finland, Sweden, Norway, Denmark, and Holland.* Trans. Clara Kappey. 1882. London: Boosey, [c. 1905]. NS

Karpeles, Maud, ed. *Folk Songs of Europe.* International Folk Song Anthologies, for the International Folk Music Council. London: Novello, 1956. New York: Oak, 1964. DFINS

Rev. Violet Alford. *Folklore* 68 (1957): 309.

Rev. Tristram P. Coffin. *Journal of American Folklore* 71 (1958): 171–72.

Rev. W. Edson Richmond. *Western Folklore* 25 (1966): 218.

Rev. S. J. Sackett. *Journal of American Folklore* 81 (1968): 79–81.

Rev. D. K. Wilgus. *Midwest Folklore* 8 (1958): 107.

Kastman, Valborg and Greta Köhler. *Swedish Song Games: A Collection of Games for School, Home, and Playground Use.* Boston: Ginn, 1913.   FN

Keightley, Thomas. *The Fairy Mythology: Illustrative of the Romance and Superstition of Various Countries.* 2 vols. London: Whittaker, Treacher, 1828.   S

————. *The Fairy Mythology: Illustrative of the Romance and Superstition of Various Countries.* Rev. and enl. ed. London: Bohn's Antiquarian Library, 1850. [Reprintings through 1910]   S

[————]. "Scandinavian Mythology." *Foreign Quarterly Review* 4 (April 1829): 102–39.   D

————. *The World Guide to Gnomes, Fairies, Elves and Other Little People.* New York: Avenel-Crown, 1978. Reprint of *The Fairy Mythology: Illustrative of the Romance and Superstition of Various Countries.* Rev., enl. ed. 1850.   S

Rev. Alison Lurie. *The New York Review of Books* 26.3 (8 March 1979): 16–19.

Kemppinen, Iivar. *The Ballad of Lady Isabel and the False Knight.* Diss. Helsinki, 1954.   D

Kenealy, Edward Vaughan. *Poems and Translations.* London: Reeves and Turner, 1864.   DS

Rev. *The Reader* 2 (19 Dec. 1864): 721–22.

————. *Poetical Works.* 3 vols. London: Englishman Office, 1875–79.   DS

————, trans. "Swedish Anthology." *Ainsworth's Magazine* 9 (1846): 111–22.   S

Ker, W[illiam] P[aton]. *Collected Essays.* Ed. Charles Whibley. 2 vols. London: Macmillan, 1925.   DIS

———. *Epic and Romance: Essays on Medieval Literature*. London: Macmillan, 1897. D

———. "On the Danish Ballads." *Scottish Historical Review* 1 (1904): 357–78; 5 (1908): 385–401. DIS

Kershaw, N[ora], trans. *Stories and Ballads of the Far Past*. Cambridge, England: Cambridge UP, 1921. [Later Nora Kershaw Chadwick] D

Rev. Francis Burrows. *The London Mercury* 4 (1921): 437–39.

Kingsley, Charles. *Historical Lectures and Essays*. London: Macmillan, 1880. F

———. *Lectures Delivered in America in 1874*. Philadelphia: Coates; London: Longmans Green, 1875. F

Kirkconnell, Watson, trans. *The North American Book of Icelandic Verse*. New York: Louis Carrier and Alan Isles, 1930. I

Knudsen, Dina, trans. *55 of the Best Known Scandinavian Songs*. Breckenridge, TX: n.p., n.d. N

Kolle, Frederick Strange, trans. *Axel and Valborg: An Historical Tragedy in Four Acts*. By Adam Oehlenschläger. New York: Grafton, [1906]. D

Krogsæter, Johan. *Folk Dancing in Norway*. Oslo: Johan Grundt Tanum, 1968. N

Krone, Beatrice Perham and Ruth Vivian Ostlund. *Songs of Norway and Denmark*. Chicago: Neil A. Kjos, 1941. DN

———. *Songs of Sweden and Finland*. Chicago: Neil A. Kjos, 1942. NS

L., D. H., trans. "The Erl-King's Daughter." *Athenæum* 3, No. 124 (March 13, 1830): 153–54. D

Leach, Henry Goddard. *Angevin Britain and Scandinavia*. Harvard Studies in Comparative Literature 6. Cambridge, MA: Harvard UP, 1921. DI

———, ed. *A Pageant of Old Scandinavia*. Princeton, NJ: Princeton UP for American-Scandinavian Foundation, 1946. Freeport, NY: Books for Libraries Press, 1968. DFI

Leach, MacEdward, ed. *The Ballad Book.* New York: A. S. Barnes, 1955. D

[Lewis, Matthew Gregory], trans. "The Erl-King's Daughter." *The Monthly Mirror* 2 (1796): 371–73. D

Lewis, M[atthew] G[regory]. *The Monk.* Ed. Howard Anderson. London: Oxford UP, 1973. Orig. pub. London, 1796. D

———. *Tales of Wonder.* 2. vols. London: W. Bulmer, 1801. D

> Rev. *Antijacobin Review* 8 (Mar. 1801): 322–37.
> Rev. *British Critic* 16 (Dec. 1800): 681. [Not seen]
> Rev. *Monthly Magazine* Suppl. vol. 8 (July 20, 1801): 605–06.
> Rev. *Poetical Register* 1 (1801): 436. [Not seen]

[———]. "The Water-King." *Scots Magazine* 59 (March 1797): 197. D

Lewis, Thomas P., ed. *A Source Guide to the Music of Percy Grainger.* White Plains, NY: Pro/Am Music Resources, 1991. D

Liestøl, Knut. *Draumkvæde: A Norwegian Visionary Poem from the Middle Ages.* Trans. Illit Grøndahl. Studia Norvegica No. 3. Oslo, 1946. FIN

> Rev. William J. Entwistle. *Modern Language Review* 43 (1948): 123–24.

Rev. of *Literature and Romance of Northern Europe,* by William Howitt and Mary Howitt. *British Quarterly Review* 15 (1852): 425–53. S

Lloyd, L. *Peasant Life in Sweden.* London: Tinsley, 1870. New York: AMS, 1982. S

Loewe, Carl. *Twelve Songs and Ballads.* Trans. Th. Baker. 2 vols. New York: Schirmer, 1903. D

Longfellow, Henry Wadsworth. *Aftermath.* Boston: James R. Osgood, 1873. D

———. *Ballads and Other Poems.* Cambridge, MA: J. Owen, 1842. [Not seen] D

———. *Complete Poetical Works.* Cambridge ed. Boston: Houghton Mifflin, 1893. D

———, ed. *Poems of Places.* Vol. 8. Boston: James R. Osgood, 1876. D

———. *Poetical Works.* New York: Wm. L. Allison, n.d. D

————, ed. *The Poets and Poetry of Europe*. Philadelphia: Carey and Hart, 1847.
DS

————. *Tales of a Wayside Inn*. Boston: Houghton Mifflin, 1873. [Earlier editions without translated ballad]   **D**

————. *Works: With Bibliographical and Critical Notes and His Life*. 14 vols. New York: AMS Press, 1966.   **D**

Lorentzen, Paul. "Folk Dances in Denmark." *American-Scandinavian Review* 18 (1930): 612–22.   **D**

Low, George. *A Tour through the Islands of Orkney and Schetland*. Kirkwall: Joseph Anderson, 1879. [Not seen]   **Shetl.**

Luboff, Norman and Win Stracke, eds. *Songs of Man: The International Book of Folk Songs*. Englewood Cliffs, NJ: Prentice-Hall; New York: Walton Music, 1965.   **D**

Lund, Engel, comp. *A Second Book of Folk-Songs: With Pianoforte Accompaniments*. Trans. Ursula Wood. London: Oxford UP, 1947.   **D**

McConathy, Osbourne, John Beattie, and Russel V. Morgan, eds. *Music Highways and Byways*. New York: Silver Burdett, 1936.   **S**

Mangan, James Clarence, trans. *Anthologia Germanica. German Anthology*. 2 vols. Dublin: William Curry; London: Longmans, Brown, 1845.   **D**

————. *Poems*. Ed. John Mitchel. New York: P. M. Haverty, 1894.   **D**

[————], trans. "Stray Leaflets from the German Oak - 2d drift." *Dublin University Magazine* 15 (1840): 625–34.   **D**

Marzo, Eduardo, ed. *Sixty Carols of All Nations for All Occasions*. Cincinnati: Willis Music, [c. 1928].   **S**

Masters, Brien, comp. and ed. *The Waldorf Song Book*. Southampton, England: Floris, 1987.   **F**

MBfD   See Smith-Dampier, E. M. *More Ballads from the Danish*.

Melby, Frida, trans. Folk Song in the Faroe Islands. By Hjalmar Thuren. Ts. U of Wisconsin-Madison Library. 1914. DF

Merry, Eleanor C., trans. *The Dream Song of Olaf Åsteson*. Ill. from paintings by author. East Grinstead, England: New Knowledge Press, 1961. N

Metcalfe, Frederick. *The Oxonian in Iceland; or, Notes on Travel in that Island in the Summer of 1860*. London: Longman, Green, Longman, and Roberts, 1861. FI

Meyer, Henry, trans. *Danish Ballads and Folk Songs*.   See Dal, Erik.

Milligan, Sophia. *Original Poems: With Translations from Scandinavian and Other Poets*. London: Hurst and Blackett, 1856. D

Moe, Moltke. *Samlede Skrifter*. Ed. Knut Liestøl. Vol. 3. Oslo: H. Aschehoug, 1927. N

Morris, May. *William Morris: Artist Writer Socialist*. 2 vols. Oxford: Basil Blackwell, 1936. S

Morris, William, trans. "Axel Thordson and Fair Walborg." May Morris papers. [Not seen. Cited in K. O. E. Anderson, "Scandinavian Elements in the Works of William Morris," diss., Harvard U. 1942, 147–48.] D

———. *Collected Works*. Ed. May Morris. Vols. 9 and 24. London: Longmans, Green, 1911, 1915. DI

———. *Poems by the Way*. Printed at the Kelmscott Press. London: Reeves & Turner, 1891. DI

———. *Poems by the Way & Love Is Enough*. London: Longmans, Green, 1896. DI

NKB See Smith-Dampier, E. M. *The Norse King's Bridal*.

Norsk Nationalalbum. English-Norwegian Edition. A Collection of Norse National Music Containing the Most Popular Folk-songs, Dances, etc., and also Compositions by Various Norse Composers. Oslo: Norsk Musikforlag, n.d. N

Den Norske Studentersangforening. The Norwegian Royal University Chorus. American Tour 1939. Oslo, n.p., n.d. NS

Norway Sings: A Collection of Norwegian Folk Music. Trans. Christopher Norman [Ragnar Christophersen]. English-Norwegian ed. Oslo: Norsk Musikforlag, 1950. N

Norwegian National Music: 50 Folk Songs, Dances, etc. and also Compositions by Various Norwegian Composers. New York: Norwegian-American Music Co., n.d. N

Nygard, Holger Olof. "The Icelandic Ásu Kvæthi: The Narrative Metamorphosis of a Folksong." *Midwest Folklore* 5 (1955): 141–51. I

Ólason, Vésteinn. "Literary Backgrounds of the Scandinavian Ballad." *The Ballad and Oral Literature.* Ed. Joseph Harris. Cambridge, MA: Harvard UP, 1991. 116–38. FN

———. "Saint Olaf in Late Medieval Icelandic Poetry." *Narrative Folksong: New Directions.* Ed. Carol L. Edwards and Kathleen E. B. Manley. Boulder, CO: Westview, 1985. 2–17. I

———. *The Traditional Ballads of Iceland: Historical Studies.* Ballads trans. Sverrir Hólmarsson. Reykjavík: Stofnun Árna Magnússonar, 1982. I

Rev. of *Old Danish Ballads,* by An Amateur. *The Literary Gazette* 38 (1856): 250–51. D

Olrik, Axel, ed. *A Book of Danish Ballads.* Trans. E. M. Smith-Dampier. Princeton: Princeton UP for American-Scandinavian Foundation, 1939. DIS

> Rev. Grover I. Cronin. *Thought* 15 (1940): 172–73.
> Rev. Gordon Hall Gerould. *American-Scandinavian Review* 27.4 (1939): 372.
> Rev. Lee M. Hollander. *Modern Language Journal* 25 (1940): 157–58.
> Rev. S[igurd] B. Hustvedt. *Journal of American Folklore* 56 (1943): 93–94.
> Rev. Kemp Malone. *Modern Language Notes* 57 (1942): 79.
> Rev. Britta Mortensen. *Folk-lore* 51 (1940): 233–36.

Olsen, Sparre. *Draumkvædet. The Dream-Lay. Op. 22.* [Trans. Illit Grøndahl.] Oslo: Norsk Musikforlag, 1952. N

————, comp. and ed. *Norske Folkevisur. Norwegian Folk Songs. Nr. 1. Fra Gudbrandsdalen*. Trans. Percy Grainger. Oslo: Norsk Musikforlag, [1946]. N

"On the Songs of the People of Gothic or Teutonic Race." *London Magazine* 3 (1821): 143–53; 4 (1821): 41–47, 412–17. D

"On the State of the Cultivation of the Ancient Literature of the North at the Present Period." *London Magazine* 1 (1820): 391–401. D

PBS See Jamieson, Robert. *Popular Ballads and Songs.*

Peed, John H. "Edvard Grieg: An Analytical Survey of the Unaccompanied Partsongs for Male Chorus." D. A. diss. U Northern Colorado, 1989. N

People's Institute, New York. *Six Centuries of Folk Songs of Europe and North America. Fifteen Concerts. Jan. 21–April 29, 1919*. Concert 9. New York: Music League of the People's Institute, 1919. S

Peterson, Frederick. *Poems and Swedish Translations*. Buffalo, NY: P. Paul, 1883. S

Piø, Iørn. "'Ebbe Skammelsøn' (DgF 354): A Sixteenth-Century Broadside Ballad." *Narrative Folksong: New Directions*. Ed. Carol L. Edwards and Kathleen E. B. Manley. Boulder, CO: Westview, 1985. 18–57. D

PoP See Longfellow, Henry Wadsworth. *Poems of Places.*

Rev. of *Popular Ballads and Songs*, by Robert Jamieson. *Literary Panorama and National Register* 1 (Dec. 1806): col. 472–81. D

Powell, F. York, trans. *The Tale of Thrond of Gate Commonly Called Færeyinga Saga*. London, D. Nutt, 1896. F

PPE See Longfellow, Henry Wadsworth. *Poets and Poetry of Europe.*

Prior, R[ichard] C[handler] Alexander. *Ancient Danish Ballads Translated from the Originals*. 3 vols. London and Edinburgh: Williams and Norgate, 1860. DFS

Rev. *Atheneum* [London] No. 1716 (15 Sept. 1860): 343–45.
Rev. Robert Buchanan. *The Fortnightly* 3 (1865): 253.
Rev. [F. M. Drummond-Davies]. *Westminster Review* 75 (1861): 1–33.
Rev. *North American Review* 92 (1861): 588–89.
Rev. [Whitley Stokes]. "Danish Ballads II." *Saturday Review* 11 (1861): 46–48.

Præstgaard Andersen, Lise. "The Development of the Genres—the Danish Ballad." Trans. Gillian Fellows Jensen. *Sumlen* 1981: 25–35.   D

Read, Donald, ed. *Songs of the United Nations Singers*. New York: Dodd, Mead, 1965.   D

Reburn, Margaret. Letter of March 6, 1882 to Francis J. Child. Child Mss. Vol. 18 (25241.47F*). Harvard College Library.   D

Reed, Edward Bliss, ed. *Swiss, English and Swedish Carols*. Arr. David Stanley Smith. Pub. of the Carol Society 11. London: Stainer and Bell, 1934.   S

Richmond, W. Edson. "'Den utrue egtemann': A Norwegian Ballad and Formulaic Composition." *Norveg: Folkelivsgransking* 10 (1963): 59–88.   N

———. "Esse est percipi: A Poetic Genre Created by Perceptions." *Inte bara visor: Studier kring folklig diktning och music tillägnada Bengt R. Jonsson den 19 Mars 1990*. Ed. Sven-Bertil Jansen, et al. Stockholm: Svenskt Visarkiv, 1990.   N

———. "From Edda and Saga to Ballad: A Troll Bridge." *Folklore Studies in Honour of Herbert Halpert*. Ed. Kenneth S. Goldstein and Neil V. Rosenberg. St. John's, Newfoundland: Memorial U, 1980. 303–13.   N

———. "*Paris og Helen i Trejeborg*: A Reduction to Essentials." *Medieval Literature and Folklore Studies*. Ed. Jerome Mandel and Bruce A. Rosenberg. Rutgers, NJ: Rutgers UP, 1970. 229–43, 369–75.   N

———. "'Stig liten fell.' An Edition of Some Previously Unpublished Texts of a Scandinavian Ballad." *ARV* 14 (1958): 33–44.   D

[Robinson, Therese Albertine L.] "Popular Poetry of the Teutonic Nations." *North American Review* 42 (1836): 265–339.   DS

Rodholm, S[øren] D[amsgaard]. *A Harvest of Song: Translations and Original Lyrics*. Des Moines: Committee on Publications, American Evangelical Lutheran Church, 1953. D

Rohrbough, Lynn, ed. *Handy Play Party Book. Singing Games and Folk Songs*. Delaware, Ohio: Cooperative Recreation Service, 1940. [Several other eds.] S

Rom. Ball. See Borrow, George. *Romantic Ballads*.

Rossel, Sven H., ed. *Scandinavian Ballads*. Wisconsin Introductions to Scandinavia II No. 2. Madison, WI: U Wisconsin Dept. Scandinavian Studies, 1982. DINS

Ruud, Martin B. "The Draumkvæde: A Norwegian Vision Poem of the Thirteenth Century." *Scandinavian Studies and Notes* 7 (1922): 52–57. N

Schach, Paul. "Tristan and Isolde in Scandinavian Ballad and Folktale." *Scandinavian Studies* 36 (1964): 281–97. D

Schlauch, Margaret. *Medieval Narrative. A Book of Translations*. New York: Prentice-Hall, 1928. I

Scott, Walter. "Herbert's Poems." Rev. of *Miscellaneous Poetry*, by William Herbert. *Edinburgh Review* 8 (1806): 211–23. D

———. *The Lady of the Lake. A Poem*. Edinburgh: John Ballantyne, 1810. [This ed. not seen] D

———. *Miscellaneous Prose Works*. Vol. 17. Edinburgh, 1835. D

———. *Poetical Works*. Ed. J. Logie Robertson. London: Oxford UP, 1904. D

SD-S See Smith-Dampier, E. M. *Sigurd the Dragon-Slayer*.

Seemann, Erich, Dag Strömbäck, and Bengt R. Jonsson, eds. *European Folk Ballads*. Trans. G. René Halkett and J. A. Arengo Jones. European Folklore Series. Vol. 2. Copenhagen: Rosenkilde and Bagger, 1967. DFINS

Rev. Alan Jabbour. *Western Folklore* 29 (1970): 207.

Rev. Felix J. Oinas. *Journal of American Folklore* 82 (1969): 284–85.
Rev. Henri Stegemeier. *Journal of English and Germanic Philology* 68 (1969): 153–55.

Semb, Klara. *Dances of Norway.* Handbooks of European National Dances. New York: Crown, 1951. N

Sevig, Mike and Else Sevig, eds. *Mike and Else's Norwegian Songbook.* Trans. Mike Sevig and John Gundersen. Minneapolis: Skandisk, 1985. N

Shekerjian, Haig and Regina Shekerjian, eds. *A Book of Christmas Carols.* Arr. Robert de Cormier. Swedish carols trans. Selma S. de Cormier and Ulla Löfgren. New York: Harper and Row, 1963. S

Simpson, Jacqueline, ed. and trans. *The Northmen Talk: A Choice of Tales from Iceland.* Madison, WI: U Wisconsin P, 1965. I

Rev. Foster W. Blaisdell. *Scandinavian Studies* 39 (1967): 186–88.
Rev. *Booklist* 62 (1 Nov. 1965): 257–58.
Rev. George Mackay Brown. *New Statesman* 70 (15 Oct. 1965): 568–69.
Rev. *Choice* 2 (Febr.–March 1966): 864.
Rev. H. R. Ellis Davidson. *Folklore* 76 (1965): 230–32.
Rev. M. A. Malkin. *Antiquarian Bookman* 36 (27 Sept. 1965): 1100. [Not seen]
Rev. W. Edson Richmond. *Journal of American Folklore* 80 (1967): 202.
Rev. Paul Schach. *Journal of English and Germanic Philology* 66 (1967): 392–95.
Rev. Archer Taylor. *Western Folklore* 26 (1967): 213–15.
Rev. *Times Literary Supplement* 8 July 1965: 575.
Rev. Francis Lee Utley. *Speculum* 42 (1967): 533–35.

Smith-Dampier, [E. M.] "The Ballad of William Curt-Nose." *Saga-Book of the Viking Society* 11 (1936): 247–49. [Published as N. Smith-Dampier] F

Smith-Dampier, E. M., *Ballads from the Danish and Original Verses.* London: Andrew   Melrose, 1910. D

———. *BDB.* See Olrik, Axel.

———. *A Book of Danish Ballads.* See Olrik, Axel.

———, trans. *Danish Ballads.* Cambridge: Cambridge UP, 1920. DI

Rev. H. M. Belden. *Modern Language Notes* 36 (1921): 381–82.
Rev. W. H. Chesson. *Bookman* 59 (1921): 168–69.

Rev. Britta Mortensen. *Folklore* 51 (1940): 172. [Not seen]

————, trans. "Dead Rides Sir Morten." *The Poetry Review* 19.1 (1928): 7–8.
D

————, trans. "The Death of Queen Dagmar." *American-Scandinavian Review*
2.4 (1914): 24–27.   D

————, trans. "A Faroëse Ballad-Dance." *American-Scandinavian Review* 20
(1932): 86–89.   F

————, trans. *More Ballads from the Danish and Original Verses*. London:
Andrew Melrose, 1914.   DIN

Rev. *American-Scandinavian Review* 3.3 (1915): 183.
Rev. Francis Bickley. "Some Recent Poetry." *Bookman* 47 (1914): 96–97.

————, trans. *The Norse King's Bridal: Translations from the Danish and Old
Norse, with Original Ballads*. London: Andrew Melrose, 1912.   D

Rev. *Bookman* 42 (1912): 272.
Rev. J. G. *Poetry Review* 1 (1912): 334.

————, trans. *Sigurd the Dragon-Slayer: A Faroese Ballad-Cycle*. Oxford:
Basil Blackwell, 1934.   DF

————, trans. "Sir Morten of Fuglsang." *American-Scandinavian Review* 20
(1932): 199–200.   D

————. "The Song of Roland in the Faroës." *Saga-Book of the Viking Society*
11 (1936): 239–46. [Published as N. Smith-Dampier]   F

————. "The Song of Roland in the Faroes." *American-Scandinavian Review*
40 (1952): 39–43.   F

Smith-Dampier, E. M., et al, trans. "A Group of Ballads." *American-Scandinavian Review* 12 (1924): 764–68.   D

Solberg, Olav. "Jocular Ballads and Carnival Culture." *ARV* 48 (1992): 17–23.
N

————. "The Norwegian Jocular Medieval Ballad: A Presentation and Some Themes." *Talking Folklore* No. 9 (1990): 34–46. N

Steenstrup, Johannes C. H. R. *The Medieval Popular Ballad.* Trans. Edward Godfrey Cox. Boston: Ginn, 1914. Intr. David C. Fowler; Bibl. Essay by Karl-Ivar Hildeman. Seattle: U Washington P, 1968. DFIN

Steiner, Rudolf. *The Festivals and Their Meaning: Christmas, Easter, Ascension and Pentecost, Michelmas.* 1955–57. London: Rudolf Steiner Press, 1981. N

[Stephens, George]. Rev. of *Svenska Folk-Visor från Forntiden*, by Gust. Geijer and Arv. Aug. Afzelius, and *Svenska Fornsånger*, by Adolf Iwar Arwidsson. *Foreign Quarterly Review* 25 (1840): 14–29; 26 (1840): 16–31. [American ed. of *FQR* has different pagination] S

Stephens, George. *Revenge, or Woman's Love. A Melodrama in Five Acts.* Copenhagen: C. G. Iversen; London: John Russell Smith, [1857]. S

Stephens, James, Edwin C. Beck, and Royall H. Snow, eds. *Victorian and Later English Poets.* New York: American Book Co., 1937. D

Stockholms Studentsångarförbund sångarfärd till Amerika 1925. Trans. Edward Adams-Ray. Stockholm: Kungl. Boktryckeriet. P. A. Norstedt, 1925. S

Stoddard, R. H., ed. *Translations.* New York: Charles Scribner's Sons, 1883. D

[Stokes, Whitley]. "Danish Ballads." *Fraser's Magazine for Town and Country* 45 (1852): 649–59. D

————. "Danish Ballads." Rev. of *Danmarks gamle Folkeviser* 1, 2, ed. Svend Grundtvig. *The Saturday Review* 6 (Aug. 28, 1858): 213–15. D

————. "Danish Ballads." Rev. of *Danmarks gamle Folkeviser* 3, ed. Svend Grundtvig and of *Ancient Danish Ballads*, trans. R. C. Alexander Prior. *The Saturday Review* 11 (Jan. 12, 1861): 46–48. D

————. "A Second Batch of Danish Ballads." *Fraser's Magazine for Town and Country* 51 (1855): 86–95. D

Strömbäck, Dag. "St. Stephen in the Ballads." *ARV* 24 (1968): 133–47. DS

Stub, Valborg Hovind, ed. *Songs from the North*. Trans. Auber Forestier [Aubertine Woodward Moore]. Boston: Oliver Ditson, 1907. D

Sveinbjörnsson, Sv. *Íslenzk þjóðlög. Icelandic Folksongs*. Edinburgh: R. W. Pentland, n.d. I

Swedish National Songs. Schwedische Volkslieder. Chants nationaux suedois avec piano. Stockholm: A. Lundquist, 1877. [Not seen] S

Syndergaard, Larry. Duplicated instructional material. Western Michigan University. 1986. D

———. "Realization of the Feminine Self in Three Traditional Ballads from Scotland and Denmark." *Michigan Academician* 20 (Winter, 1988): 85–100. D

Sångsällskapet de Svenske. *"The Singing Vikings" National Chorus of Sweden America Tour, 1927*. Trans. Edward Adams-Ray. Stockholm: Bröderna Lagerström, 1927. S

Tales See Lewis, M. G. *Tales of Wonder*.

Talvj. See Robinson.

Taube, Sven-Bertil. *Swedish Folk Songs & Ballads*. LP. New York: Folkways, 1954. Audiocassette. Washington, DC: Smithsonian Folkways, 1991. [Not seen] S

Thomas, Edith Lovell, comp. *The Whole World Singing*. New York: Friendship Press, 1950. S

Thomas, Margaret. *Denmark, Past and Present*. London: Anthony Treherne, 1902. D

Thorpe, Benjamin. *Northern Mythology*. Vol. 2. *Scandinavian Popular Traditions and Superstitions*. London: Edward Lumley, 1851. D

Tobitt, Janet Evelyn, comp. *The Ditty Bag*. New York: Janet Tobitt, 1946. S

UNEF Song Book: International Songs Dedicated to the Men of the United Nations Emergency Force. Delaware, Ohio: Cooperative Recreation Service, 1958. N

Vanberg, Bent. *Of Norwegian Ways.* Minneapolis: Dillon, 1990. N

Van Cleve, Cecilia. *Folk Dances for Young People: With Explanatory Text Diagrams and Photographic Illustrations.* Springfield, MA: Milton Bradley, 1916. FN

Van Doren, Mark, ed. *An Anthology of World Poetry.* New York: Literary Guild of America, 1928. [Many other editions] D

———, ed. *An Anthology of World Poetry.* Rev. ed. New York: Blue Ribbon Books, 1935. [Many other printings] D

Van Doren, Mark and Garibaldi M. Lapolla, eds. *An Anthology of World Poetry.* High School edition. New York: Abert & Charles Boni, 1929. D

———, eds. *The World's Best Poems.* Cleveland: World, 1928. D

Vornholt, Dan, comp. and ed. *The Folk Singer.* Madison, WI: U Wisconsin Extension Service of College of Agriculture, 1943. NS

Warmuth's Collection. Norwegian National Music. Christiania: Carl Warmuth, n.d. N

Warner, Dudley, ed. *Library of the World's Best Literatures: Ancient and Modern.* 46 vols. New York: J. A. Hill, 1902. D

Warnock, Robert and George K. Anderson, eds. *The World in Literature.* Chicago: Scott, Foresman, 1959. D

Weber, Henry, R[obert] Jamieson, and W[alter] S[cott], eds. *Illustrations of Northern Antiquities, from the Earlier Teutonic and Scandinavian Romances . . . with Translations of Metrical Tales from the Old German, Danish, Swedish and Icelandic Languages.* London: Longman, Hurst, Rees, Orme, and Brown; Edinburgh: John Ballantyne, 1814. DS

West, John F. "Ballad-Dancing in the Faroe Islands." *Co-Scan Newsletter.* Issue 1 (Winter 1983/84): 19–21. F

Widén, Albin. "Scandinavian Folklore and Immigrant Ballads." *Bulletin of the American Institute of Swedish Arts, Literature and Science* ns 2 (March 1947): 2–44. s

Wilson, James Grant, ed. *The Poets and Poetry of Scotland: From the Earliest to the Present Time*. 2 vols. London: Blackie, 1876–1877. D

With, Mogens. "Danish." *Eos: An Enquiry into the Theme of Lovers' Meetings and Partings at Dawn in Poetry*. ed. Arthur T. Hatto. The Hague: Mouton, 1965. 562–67. D

Woods, George B., ed. *Poetry of the Victorian Period*. Chicago: Scott, Foresman, 1930. D

A World of Song. 11 Parts. Des Moines: Danish American Young People's League, Grand View College, 1941–43. D

A World of Song. Rev. Ed. Des Moines: American Evangelical Lutheran Youth Fellowship, 1958. D

Wright, Herbert G. "George Borrow's Translations from the Scandinavian Languages." *Edda* 16 (1921): 137–45. D

Wylie, Jonathan and David Margolin. *The Ring of Dancers: Images of Faroese Culture*. Phildelphia: U Pennsylvania P, 1981. F

Young Women's Christian Association Music Committee. *Sing Along the Way*. New York: Woman's Press, 1947. [Several other eds.]   s

Zanzig, Augustus Delafield, comp. *Singing America, Song and Chorus Book*. Boston: C. C. Birchard for the National Recreation Association, 1941. s

BIBLIOGRAPHY OF TRANSLATORS' SOURCES

The bibliography includes some standard works that are the near-equivalent of sources used for certain translations even if not demonstrably the sources themselves. (These have been indicated by = or ≅ in the "Translator's Source" column in the tables.) The capital letters in bold-face following the entries indicate the language in which the source ballads *originate*. This is not always the language of the ballads in the source itself, because some books of translations become sources for other translations (see the "Notes" column in the tables). Works not seen or seen in other editions of the work cited are so indicated in brackets.

Abrahamson, [W. H. F.], [Rasmus] Nyerup, and [K. L.] Rahbek, eds. *Udvalgte Danske Viser fra Middelalderen.* 5 vols. København, 1812–14. **D**

Andersson, Otto, ed. *Finlands svenska folkdiktning.* Vol. 5 *Folkvisor. 1. Den äldre folkvisan.* Helsingfors: Svenska Litteratursällskapet i Finland, 1934. **S**

ANR. See Abrahamson, Nyerup, and Rahbek.

Arwidsson, Adolf Iwar, ed. *Svenska Fornsånger: En Samling af Kämpavisor, Folk-Visor, Lekar och Dansar, samt Barn- och Vall-Sånger.* 3 vols. Stockholm: P. A. Norstedt, 1834–42. **S**

Berge, Richard, comp. and ed. *Norsk Visefugg: Med Tonar.* Melodies comp. Arne Eggen. Kristiania: Olaf Norlis, 1904. **N**

Berggreen, A[ndreas] P[eter], comp. and ed. *Folke-Sange og Melodier, fædrelandske og fremmede.* Vol. 3. København: G. H. Jæger, 1845. **I**

———, comp. and ed. *Folke-Sange og Melodier, fædrelandske og fremmede.* 2nd ed. Vol. 1. København: Gyldendal, 1860. **D**

———, comp. and ed. *Folke-Sange og Melodier, fædrelandske og fremmede.* 3rd ed. Vol. 1. København: Reitzel, 1869. **DI**

Blom, Ådel Gjøstein and Olav Bø, eds. *Norske balladar i oppskrifter frå 1800–talet*. Oslo: Det Norske Samlaget, 1973. N

Blom, Ådel Gjøstein, Øystein Gaukstad, and Nils Schiørring, eds. *Norske mellomalderballadar*. Vol. 1. *Legendeviser*. Oslo: Universitetsforlaget, 1982. N

Boisen, P. O. *Nye og gamle viser af og for danske folk*. København: ?Thiele, 1849. [This ed. not seen] D

Bragur 3: 292. [Not seen] S

Briem, Ólafur, ed. *Fornir Dansar*. Reykjavík: Hlaðbúð, 1946. I

Bugge, Sophus, ed. *Gamle norske Folkeviser*. Kristiania: Feilberg & Landmark, 1858. N

CCF See Grundtvig, Svend and Jørgen Bloch. *Føroya Kvæði. Corpus Carminum Færoensium.*

Danske Tilskuer 1793 No. 99–100. [Not seen] D

DgF. See Grundtvig, Svend, et al. *Danmarks gamle Folkeviser.*

Erk, Ludwig Christian, and Franz M. Böhme. *Deutscher Liederhort: Auswahl der vorzüglicheren deutschen Volkslieder*. Vol. 3. Leipzig: Breitkopf und Härtel, 1894. [Not seen] D

ETK See Kristensen, Evald Tang, ed. *Et hundrede gamle danske Skjæmteviser.*

Fagerlund, Lars Wilhelm. *Anteckningar om Korpo och Houtskärs Socknar. Bidrag til Kännedom af Finlands Natur och Folk*. 28. Helsingfors: Finska Vetenskaps-Societien, 1878. [Not seen] S

FAnth See Hammershaimb, V[enceslaus] U. *Færøsk Anthologi.*

FKvr See Hammershaimb, V[enceslaus] U. *Færöiske Kvæder.*

Folkminnen och folktankar (1916): 15–16. [Not seen] S

Frydendahl, H[ans] C[hristian], comp. and ed. *Fynske folkeminder*. 1. Krarup, Denmark: Fynsk Hjemstavns Forlag, 1945. D

FSF See Andersson, Otto. *Finlands svenska folkdiktning.*

GA See Geijer, Er. Gust. and Arv. Aug. Afzelius, eds. *Svenska Folk-visor från forntiden.*

GAB See Geijer, Er. Gust. and Arv. Aug. Afzelius, eds. *Svenska Folkvisor.* Rev ed. R. Bergström and L. Höijer.

Garborg, Hulda. *Norske Dansevisur.* 3rd ed. Kristiania: H. Aschehoug, 1920. [Other editions not seen] N

———. *Song-Dansen i Nord-Landi.* Kristiania: H. Aschehoug, 1903. F

Geijer, Er. Gust. and Arv. Aug. Afzelius, eds. *Svenska Folk-visor från Forntiden.* 3 vols. Stockholm: Strinnholm och Häggström, 1814–18. S

———. *Svenska Folkvisor.* Rev., enl. ed. Ed. R. Bergström and L. Höijer. 3 vols. Stockholm: Z. Hæggström, 1880. S

Grieg, Edvard. *Album for Mandsang (Kor og Soli) frit efter norske Folkeviser, Op. 30.* Kristiania: Carl Warmuth, [1878]. [Other ed. seen] N

———. *Der Bergentrückte. Den Bergtekne. Den Bjærgtagne: Ältnordische Volkspoesie.* Kopenhagen: Vilhelm Hansen; Leipzig: B. Hermann, [1882]. N

———. *Samlede Verker. Gesamtausgabe. Complete Works.* Vol. 17. Ed. Dan Fog. Frankfurt: C. F. Peters, 1985. N

Grimm, Wilhelm Carl, trans. *Altdänische Heldenlieder, Balladen und Märchen.* Heidelberg: Mohr und Zimmer, 1811. D

GrN see Grüner Nielsen, H.

Grundtvig, F[rederik] L., ed. *Sangbog for det danske Folk i Amerika.* Clinton, Iowa: Dansk Folkesamfund, 1889. [Several later eds.] D

Grundtvig, Nik[olai] F. S., ed. *Danske Kæmpeviser til Skole-brug.* København: Reitzel, 1847. D

Grundtvig, Svend. Communications to Francis J. Child cited in *The English and Scottish Popular Ballads.* 5 vols. Boston: Houghton Mifflin, 1882–98. D

———, ed. *Danmarks Folkeviser i Udvalg.* København: P. G. Philipsens, 1882. D

———, ed. *Danske Kæmpeviser og Folkesange fra Middelalderen*. København: Gad, 1867. D

———, ed. and trans. *Engelske og skotske Folkeviser, med oplysende Anmærkninger*. 4 vols. København, 1842–46. [Not seen] D

Grundtvig, Sv[end] and J[ørgen] Bloch, comps. *Føroya Kvæði: Corpus Carminum Færoensium*. Ed. N. Djurhuus and Chr. Matras. 6 vols. Kopenhagen: Ejnar Munksgaard, for Universitets-Jubilæets danske Samfund, 1941–72. F

Grundtvig, Svend, Axel Olrik, H. Grüner Nielsen, Erik Dal, et al, eds. *Danmarks gamle Folkeviser*. 12 vols. København: Samfundet til den danske Literaturs Fremme and Universitets-Jubilæets danske Samfund, 1853–1976. DFNS

Grundtvig, Svend and Jón Sigurðsson, eds. *Íslenzk fornkvæði*. 2 vols. København: Det nordiske Literatur-Samfund, 1854–85. I

Grüner Nielsen, H., ed. *Danske Folkeviser fra Riddersal og Borgestue*. København: Martins Forlag, 1925. D

———, ed. *Danske Skæmteviser (Folkeviser og litterær Efterklang) efter Visehaandskrifter fra 16.–18. Aarh. og Flyveblade*. 2 vols. København: Universitets-Jubilæets danske Samfund, 1927–28. D

———, ed. *Danske Viser fra Adelsvisebøger og Flyveblade 1530–1630*. 7 vols. København, 1912–31. [Not seen] D

Hammershaimb, V[enceslaus] U. "Faðir og dottir." *Antiquarisk Tidsskrift* 1849–51: 88–91. [Not seen] F

———. "Frísa Vísa." *Antiquarisk Tidsskrift* 1849–51: 95–96. [Not seen] F

———, ed. *Færøsk Anthologi*. 2 vols. København: S. L. Møller, 1891. F

———, ed. *Færöiske Kvæder*. 2 vols. København: Det nordiske Literatur-Samfund, 1851–55. Vol. 1 originally *Sjúrðar Kvæði*. F

———. "Rudisar vísa." *Dansk Kirketidende* 1852 No. 344. [Not seen] F

Helgason, Jón, ed. *Íslenzk fornkvæði. Islandske folkeviser*. 8 vols. København: C. A. Reitzel, 1962–81. I

Hellgren, Otto, ed. and comp. *Sånglekar från Nääs*. Stockholm: Abr. Lundquist:s Kongl. Hof-Musikhandel, 1906. [First publ. 1905]   FN

Herder, Johann Gottfried. *Volkslieder*. 2 vols. Leipzig, 1778–1779.   D

Hollmérus, Ragnar, and Otto Anderson. *Du sköna sång*. Åbo: Forlaget Bro, 1946. [Not seen]   S

Hægstad, Marius, ed. *Hildinakvadet: med utgreiding um det norske maal paa Shetland i eldre tid*. Videnskabsselskabets skrifter. II. Historisk-filosofiske klasse. 1900. No. 2. Christiania: Jacob Dybwad, 1900.   **Shetl.**

ÍF   See Helgason, Jón. *Íslenzk fornkvæði. Islandske folkeviser.*

Ífkv   See Grundtvig, Svend and Jón Sigurðsson. *Íslenzk fornkvæði.*

Jonsson, Bengt, ed. *Svenska Medeltidsballader: Ett Urval*. Stockholm: Natur och Kultur, 1962. 2d ed. 1966. [Not seen]   S

Jonsson, Bengt R., Margareta Jersild, and Sven-Bertil Jansson, eds. *Sveriges Medeltida Ballader*. 3 vols. to date. Stockholm: Almqvist and Wiksell for Svenskt Visarkiv, 1983– .   S

Karpeles, Maud, ed. *Folk Songs of Europe*. International Folk Song Anthologies for the International Folk Music Council. London: Novello, 1956. New York: Oak, 1964.   D

Kristensen, Evald Tang, ed. *Et hundrede gamle danske Skjæmteviser, efter Nutidssang*. Århus: Jacob Zeuners, 1901.   D

———, ed. *Jydske Folkeviser og Toner, samlede af Folkemunde, især i Hammerum-Herred*. Jy(d)ske Folkeminder 1. København, 1871. [Not seen.]   D

Lammers, Thorvald, ed. *Norske Folkeviser: Tekst og Toner*. Christiania, H. Aschehoug, 1901–02. [Not seen]   N

Landstad, M[agnus] B., ed. *Norske Folkeviser*. Christiania, 1853. Oslo: Norsk folkeminnelag/Universitetsforlaget, 1968.   N

Levn. 1   See Sandvig, Bertel Christian.

Liestøl, Knut and Moltke Moe, eds. *Norske Folkevisor*. Folkeutgave. 3 vols. Kristiania: Jacob Dybwad, 1920–24.   N

Liestøl, Knut and Klara Semb. *Norske Folkedansar. I. Danseviser*. 7th ed. Oslo: Noregs Boklag, 1951. [Earlier eds. not seen]   N

Lindeman, Ludvig M. *Ældre og nyere Norske Fjeldmelodier: Samlede og bearbeidede for Pianoforte*. Christiania: P. T. Mallings Forlag, 1853–1867 and C. Warmuth, 1907. Facsimile ed. Oslo: Universitetsforlaget, 1963.   N

"Liten Kerstins Förtrollning." *Svenska Fornminnesforeningens Tidskrift* 2 (1873–74): 72 ff. [Not seen]   S

Loewe, Carl. *Schottische, englische und nordische Balladen*. Leipzig: Breitkopf & Härtel, 1899. Vol. 3 of *Carl Loewes Werke*. Ed. Max Runze. 17 vols. 1899–1904.   D

Lyngbye, Hans Christian, ed. *Færøiske Qvæder om Sigurd Fofnersbane og hans Æt*. Randers, Denmark: 1822.   F

Magnússon, Gísli and Jón Þórðarsson, eds. *Snót: Nokkur Kvæði eptir ýmiss Skáld*. København, 1850. [Not seen]   I

Moe, Moltke. *Samlede Skrifter*. Ed. Knut Liestøl. Vol. 3. Oslo: H. Aschehoug, 1927.   N

Mortensson-Egnund, Ivar. *Gjallarbrui: Ei Diktbok om Draumkvede-skalden (ein mystikar i millomalderen)*. Oslo: Cammermeyer, 1926.   N

NMB   See Blom, Ådel Gjøstein, et al. *Norske mellomalderballadar*.

Noreen, Adolf and J. A. Lundell, eds. *1500- och 1600-talens Visböcker*. Vol. 8. Uppsala: Svenska litteratursällskapet, 1913–15. [Not seen]   S

NR. See Nyerup and Rasmussen.

Nyerup, R[asmus] and P. Rasmussen, eds. *Udvalg af Danske Viser fra Midten af det 16de Aarhundrede til henimod Midten af det 18de*. 2 vols. København: Schultz, 1821.   D

Oehlenschläger, Adam G. *Axel og Valborg; et Sörgespil*. København: A. Seidelin, 1810.   D

————, ed. *Gamle danske Folkeviser*. København: Andr. Fred. Høst, 1840. D

Olrik, Axel and Ida Falbe-Hansen, eds. *Danske Folkeviser i Udvalg*. København: Gyldendal, for Dansklærerforeningen, 1899. DI

————, eds. *Danske Folkeviser i Udvalg: Anden Samling*. København and Christiania: Gyldendal, for Dansklærerforeningen, 1909. D

"Om Edda-Mythernes allmånlighet." *Iduna* 8 (1820): 122–27. S

Patursson, Jóannes, ed. *Kvæð(a)bók*. Vols. 1, 2. Tórshavn: Föroya Lögting, 1922–23. [Not seen] F

Rafn, Carl Christian. *Antiqvitates Americanæ; sive, scriptores septentrionales rerum ante-columbian arum in America. Samling af de i nordens oldskrifter indeholdte efterretninger om de gamle nordboers opdagelsesreiser til America fra det 10de til det 14de aarhundrede*. København: Schultz, 1837. F

Rancken, J[ohan] O[skar] I., ed. *Några Prof af Folksång och Saga i det svenske Österbotten*. Helsingfors: the author, 1878. S

Ranke, Friedrich, ed. *Tristan und Isold*. Bücher des Mittelalters. München: F. Bruckmann, 1925. I

Ravn, Hans M. (Corvinus). *Ex Rhytmologia Danica Epitome Brevissima*. Sorø, 1649. [Not seen] D

Recke, Ernst von der, ed. *Danmarks Fornviser*. 4 vols. København: Møller og Landschultz, 1927–29. D

Sandvig, Bertel Christian, ed. *Levninger of Middel-Alderens Digtekunst*. 1. København: Godiches Arvinger, 1780. D

Säve, P. A., comp. *Götlandska visor*. Ed. Erik Noreen and Herbert Gustavson. 3 vols. Uppsala and Stockholm: Kungl. Gustav Adolfs Akademien, 1949–55. S

Schrøter, J. H. *J. H. Schrøters Optegnelser of Sjúrða Kvæði*. Ed. Christian Matras. Færoensia 3. København, 1951–53. [Not seen] F

SF See Arwidsson, Adolf Iwar. *Svenska Fornsånger*.

SMB   See Jonsson, Bengt, et al, eds. *Sveriges Medeltida Ballader.*

Sneedorff-Birch, Fr., comp. *Danske Folkeviser og Melodier: Første Pentade, indeholdende fem jydske Viser med Melodier.* København, 1837. New ed. with notes by Erik Dal and A. P. Berggreen. Meddelanden från Svenskt Visarkiv 36. Stockholm: Svenskt Visarkiv, 1976.   D

Svenska Fornminnesforeningens Tidskrift 2 (1873–74): 72f. [Not seen]   S

Syv, Peder, ed. *Et Hundrede udvalde Danske Viser . . . Forøgede med det Andet Hundrede Viser om Danske Konger, Kæmper og Andre.* København, 1695. [Seen only in *Dgf* reprintings]   D

Thuborg, Karen. *Det gamle Harboøre.* Ed. Henrik Ussing. Danmarks Folke-minder No. 36. København: Schønbergske Forlag, 1928.   D

Thuren, Hjalmar. *Folkesangen paa Færøerne.* Folklore Fellows Publications. Northern ser. 2. København, 1908. [Not seen]   DF

———. "Tanz, Dichtung und Gesang auf den Färöern." *Sammelbände der Internationalen Musik-Gesellschaft.* Vol. 3. Ed. Oskar Fleischer and Johannes Wolf. Leipzig: Breitkopf & Härtel, 1901–02. 222–69.   F

Thyregod, S. Tvermose, ed. *Danmarks Sanglege.* København: Schønbergske Forlag, 1931.   D

Trummler, Erich, trans. *Traumlied des Olav Aasteson.* 1927. [Not seen.]   N

Vedel, Anders Sørensen, ed. *It Hundrede Vduaalde Danske Viser.* Ribe, 1591. [Several later editions. Seen only in *DgF* reprintings.]   D

Winding, A. F., ed. *Kjæmpeviser, utgivne som Text til 2det Hefte af Prof. Ridder Weyses Melodier.* København: Klein, 1843.   D

Winther, Christian, ed. *Kjæmpeviser, utgivne som Text til 1ste Hefte af Prof. Ridder Weyses Melodier.* København: Klein, 1840.   D

Woll, Carsten, comp. *Sangbog for Sønner af Norge. I. Melodi- og Tekstutgave.* Minneapolis: Sønner af Norges Forlag, 1926. [Not seen]   N

Appendix A

SCHOLARLY WORKS DEALING WITH ENGLISH TRANSLATIONS OF
THE SCANDINAVIAN BALLADS

A sustained scholarly discourse in this area has yet to develop. Thus works are included which discuss the translations of Scandinavian ballads only in passing, so long as that discussion is serious. Discussions by translators of others' translations are not cited; see the Bibliography of Works Including Translations.

Bredsdorff, Elias. *Danish Literature in English Translation, with a Special Hans Christian Andersen Supplement: A Bibliography.* Copenhagen: Ejnar Munksgaard, 1950.

———. "The Medieval Danish Ballads." *Denmark* Oct. 1949: 13–15.

———. "Sir Alexander Gray, skotsk oversætter af danske folkeviser." *Hvad fatter gjor–: Boghistoriske, litterære og musikalske essays tilegnet Erik Dal.* Herning, Denmark: P. Kristensen, 1982. 92–107.

Dal, Erik. *Nordisk folkeviseforskning siden 1800: Omrids af text- og melodistudiets historie og problemer især i Danmark.* København: J. H. Schultz, 1956.

———. "Oversættelser af nordiske folkeviser." *Samlet og spredt om folkeviser: Fagmandens, bibliografens og samlerens efterskrift til Nordisk folkeviseforskning siden 1800 (1956).* C. C. Rafn Forlæsning 4. Odense: Odense Universitetsforlag, 1976. 9–29.

———. "Tyske, franske og engelske oversættelser af færøkvæder." *Fróðskaparrit* 18 (1970): 77–92. Issue = *Meddelanden fra Svenskt Visarkiv* 30.

Holst, Olaf. "Engelske oversættelser af danske folkeviser." *Danske Studier* 1941: 113–20.

Hustvedt, Sigurd Bernhard. *Ballad Books and Ballad Men: Raids and Rescues in Britain, America, and the Scandinavian North since 1800.* Cambridge, MA: Harvard UP, 1930.

————. "George Borrow and His Danish Ballads." *Journal of English and Germanic Philology* 22 (1923): 262–70.

Malmin, Marie Helene. "A Bibliography of the Translations and Criticism of Norwegian, Swedish, and Danish Literature in England and America." Diss. U Minnesota, 1929.

Meisling, Peter. *Agnetes latter: En folkevise-monografi.* København: Akademisk Forlag, 1987.

Roos, Carl. "Die dänische Folkevise in der Weltliteratur." *Forschungsprobleme der vergleichenden Literaturgeschichte.* Ed. Kurt Wais. Tübingen: Max Niemeyer, 1951.

Schroeder, Carol L. *A Bibliography of Danish Literature in English Translation 1950–1980: With a Selection of Books about Denmark.* [Copenhagen]: Det danske Selskab, 1982.

Syndergaard, Larry. "'An Amateur' and His Translations of the Danish Ballads—Identity and Significance." *Danske Studier* 85 (1990): 80–93.

————. "The Translations of the Danish Ballads Seen as Intercultural Communication." *Scandinavian Literature in a Transcultural Context: Papers from the XV. IASS Conference.* Ed. Sven H. Rossel and Birgitta Steene. Seattle: U Washington, 1985. 222–25.

Wright, Herbert. "George Borrow and Scandinavia." *Studies in Anglo-Scandinavian Literary Relations.* Bangor, 1919. 18–48.

————. "George Borrow's Translations from the Scandinavian Languages." *Edda* 16 (1921): 137–45. [An adaptation of preceding work]

APPENDIX B

SCANDINAVIAN BALLADS WITH COGNATES IN ENGLISH

The information here is based on the concordance of Danish ballads and cognates in English in *Danmarks gamle Folkeviser* 12:112. That material has been indexed to pan-Scandinavian (TSB) ballad type designations in *The Types of the Scandinavian Medieval Ballad* and arranged in order of TSB types. "Child" is Francis J. Child's *The English and Scottish Popular Ballads*, the central edition in English. The coverage of the appendix is incomplete; it will indicate cognates in English for only those Faroese, Icelandic, Norwegian, and Swedish ballads that have Danish counterparts. No attempt is made to limit the Scandinavian ballad types listed to those that have been translated.

The term "cognates" means only that significant portions of the two narratives are similar; it does not imply a genetic relationship in all cases. The asterisk * marks eight of the closest equivalencies, cases in which one unequivocally can speak of the same narrative in English and in one or more Scandinavian languages.

Many partial echoes, broader parallels, and shared motifs are not indicated here. Child discusses such cases, as does *DgF*, for those who can read Danish. Ólason, *The Traditional Ballads of Iceland*, discusses the most important cognates in English of the Icelandic ballads.

TSB	DgF	Child		TSB	DgF	Child
A 11	81	43		D 36	408	25
A 38	95	10*		D 37	409	25*
A 40	84	6*		D 69	416	71
A 40	85	6		D 72	218	52
A 41	82	7*		D 97	231	112
A 44	68	270		D 98	230	112
A 54	37	41		D 136	68	270
A 63	47	42		D 145	224	268
A 67	90	77		D 150	230	112
				D 178	314	110
B 8	96	22		D 179	314	110
B 16	98	21		D 231	13	59
B 21	338	14		D 239	208	68
B 27	94	269		D 245	210	73
B 27	305	269		D 259	255	253
B 36	529	20*		D 279	446	75

241

TSB	DgF	Child		TSB	DgF	Child
D287	270	15		D391	486	95
D288	271	15		D392	468	266
D289	272	15		D396	267	63
D290	273	15		D399	238	110
D320	340	13*		D410	249	9
D321	341	12		D411	183	4*
D324	304	69		D421	274	5*
D346	126	64				
D360	375	58		E 96	298	89
D361	376	57				
D390	305	269		Later Ballad German	258	62